ROUTLEDGE LIBRARY EDITIONS:
MULTINATIONALS

Volume 2

HOW PARTICIPATORY EVALUATION RESEARCH AFFECTS THE MANAGEMENT CONTROL PROCESS OF A MULTINATIONAL NONPROFIT ORGANIZATION

HOW PARTICIPATORY EVALUATION RESEARCH AFFECTS THE MANAGEMENT CONTROL PROCESS OF A MULTINATIONAL NONPROFIT ORGANIZATION

GAIL J. FULTS

Routledge
Taylor & Francis Group

LONDON AND NEW YORK

First published in 1993 by Garland Publishing, Inc.

This edition first published in 2017
by Routledge
2 Park Square, Milton Park, Abingdon, Oxon OX14 4RN

and by Routledge
711 Third Avenue, New York, NY 10017

Routledge is an imprint of the Taylor & Francis Group, an informa business

British Library Cataloguing in Publication Data
A catalogue record for this book is available from the British Library

ISBN: 978-1-138-28116-5 (Set)
ISBN: 978-1-315-27111-8 (Set) (ebk)
ISBN: 978-1-138-28105-9 (Volume 2) (hbk)
ISBN: 978-1-315-27135-4 (Volume 2) (ebk)

Publisher's Note
The publisher has gone to great lengths to ensure the quality of this reprint but points out that some imperfections in the original copies may be apparent.

Disclaimer
The publisher has made every effort to trace copyright holders and would welcome correspondence from those they have been unable to trace.

How Participatory Evaluation Research Affects the Management Control Process of a Multinational Nonprofit Organization

GAIL J. FULTS

Garland Publishing, Inc.
New York & London
1993

Reprint Permissions

Thompson's Decision Matrix is reprinted, by permission, from J. D. Thompson, *Organizations in Action*, page 134, ©1967, McGraw Hill Book Company.

Sewell and Phillips' Trade-Off Between Equity and Efficiency by Degree of Citizen Involvement is reprinted, by permission, from Volume 29 *Natural Resources Journal*, pages 356-58, 1979.

Anthony and Dearden's Phases of Management Control is reprinted, by permission, from Robert N. Anthony and John Dearden, *Management Control Systems—Text and Cases*, page 21, ©1976 Richard D. Erwin, Inc.

Anthony and Dearden's Control Process is reprinted, by permission, from Robert N. Anthony and John Dearden, *Management Control Systems—Text and Cases*, page 102, ©1976 Richard D. Erwin, Inc.

Ritchie's Classification of Research Methodologies According to Three Dimensions of the Management Process is reprinted, by permission, from *MSU Business Topics*, pages 13-22, Summer 1976.

Dermer's Three-Cycle Planning and Control Process is reprinted, by permission, from Jerry Dermer, *Management Planning and Control Systems*, page 40, ©1977, Richard D. Erwin, Inc.

Maciariello's Control Hierarchy: The Structure of Control is reprinted, by permission, from Joseph A. Maciariello, *Management Control Systems*, ©1984, page 14. Adapted by permission of Prentice Hall, Englewood Cliffs, New Jersey.

Hopwood's Measurement-Reward Process with Imperfect Measurement is reprinted, by permission, from Anthony Hopwood, *Accounting and Human Behavior*, ©1974 Haymarket Publishing, page 108. Reprinted by permission of Prentice Hall, Englewood Cliffs, New Jersey.

Tannenbaum's Control Graph is reprinted, by permission, from Arnold S. Tannenbaum, *Control and Organizations*, pages 12-14, ©1968, McGraw Hill Book Company.

Stone's Comparison of Empirical Research Strategies is reprinted, by permission, from Eugene F. Stone, *Research Methods in Organizational Behavior*, Table 7-1, page 116, ©1978, Good Year Publishing Company.

Library of Congress Cataloging-in-Publication Data

Fults, Gail J., 1946–
    How participatory evaluation research affects the management control process
of a multinational nonprofit organization / Gail J. Fults.
        p.   cm. — (Nonprofit institutions in America)
    Includes bibliographical references and index.
    ISBN 0–8153–0946–5 (alk. paper)
    1. Nonprofit organizations—United States—Management.   2. International
agencies—United States—Management.   3. Evaluation research (Social action
programs)—United States—Utilization.   I. Title.   II. Series.
HD62.6.F85 1993
658'.049—dc20
                                                            92–40628
                                                            CIP

Printed on acid-free, 250-year-life paper
Manufactured in the United States of America

Dedication

To Sarah and Daniel,
thank you for the joy.

This dissertation was dedicated to three men who influenced my work greatly.

Robert Johnson, the man who encouraged me to pursue my dreams and give them my very best;

Peter Drucker, the man who encouraged me to think differently, especially for an accountant;

Herb Fults, the man who encouraged me to "get the 'damn' thing done."

To all of these men, I can now say, "I have."

Contents

Figures

Tables

Foreword

Accountability is a critical issue for administrators in non-profit organizations because they administer operations that have no inherent measure of performance. These organizations are driven by their own objectives, not by market forces. Administrators and managers have no owners' interest to maintain or maximize; instead they have donors, granting agencies, or governments supplying their capital without expecting a direct return. The organization's goods and services are provided in a non-exchange market without customers paying a price that includes any return to the organization like profit. Management has few ways to measure the organization's performance and their stewardship of the resources.

Accountants recognize that both non-business and business entities need to report outcomes from operations. The Financial Accounting Standards Board (FASB) includes non-profit organizations in their conceptual statements. The FASB and the Government Accounting Standards Board (GASB) are working currently on the form, content, and display of financial statements for non-profit organizations. Service accomplishment elements still need to be developed; the FASB has suggested that research be conducted on service effort and accomplishment measures which focus attention on achieving the organization's goals. This research seeks to improve accountants' understanding of service accomplishment by examining evaluation research findings as a potential measure.

Evaluation research is a method many non-profit organizations use to assess their policies and programs. Evaluation research methodologies and techniques have expanded greatly in the last twenty-five years and have been refined to incorporate a variety of program components. Most evaluation components complement the management control functions and parallel the management control process. While evaluation research is used unevenly by non-profit and government organizations, a sufficient number of organizations and agencies use it to suggest that administrators perceive a benefit and that the findings enhance an organization's survivability.

This was initial research towards building an interdisciplinary theory between accounting and evaluation research. Even if the two disciplines could not be merged to develop a service accomplishment measure for public disclosure in financial reporting, administrators in non-profit organizations could benefit from research which helped them learn how to use their evaluation research findings more effectively, both in the organization's operations and in their management disclosures about the organization. The research could then contribute to improved accountability by using evaluation research findings more fully.

This research uses common management research techniques. It examines each management control process function to determine how it was affected by one type of evaluation research. The research itself only identifies the outcomes and consequences; readers can give their own assessment of why each condition found in the research is present and how it can be addressed. While the operating consequences are interesting, the purpose of this research was new knowledge on the operating relationship between evaluation research and the management control process to determine if evaluation research findings provide sufficient self-control within the organization to be deemed a potential service accomplishment element in financial reporting.

The participatory evaluation process studied in this research was developed by one multinational non-profit organization for its own purposes and needs. I was fortunate to be examining the process from its inception and to make this initial analysis. The management control process and functions were used to structure the analysis because they complement the evaluation research process and they are well recognized in the accounting and management literature. They also indicate if the evaluation findings are relevant to and reliable for internal, corporate information users. If evaluation research information is useful to internal decision makers in assessing programs and goal attainment, then it could be considered a potential service accomplishment element.

The results show that evaluation research affects positively the management control process functions (planning, programming, budgeting, considering feedback information, and controlling operations) by making internal users more aware of service efforts and accomplishments in programs. Unlike standard financial reporting, the evaluation findings could not be complied, classified, and reported aggregately; percentage of goal attainment can be calculated, however, from the evaluation findings. Footnote or management disclosure is possible, therefore, and would enhance the usefulness of financial information reported on non-profit organizations by providing data on goal attainment and fund commitments. Further research is needed to examine if this information would be relevant to the decision processes of donors, creditors, funding agencies, and other external users of accounting information on non-business entities.

Beyond the accounting implications, several other aspects of this work are interesting and applicable to readers from different disciplines. First, it demonstrates that modern management techniques can be applied in non-profit organizations. Second, these techniques allow a researcher to see different outcomes from the same process in different locations in multinational organizations. Third, the results focus operating managers' and administrators' attention on individual evaluation process components to improve the process and subsequently their operations. Finally, the research shows the potential for executive administrators to enhance the organization's accountability and their stewardship of resources by using evaluation research findings more fully as well as to disclose service accomplishment. I hope all readers enjoy the eclectic nature of this work.

Arcata, California
September 23, 1992

Preface

Eleemosynary organizations operate in a non-exchange market environment for their goods and services where organizational objections not market orientation drives their production processes. No single established indicator of performance, like profit, exists in this environment so other indicators of performance are needed. The Financial Accounting Standards Board (FASB) asserts that service accomplishment elements, particularly measurement of program results, are generally underdeveloped and that research is needed to determine if measures can be developed for accounting information.

Problem

Evaluation research parallels the management control process and complements many management control functions. Evaluation research should, therefore, be examined as a possible service effort and accomplishment measure for financial reporting. For this dissertation, initial research was conducted on one form of evaluation research—participatory evaluations—to determine if it has the potential to function as a surrogate market to measure and report service effort and accomplishment for non-profit organizations. Three major research questions were addressed. First, can host communities (where the goods or services are being provided) design and use their own project evaluation plan? Second, can evaluation findings be incorporated into the formal management control system of a multinational, non-profit organization? And third, does participatory evaluation provide the benefits attributed to management by objectives and self-control in a decentralized organization?

Methodology

A field study was conducted on one multinational, non-profit organization which was installing a participatory evaluation process into its development projects. Answers to all three questions were sought from survey data elicited from its employees in thirty-three countries.

Findings

First, the host community members were able to design and use their own project evaluation plan, thereby partially creating an open-system environment.

Second, the information provided by the participatory evaluation process served the needs of project-level management, but it could not presently be incorporated into the formal management control system of the organization.

Third, the behavioral aspects (e.g., alignment of functional tasks nearest the point of performance, enhancement of staff performance and project effectiveness) of management by objectives and self-control in decentralized operations were present but the technical aspects (e.g., efficient resource allocation in both the long-run and the short-run) were not.

Implication

Internal and external users of accounting information need a service accomplishment measure to assess project performance. For external reporting, the FASB requires a good measure to be both relevant and reliable. This research suggests that participatory evaluation provides relevant data, but further development is needed for it to be considered a useful service effort and accomplishment measure.

Acknowledgments

A study of this size requires the support and assistance of many people. Likewise, the publication of a book involves a number of people to whom the author is indebted. I acknowledge the work of others to make this study and its publication possible; I appreciate their support. Responsibility for the content, however, rests with me. Errors of omission or commission in the analysis and interpretations are mine.

Original Research

I want to thank several people who have been extremely helpful in the completion of this thesis. My interest in the management control process and evaluation research in non-profit organizations was first stimulated in graduate course work. As my thesis chairman, Joseph Maciariello helped me organize and refine the management arguments made in this thesis. The critical comments and guidance of Mark Lipsey were also very important to the data analysis and to the assessments made on participatory evaluation research. He has been very supportive throughout the long process of completing this project in the management discipline. More generally, this research benefitted greatly from the management and accounting questions raised by Keith Ehrenreich and James Giles.

I am especially grateful to the organization studied in this thesis for their cooperation. The participatory evaluation process examined in this thesis was designed, developed, and implemented by them to fulfill their organizational needs for program assessment. They were receptive to analysis of their process from a management control perspective for the purpose of examining evaluation research's potential to be a service effort and accomplishment measure in published financial reporting. They generously allowed me access to their administrative and operational employees. Discussions with their staff were helpful throughout this project, especially in the early stages of its formation, I am indeed fortunate for their willingness to open their organization to outside scrutiny by an academic researcher.

My Pomona College colleague, Marian Brown, graciously read the manuscript and offered helpful suggestions which improved the content and exposition of the thesis. I also want to thank my typist, Mrs. Joyce Partin. She was a careful typist, a conscientious editor for style requirements, and genially retyped the manuscript as improvements were made.

Finally I want to thank my children, Sarah and Daniel Fults, for sharing their mother with this project for five years in their early life. The emotional support and personal encouragement of these many friends allowed me to completed my education.

Publication of This Book

I acknowledge the work of Judy Hutchinson, Director of Evaluation and Training, at World Humanitarian Aid (WHA) during the time of this study. The participatory evaluation process was her vision. Along with her staff, they designed the evaluation process, the training curriculum for WHA's staff, and participatory techniques used to conduct individual project evaluations. I appreciate her support within WHA for the approvals to conduct this research, for access to WHA's staff and procedures while conducting the research, and for complete freedom to analyze the accounting and management issue of interest to me. I am grateful to her and to WHA for their cooperation and candor.

In transforming this dissertation into a book, I appreciate the assistance of all the colleagues at Humboldt State University who gave me assistance. In particular, I thank Judy Kirsch, our typographer, for creating this manuscript graciously and skillfully. My colleague, Peter Kenyon, read the manuscript and offer helpful suggestions which improved the content and exposition of the book. I thank Patty Olson and Maureen Reiner for preparing Appendix B. Joan Grytness gave me advice and help with graphic design. I am grateful to my family, friends, colleagues, and students for allowing me the time to prepare this book. Their support, encouragement, and tolerance allowed the book to become a reality.

Finally, I give God glory for the miracle of this project, from its inception twelve years ago, to its publication as a book, and for how it is used in the future.

How Participatory Evaluation Research Affects the Management Control Process of a Multinational Nonprofit Organization

CHAPTER I

Introduction

Kenneth Boulding once wrote that the earth is a spaceship traveling through time with a limited supply of resources. Man has been given the task to manage these resources for their greatest potential benefit and then distribute the wealth so all mankind may survive and prosper. Multinational organizations are the dominant emerging institutional form, and they play a major role in the distribution and re-distribution of the world's resources.

Multinational non-profit organizations are a major subsection of these institutions. In both the public and private sector, they provide goods and services for the creation and redistribution of wealth.

Public sector non-profit organizations are the largest and most well known. The World Bank and the International Monetary Fund (IMF) work in mutual cooperation to secure funds from first world member nations and provide loan funds and banking services to developing nations. The World Bank finances high priority development projects, provides technical assistance, and facilitates economic dialogue and discussions for 144 member countries. In the poorest countries they make loans for macro-development projects at concessional rates; in more developed countries, they promote emerging private enterprise through equity participation programs and loans.[1]

The IMF provides funds for individual countries having short-term and medium term payment difficulties, and it works to improve the economic relationships between member nations. In order to provide these services, very large organizations with complex operating structures have been created. The Managing Director of the IMF supervised a staff of over 1500 people, in 1984.[2]

Likewise, the United Nations oversees the funding and operations of subsidiary redistributive institutions. These include the United Nations Educational, Scientific, and Cultural Organization (UNESCO) and the United Nations Children's Fund (UNICEF). UNESCO promotes collaboration between 160 member nations to extend, improve and promote education, to facilitate international cooperation in scientific projects, and to disseminate cultural information between countries. Its 1984 budget was $374,410,000 (all amounts are given in U.S. dollars); its administration and oversight duties are conducted on four continents.[3] UNICEF develops activities aimed at improving the quality of life for children and mothers in developing countries. During 1983 it operated in over 110 countries, providing basic services such as health care, nutrition, sanitation, and education for over 1,300,000,000 children and their mothers. It is funded by contributions from governments, private organizations, and individuals; in 1984 its budget was $297,000,000.[4] These are but two examples of the very massive U.N. organizational structure.

Individual governments provide aid and assistance to other nations through their own agencies as well. The United States government funds various projects and programs through the Agency for International Development (U.S. AID). Created in 1961, the agency makes non-military loans and grants to developing, third world nations. Its strategic objectives are to address severe economic problems, health, population planning, energy, and education. To accomplish these objectives it supports traditional aid programs, development of private enterprise, transfer of technology, long-range development planning, self-help programs, and private investment in development.

In fiscal year 1984-85, its budget was $5.6 billion dollars. The agency is headed by an Administrator and a Deputy Administrator in Washington, D.C.. Field operations are directed by Assistant Administrators in four regional bureaus and carried out by field missions in various countries. In 1984, the agency had over 4,850 employees in Washington, D.C. and over 3,500 employees overseas.[5]

Private sector agencies are smaller and perhaps less well known, but they too provide goods and services for the creation and redistribution of wealth. The International Red Cross is located in Geneva, Switzerland and operates throughout the world to provide emergency aid, relief, rehabilitation, and public services. In the United

States, the American Red Cross has headquarters in Washington, D.C.; its administration is coordinated by four field offices which are segmented into sixty divisions. In these divisions, the work is carried out by 3,100 local chapters. Each member country of Red Cross International has a similar organizational structure to coordinate their work efforts.[6]

Other private agencies administer their work in one country and perform their services throughout the world. The Oxford Committee for Famine Relief (OXFAM) began as a small group of individuals concerned for people in Greece after World War II. In 1984, it was funding over 1850 projects in 77 countries. The projects which it funds provide immediate, vital disaster relief and support long-term development projects.

OXFAM funds projects carried out through appropriate, local agencies. The international headquarters is located in Oxford, England, where the Directors, executives, and administrative staff direct the operations. Field Directors in individual countries oversee national funding operations using local assistants and technical directors.[7]

All of these institutions share some common characteristics. Their organizational units are geographically dispersed in several nations. Their operations are functionally diverse; they provide many different goods and services at the same time, each of which may require a different specialization or comparative advantage. Their individual projects and programs must be culturally contextual to be utilized and responsibly accepted by the host country and their people. Furthermore, none of these organizations function in an exchange environment to measure and assess their performance. Nevertheless, they all need a management control process and a management information system to coherently guide their organizational performance. Moreover, non-profit organizations operating in the United States also need to provide annual published financial statements reporting their resources, obligations, accumulated funds, and operating performance.

PROBLEM ORIENTATION

Considerable attention has been given to the management control and the financial accounting processes of non-profit organizations.

Several desirable, pervasive characteristics are well established in the accounting literature.

In 1966, the American Accounting Association published *A Statement of Basic Accounting Theory* (ASOBAT) in which it identifies internal management as a primary user of accounting information. It states,

> The objective of accounting for internal use is to provide information to persons within an organization that enables them to make informed judgments and effective decisions which further the organization's goals. These judgments and decisions relate to a large and widely varied collection of issues and problems, and the information needed for their proper resolution is extensive and enormously diverse in nature and in classification.[8]

Management must make decisions and judgments about both planned and unplanned occurrences. The monograph goes on to divide the management function into the planning process and the control process, which together provide a degree of structure to guide the decisions and actions management must take. A variety of information is needed to aid in this decision making. The characteristics of the planning and control processes have had considerable influence on accounting information.

> The complete and systematic manner in which accounting has responded to the requirements of organization control has caused the information it furnishes to be widely used but at the same time severely criticized for being inappropriate to all the uses it has been put. Planning and decision making is one aspect of management and feedback and control the other. Information on what has occurred and what areas need investigation is useful for considering what succeeding actions should be, but it is not necessarily the best guide in the evaluation of possible alternatives.[9]

Thus, while accounting should respond to the evolving needs of management for information, the characteristics of that information should remain relevance, verifiability, freedom from bias, and quantifiability. In assessing the future needs of management for information, the Association contended that accounting must continue to evolve and incorporate new types of information.

> Examining the needs of management for quantitative information reveals both the importance of the information produced through the conventional accounting system and the necessity for expanding this concept to include information that meets the standards of accounting but which is often viewed as falling outside of the conventional model. . . . Although the conventional accounting model serves the financial control functions of management reasonably well, new developments in technology are altering the organizational structure with consequent effects upon the control process and the information it requires . . . There is no question but that accounting information will continue to be involved in these and in other mentioned developments. The major problem is that of providing an orderly growth toward the future without losing the value of established practices and the lessons of the past.[10]

ASOBAT established qualitative characteristics for accounting information and demonstrated that these characteristics applied to all accounting information, whether it is intended for external or for internal users. The study argued that orderly growth could only occur through research efforts to identify, measure, and classify new elements of accounting information.

In 1973, the Trueblood Report on the *Objectives of Financial Statements*, which was commissioned by the American Institute of Public Accountants (AICPA), incorporated non-profit organizations in their study. They concluded that the objective of accounting information for both profit and non-profit organizations was the same: to provide information that serves users' needs.

The Trueblood Commission argued that decision-makers are interested in predicting, comparing, and evaluating benefits and sacrifices of alternative actions in terms of their amount, timing, and uncertainty. Even though non-profit organizations seek nonmonetary benefits, and these benefits are not easily quantified, the decision process is essentially the same for both external and internal uses.

The Commission went on to contend that useful indicators of performance for non-profit organizations are those based upon the organization's goals. These will vary widely and be difficult to measure, but accounting information should be expanded to provide indicators from which external users can compare and evaluate the organization's performance. They suggested that accounting information should provide users needed information for assessing: (1) past attainment of the organization's goals, (2) the status of present efforts to attain goals, and (3) the probability of future goal attainment.

> Managers of government and eleemosynary organizations are also accountable for their performance and goal attainment. . . . An objective of financial statements for government and not-for-profit organizations is to provide information useful for evaluating effectiveness of the management of resources in achieving the organization's goals. Performance measures should be quantified in terms of identified goals.[11]

The Trueblood report established that the accounting information of non-profit organizations had the same objectives as accounting information from other organizations. These organizations have special needs due to the nature of their business; but the nature of accounting information should expand to incorporate alternative forms of reporting for these entities while maintaining its qualitative characteristics.

In 1980, the Financial Accounting Standards Board (FASB) set forth its Statements of Financial Accounting Concepts. The qualitative characteristics of accounting information are presented in Concepts Statement No. 2. The Board states that all financial reporting is concerned in varying degrees with decision making. This central role assigned to decision making leads straight to the overriding criterion by which all accounting choices must be judged: usefulness for decision making. Finally, the Board contends that relevance and reliability are the two primary qualities that make accounting information useful for decision making.

> The primary qualities are that accounting information shall be relevant and reliable. If either of these qualities is completely missing, the information will not be useful. . . . To be relevant, information must be timely and it must have predictive value or feedback value or both. To be reliable, information must have representational faithfulness, and it must be verifiable and neutral . . . comparability, including consistency, is a secondary quality that interacts with

relevance and reliability to contribute to the usefulness of the information.[12]

In Concepts Statement No. 4, Objectives of Financial Reporting by Nonbusiness Organizations, the Board extends these characteristic to non-profit organizations. The Board argues that three distinguishing characteristics heavily influence the operations of these entities:

1. Receipts of significant amounts of resources from resource providers who do not expect to receive either repayment or economic benefits proportionate to resources provided.
2. Operating purposes that are other than to provide goods or services at a profit or profit equivalent.
3. Absence of defined ownership interest, that can be sold, transferred, or redeemed, or that convey resources in the event of liquidation of the organization.[13]

These distinctions require that the objectives of financial reporting be expanded to cover a non-business relationship between providers and users of accounting information. Those who provide resources to a non-profit organization have a dual interest in the current services which the organization provides and in its continuing ability to provide services. However, these organizations have no single established indicator of performance, like profit, so other indicators of performance are needed. In addition these organizations are not subject to the efficiency test of direct competition in markets. Therefore the Board argues,

> Other kinds of controls introduced to compensate for the lesser influence of markets are a major characteristic of their operations and affect the objectives of their financial reporting. Controls, such as formal budgets and donor restrictions on the use of resources, give managers a special responsibility to ensure compliance. Information about departures from those mandates that may impinge upon an organization's financial performance or its ability to provide a satisfactory level of service is important in assessing how well managers have discharged their stewardship responsibilities.[14]

Therefore the Board established three additional objectives of financial reporting for non-business organizations. Besides providing information that is useful in making rational resource allocation decisions, non-business organizations should provide information: (1) useful in assessing the services provided and the ability to continue to provide services, (2) useful in assessing management's stewardship and performance, and (3) about economic resources, obligations, net resources, and changes to these.

Two indicators of performance were also established for non-businesses. One is information about the nature of and relationship between inflows and outflows of resources. The second is information about service efforts and accomplishments. Finally the Board concludes,

> Information about service accomplishments in terms of goods or services produced (outputs) and of program results may enhance significantly the value of information provided about service efforts. However, the ability to measure service accomplishments, particularly program results, is generally underdeveloped. At present, such measures may not satisfy the qualitative characteristics of accounting information identified in Concepts Statement 2. Research should be conducted to determine if measures of service accomplishments with the requisite characteristics of relevance, reliability, comparability, verifiability, and neutrality can be developed. If such measures are developed, they should be included in financial reports. In the absence of measures suitable for financial reporting, information about service accomplishments may be furnished by managers' explanations and sources other than financial reporting[15]

Evaluation research conducted on projects and programs is another source of information about service efforts and accomplishment in a non-profit organization. The introduction of international and multiple intra-national operations compounds the Board's appeal to introduce a service accomplishment element into financial reporting on non-profit organizations. In the multinational case, financial reporting must be relevant to local and national information users as well as to executive administrators located at a central headquarters. The operative question is: can evaluation research serve as a surrogate market to measure and assess operating performance?

Before the value of including evaluation research as a service effort and accomplishments measure in published financial reports can be determined, prerequisite conditions internal to the organization must be present. The evaluation research process used by a non-profit organization must be functioning effectively; in addition, the information produced on evaluation research findings must be processed and recycled by the organization's reporting systems; and finally, the conditions necessary for control must be present in the evaluation of the process.

Then evaluation research findings could not only be used to assess performance but they could also be used to evaluate decisions, thereby allowing managers to improve goals, perceptions, and performance in their responsiveness to various environments.

This dissertation will study one form of evaluation research, participatory evaluation; and it will focus on how participatory evaluation affects the management control process in a multinational non-profit organization. Knowledge acquisition and theory building for incorporating evaluation research findings into the control function of a non-profit organization's management process should provide a general frame of reference from which future accounting practice can evolve, be evaluated, and set guidelines for new management and accounting procedures. Providing initial descriptions and measurements and identifying operating relationships are the first steps to providing greater objectivity for subsequent research that seeks to determine how evaluation research can be incorporated as a service accomplishment element in accounting information and financial reporting.

PURPOSE OF THE DISSERTATION

The need to incorporate service accomplishment elements into the published accounting information of non-profit organizations has been established by the Financial Accounting Standards Board, in Concepts Statement 4. In the absence of a market environment, surrogates must be found from which to assess the organization's performance. The Board stated,

> . . . the ability to measure service accomplishments, particularly program results, is generally undeveloped. . . . Research should be conducted to determine if measures of

service accomplishment with the requisite characteristics of relevance, reliability, comparability, verifiability, and neutrality can be developed.[16]

The purposes of this dissertation are to conduct initial research on participatory evaluation, to examine how it affects the management control process of a multinational non-profit organization, and to discuss if it has the potential to be a service accomplishment element in published financial statements on non-profit organizations.

To accomplish these objectives, the following sub-objectives have been established:

1. To review contemporary literature and related research in order to assess the current relationship between evaluation research and the management process.
2. To study a multinational, non-profit organization in which a participatory evaluation process is being used to determine if relevant and reliable assessments are being produced by the process.
3. To examine if the characteristics attributed to self-control in the management literature are present in a participatory evaluation research process. These characteristics would help identify the operational relationships present in participatory evaluation and help develop an interdisciplinary theory of service accomplishment in non-profit organizations between accounting and evaluation.

STATEMENT OF THE PROBLEMS

This dissertation addresses two questions: Can evaluation research function as a surrogate market in non-profit organizations to measure, value, and assess the goods and services they provide? And second, can the findings from an evaluation process be incorporated as a service accomplishment element into the accounting information published by non-profit organizations? Various evaluation research models have been developed. Scientific evaluation research models use experimental and quasi-experimental research designs to assess program results. Pluralistic evaluation research models use behavioral research designs and incorporate various stakeholders in the program to assess program results.

Participatory evaluation research is a pluralistic form of evaluation which incorporates more pragmatism than other models. In participatory evaluation, the evaluation research design and implementing process are developed, used, and reported by the host community members and the intervening organization's staff, without the inclusion of an evaluation research specialist.

The desirable characteristics of relevance and verifiability should be enhanced by such a process. However the characteristics of reliability and comparability would be in doubt when no absolutes are invoked on the process. The pragmatism of John Dewey makes inquiry the essence of logic while truth is found in the current human experience. Here human beings and their immediate context occupy the imagination and it is the power of the community that is valuable. This philosophy of instrumentalism propels the strong sense of the collective power of human communities, absent of constant or absolute values.

Bertrand Russell warned of the limits of pure pragmatism, "In all this I feel a grave danger, the danger of what might be called cosmic impiety."[17] Most probably, however, the combined values of all constituent groups would limit the evaluation parameters considered acceptable. Thus the upper limit of what is included in the evaluation process would be set by the values in the community and in the intervening organization.

Therefore, the first major problem addressed by this research is related to the abilities of host community members to perform evaluation research functions. Allowing stakeholders to assess their own environment, identify needs, and determine an action program, opens the organization to its total environment. It also allows intercourse and reciprocation between the organization and its constituents. These people have the requisite knowledge to determine if the goods and services provided by the program are accomplishing desirable results; but can they adequately carry out technical evaluation tasks? If they can, then the next issue is whether the organization can capitalize on that knowledge and the resulting evaluation findings by incorporating the evaluation information into their management process and information system.

The second major problem addressed by this research is related to the capability of a management process to incorporate indigenous evaluation research findings into its reporting and control functions.

Management processes provide structure and impetus to the management tasks of initiation, coordination, and control. Structure often requires rigidity and standardization. Events must be classified in taxonomies or quantified by measurement to be included in the reporting system. Therefore, two important issues to investigate are whether a management information and control system can be flexible enough to incorporate alternative forms of information, or alternatively, if constituents' activities in programs can be quantitatively measured for inclusion in a formal management system.

The third major problem addressed by this research is related to the ultimate issue of self-control. Letting stakeholders establish their own goals and assess their own outcomes allows them to practice management by objectives. Each individual and work group sets their plans and objectives relative to the overall objectives of the community and the organization. Therefore, this initial examination of participatory evaluation and its effects on the management control process investigates if the benefits of management by objectives and self-control are present in the process.

Only if all three of these questions can be answered affirmatively, would participatory evaluation research be considered a potential service accomplishment element for accounting information. Therefore, the initial problem for accountants is to determine how participatory evaluation affects the management control process in a multinational non-profit organization by seeking answers to these prerequisite questions. Only when it is ascertained (1) that the participatory evaluation process is functioning at the indigenous locations, (2) that information from the process is being incorporated into the management control process and information system for distribution and utilization, and finally, 3) that self-control is occurring in both the indigenous location and the organizational hierarchy, can any further potentials for the process be discussed.

To begin examining these problems, Chapter II will explore the theories underlying these problems and their critical issues and demonstrate that a difference in perceptions exists on evaluation research as a tool for assessment and control between several dominant evaluation and management control models. This research seeks to reconcile those differences by studying, acquiring knowledge of, and beginning to measure the common elements between participatory evaluation research and the management control process. This reconciliation will be used to show the potential for evaluation research findings to augment financial information in organizational reporting for non-profit entities.

LIMITATIONS

A study of this type is subject to many limitations of both scope and results. The scope limitations include the specification of one type of evaluation research, the restriction of the study to one multinational organization, albeit large, and the inherent problems of field-based research. Boundaries on interpreting the results were imposed by both the inductive nature of the study and methodology limitations. These issues will be discussed further in Chapter III.

ORGANIZATION OF THE PAPER

This dissertation consists of seven chapters, as well as a bibliography and appendices. In Chapter I the elements of the empirical research are presented. These elements include a problem orientation, purposes of the dissertation, statement of the problems, limitations, and the organization of the paper.

Chapter II is a review of the contemporary literature. It attempts to synthesize modern management, evaluation, and management process theories as they relate to the management control process of a multinational non-profit organization. Open-system and rationality theories are discussed with some of the assessment decision implications for the management process. Evaluation models are reviewed to show the alternative approaches to this specialty. The philosophy of management by objectives and self-control is reviewed to show its relationships to participatory evaluation. Approaches to the management process and current alternative models are reviewed for their perceptions on evaluative assessments and control.

Chapter III outlines the research methodology utilized. The discussion of methodology includes general analysis, research setting, research design, research observations, research instrument construction, data collection, data analysis, summary of the methodology, and conclusions.

In Chapters IV and Chapter V the findings of the questionnaires are presented. The compilation of the data collected are displayed and the results of the statistical analysis are discussed. Chapter VI analyzes these findings to address the research questions asked in Chapter II. The concluding chapter, Chapter VII, summarizes the results of the dissertation, the emperical propositions for operational relationships of the participatory evaluation process, with recommendations for possible future research.

NOTES

1. *The International Year Book and Statesman's Who's Who*, (West Sussex, England: Thomas Skinner Directories, 1985), pp. XXIX-XXXI.

2. John Paxton, *The Statesman's Year Book*, (New York, New York: St. Martin's Press, 1985), pp. 18-20.

3. Paxton, pp. 15-16.

4. Paxton, pp. 9-12.

5. *The International Yearbook*, p. XXXIII.

6. *Encyclopedia Americana*, (Danbury, Conneticutt: Grolier Incorporated, 1985), Vol. 23, pp. 303-4.

7. *The International Year Book*, p. XXXIII.

8. American Accounting Association, *A Statement of Basic Accounting Theory*, (Sarasota, Florida: American Accounting Association, 1966), p. 38.

9. Ibid, p. 51.

10. Ibid, pp. 56-62.

11. *Objectives of Financial Statements*, (New York, New York: American Institute of Certified Public Accountants, 1973), pp. 50-51.

12. Financial Accounting Standards Board, *Accounting Standards Original Pronouncements July 1973-June 1,1984*, (New York, New York: McGraw-Hill Book Company, 1984), p. 4047.

13. Ibid, pp. 4114-4115.

14. Ibid, p. 4116.

15. Ibid, p. 4124.

16. Ibid, p. 4124.

17. Bertrand Russell, *A History of Western Philosophy*, (New York, New York: Simon and Schuster, 1945), p. 828.

CHAPTER II

Review of Literature and Related Research

Reviews of the contemporary literature concerning management theory, evaluation research, and the accounting literature devoted to the management control process were undertaken. The primary emphasis was placed upon formulating an understanding of management control concepts within the parameters suggested by modern evaluation and management thinking.

The first section of this chapter is devoted to open system theory. Contemporary management literature contends that the remainder of this century will be a dynamic time of adjustment and change. Open-systems theory suggests that organizations can be managed to adapt to these changes. Information flow and the decision process are central elements in open-systems theory. Throughout this study, emphasis is placed on these two elements for several reasons.

Principally, open system logic suggests rationality theory which builds upon different assumptions than traditional economic and management models; these assumptions have a profound effect upon how decisions are made and organizations are managed. Additionally, different values and different normative possibilities emerge for information used by management when viewing organizations from an open systems perspective; these new possibilities affect greatly the management control process. Lastly, open systems theory has an impact upon research designs appropriate for studying new techniques introduced into management systems.

The description of open systems thinking, including the underlying assumptions, value structures, and decision rationale, lays the groundwork for a synthesis of systems thinking with evaluation research and the management control process. This synthesis is important for a full analysis of participatory evaluation as a management tool. This conclusion is tentatively reached because:

1. Participative evaluation is an information feedback mechanism which:
   a. allows an organization to be aware of its diverse environmental settings
   b. acts as a corrective device to aid in keeping an organization on course.
2. This corrective mechanism may help ensure organizational responsiveness, growth, and survival in dynamic environments.

The second section of this chapter discusses evaluation research. Emphasis is placed upon understanding evaluation research: what it is, how it relates to other evaluative methods for management control, and the alternative sources of data and documentation suggested for this work. The possibility for pluralistic evaluation methods to allow self-assessment and self-control is then introduced.

The correspondence between participatory evaluation and self-control in management theory is discussed in the third section. A homogeny of the benefits attributed to self-control and decentralized operations by Drucker is presented. The possibilities for participatory evaluation methods to allow self-assessment and self-control are then explored, with examples from contemporary studies. The implications for the management control process are then discussed with difficulties cited from publications and case studies.

The fourth section presents Robert Anthony's framework for a planning and control system; several alternatives and modifications from the management accounting literature are discussed.Different approaches to evaluation in the various functions of the management control process and decision making are described. The need for the management control process of a multinational organization to encompass both providing and using various forms of information is described.

In the final section of this chapter, attention is given to why the current study explores a new management technique through empirical research.

OPEN SYSTEMS THEORY

One purpose of this chapter is to explore the importance of environmental considerations to organizational survival and growth. Greater understanding and appreciation of how the organization and its environment interrelate to one another will help us understand how participatory evaluation affects the management control process of a multinational organization. To begin the discussion of open-systems theory, the contemporary management literature is reviewed to identify major trends facing organizations.Then the open system concept is discussed with its implications for value-rational choice based on a variety of possible norms. This section will conclude with a discussion of how participatory evaluation may be a partial solution in dealing with dynamic organizational environments.

Contemporary Management Literature

Currently, the relationship of organizations to people and society has captured the popular press. *In Search of Excellence* has sold five million copies in fifteen languages.[18] Its sequel, *A Passion For Excellence*, was published in May 1985 and gave several ideas for engendering human characteristics of passion, persistence, zest, energy, care, love, and enthusiasm into an organization as sources of long-term distinction.[19] These books identify successful organizations as responsive, adaptive, innovative, and entrepreneurial.

John Naisbitt, in his best seller, *Megatrends*, presents major ways the United States is restructuring. He identifies the critical restructuring as:

> (1) We have shifted from an industrial society to one based on the creation and distribution of information. (2) We are moving in the dual direction of high-tech/high touch, matching each new technology with a compensatory human response. (3) No longer do we have the luxury of operating within an isolated, self-sufficient, national economic system; we now must acknowledge that we are part of a global economy. We have begun to let go of the idea that the United States is and must remain the world's industrial leader as we move on to other tasks. (4) We are restructuring from a society run by short-term considerations and rewards in favor

of dealing with things in much longer-term time frames. (5) In cities and states, in small organizations and sub-divisions, we have rediscovered the ability to act innovatively and achieve results—from the bottom up. (6) We are shifting from institutional help to more self-reliance in all aspects of our lives. (7) We are discovering that the framework of representative democracy has become obsolete in an era of instantaneously shared information. (8) We are giving up our dependence on hierarchial structures in favor of informal networks. This will be especially important to the business community. . . . [20]

The essence of these trends is not confined to the United States. The World Bank, in its *1983 World Development Report*, examines the economic, political, social, and managerial difficulties facing most developing countries. Over the past two decades, governments in most developing countries have played an activist role in development, building infrastructure and often engaging directly in productive activities. These policies have been critical in determining the environment in which the public and private sectors operate. Much of this activism has produced encouraging progress; however, in relation to expectation and potential, progress in many counties has been unsatisfactory.

In a hostile world environment of modest growth, high interest rates, and fluctuating exchange rates, the macroeconomic policies of developing countries will continue to be critical in ensuring price stability, balance of payments equilibrium, and conditions conducive to growth.[21]

The report goes on to emphasize the need for careful management of long-term development: the need to have efficient, price setting markets; the need to develop human resources and reverse the "brain-drain" of skilled workers leaving their native countries; and the need to develop comprehensive management systems which identify and reward performance.

In *The Changing World of the Executive* Peter Drucker similarly outlines five separate yet interrelated threats or obstacles facing executives, which can be turned into opportunities for developing an interdisciplinary theory between evaluation and accounting, especially in a multinational setting.

First, there is presently a fundamental discontinuity in technology. Formerly, technology was well described by mechanical models, but modern technology is based on a biological model. Information is the formative principle of all processes, and organizations need to change their structures and management processes to accommodate information driven technology.

Secondly, there is a major demographic discontinuity in population patterns. In developing countries there is a tremendous increase in the number of young people. Their survival will depend on creating jobs when they have very little training or formal education. Management procedures need to be simple enough for safe and reliable use by this labor force, and management techniques need to facilitate on-the-job training and learning through non-formal educational experiences.

Thirdly, there is an economic discontinuity of increasing economic integration in a world divided by national fragmentation. The emergence of the world economy as the dominant economy has produced new dynamics in economic markets. An organization's policies and its management process need to guide productive activities on a global basis. In a world market, innovations, efficiencies, and service market share will be found in both the developed and underdeveloped countries; all the functions of the management control process need to adapt themselves to various contexts, cultures, and conditions. Both for profit and non-profit entities need to organize themselves to use indigenous information effectively in their production technology to allow employees all over the world to work together for their common corporate good.

Further, economic theory and economic policy must increase the share of wealth that goes into savings for capital formation in contrast to the prevailing practice of increasing present consumption. In developing countries where the need for immediate consumption is greatest, management practices need to require economic savings and reinvestment in all resources and factors of production. The management control process needs to allocate these resources to the locations where they are needed most and where they will be utilized most productively throughout the world.

Finally, there is a discontinuity between the need for a working economic theory and a working political theory.Under the current state of economic and political theory, they are not integrated and therefore not workable.

> Business is thus caught between two realities. In its own work—that is, in the economic sphere—the world is becoming increasingly integrated. Today even a small business has to operate in the world economy, is dependent on exports, has to go multinational, has to manage foreign exchange, and so on. And yet, in its other reality—that of the political sphere—the world is becoming increasingly splintered, increasingly, protectionist, increasingly nationalist."[22]

Drucker concludes that in a time of redirection, in a world society of organizations, in relationships of interdependence, "it is the mutuality of obligations that creates true equality, regardless of differences in rank, wealth, or power."[23] Mutual obligations to one another will create new roles for workers, managers, and organizations. Workers need to become more independent, innovative, initiatory, self-controlled, and self-confident about governing themselves. Managers must, correspondingly, begin to orchestrate, direct, facilitate, serve, and protect these workers and their environment. Organizations need to evolve into more flexible, participative, democratic, entrepreneurial networks that are responsive to their constituents, that adapt to their environments, and that are aware of all their relationships. William Christopher, in his book, *Management for the 1980's*, argued that executives must lead their organizations to develop a management process and a management information system which: (1) establishes networks of integrative planning and programming to cope with transnational problems, (2) develops budgeting systems that translate plans into resources allocated for action, and (3) incorporates performance measurement and achievement reporting for control.[24] Such expanded concepts of organizations as open systems which integrate productive tasks worldwide will demand new techniques for management as well.

Open Systems Thinking

Several different perceptions of open systems have been proposed within General Systems Theory. Ludwig von Bertalanffy, a biologist, is considered the originator of general systems theory. "The notion of a 'system' being defined as any arrangement or combination, as of parts or elements, in a whole, applies to a cell, a human being, a society, as well as to an atom, a planet or a galaxy."[25] Kenneth Boulding structures nine levels of systems and describes open systems as a self-maintaining structure in "the midst of a throughput of materials and energy."[26] Organizations are envisioned as "living (organic) systems," open to their environment, and maintaining themselves by exchanging materials and energy in an input, processing, output relationship. For the purpose of this study, a multinational non-profit organization is perceived to be an open system of interrelated sub-systems working together for a common goal.

Common Characteristics of Open Systems In Multinational Organizations

The view of open systems maintaining themselves through "constant commerce with their environment" was applied by Katz and Kahn to social organizations.[27] They describe social organization as a structuring of repetitive events which takes place when a collection of human beings, machines, money, and other resources combine in a productive process. It is a contrived means or tool, created by men to allow organizations to survive, adapt, and grow through integration and transformation.

Open systems both import some forms of energy from and export other forms to their external environment. The multinational non-profit organization is continually dependent upon supplies of resources from other institutions, people, or materials. They create new products, process materials, train people, or provide services which are then exported into the environment. Multinational organizations furnish sources of energy for the repetition of activity cycles by the goods and services they exchange with the external environment worldwide.

To survive, open systems must arrest the entropic process; they must acquire negative entropy. Since multinational non-profit organizations can import more resources from their environment than they expend, they can store resources to improve their own survival position while at the same time acquiring a comfortable margin of operation from efficient use of the resources they consume.

Organizations can retard the natural decaying process of their entity by economic savings and reinvestment of stored resources. Information is the impulse, or wave of excitation, transmitted through an organization. The management process allows administrators to gather information and then respond to the stimuli they are receiving. This information furnishes signals to the organization about the environment and about its own functioning in relation to the environment. Positive, negative or new feedback enables an organization to correct or to create a new direction for its course. Multinational non-profit organizations can develop intelligence feedback functions to acquire information about changes in environmental forces and internal operations to ensure future stability, survival, and growth.

Survival of large, complex, multinational organizations is characterized by a steady state of importing energy continuously in the form of resources from the external environment and exporting products or services continuously to the external environment. The equilibrium which these complex organizations approach is quasistationary; adjustments and counter-adjustments approximate rather than equate one another, allowing the excess resources to be lost or stored. They incorporate external resources essential to survival within their boundaries, resulting in expansion and growth.

Such an organization grows by adding more ways to acquire funding resources and by adding more and more services of the same essential type it already provides. This process continues until quantitative growth calls for supportive, specialized activities, necessary for the organization's new, larger size. There is a point where these quantitative changes produce qualitative differences in the functioning of the organization. Just as a small college which triples in size is no longer the same institution, a child support program which expands to include adults is no longer the same aid or development program.

These organizations have moved in the direction of specialization and elaboration; multiplication and elaboration of roles with greater specialization and differentiation of functions is needed to support their activities. In general terms, von Bertalanffy calls this growth "progressive mechanizations,";[28] applying it to a multinational organization shows how managing growth becomes very difficult. An organization achieves an early steady state by dynamic interaction of various forces in its environment. Later development entails the use of a regulatory feedback mechanism for communications, which diminishes its opportunities for uniform potential throughout its many parts. Von Bertalanffy describes it this way,

> ...biological, psychological, or social—are governed by dynamic interaction of their components; later on, fixed arrangements and conditions of constraint are established

which render the system and its parts more efficient, but also gradually diminish and eventually abolish its equipotentiality.[29]

Fortunately, an organization can reach its final or current state of operation from different initial conditions and by a variety of paths. Therefore feedback and adjustments will continue; multinational non-profit organizations use coordination and control as adjusting mechanisms to adapt to their environments, recognizing that there is more than one way to produce a given outcome.[30]

Paradoxically, open systems theory suggests contradictory conditions for an organization: (1) a stable operating environment for efficiency; and (2) responsive change to new conditions in the environment for effectiveness, survival, and growth. The previous section of this chapter contended that major consideration should be given to the global nature of environments to explain how organizations are changing, and to the appropriate responses by multinational organizations to current conditions. Von Bertalanffy's statement that differentiation processes cause an open system first to become ". . . more efficient, but gradually diminish and eventually abolish its equipotentiality," is both poignant and relevant to the state of multinational non-profit organizations at a time of pervasive social redirections. It is vital that their efforts to "do more" result in purposeful growth rather than the mere expansion of bureaucracy. Therefore, these enterprises are looking for management techniques to "tap" their innovative, adaptive, entrepreneurial potentials on a global scale.

Theory of Rational Choice

Central to open-systems theory is the importance of feedback, decisions and control. Choice and decision-making are the very core of the management process. The sub-systems of an open-system enterprise are a chain or inter-linked pattern of decision-making points. Management actions to influence and control an organization are means to put their decisions into effect. Decisions were described by Herbert Simon like this:

> A real life decision involves some goals or values, some facts about the environment, and some inferences drawn from the values and facts. The goals and values may be simple or

> complex, consistent or contradictory; the facts may be real or
> supposed, based on observation or the reports of others; the
> inferences may be valid or spurious. The whole process may
> be viewed, metaphorically, as a process of 'reasoning,' where
> the values and facts serve as premises...without being
> bounded by the assumptions of rationality that limit the
> classical theory of choice.[31]

Rationality is seldom complete. It is limited by an individual's, or a group's, subconscious skills, habits, reflexes, values, concept of purpose, and by the relevance of their knowledge. The aim of the organization is rationality, but it is limited or bounded rationality because of the limits of the people who make decisions. In actual practice, ". . . rationality is concerned with the selection of preferred behavior alternatives in terms of some system of values whereby the consequences of behavior can be evaluated."[32]

Simon's theory of bounded rationality led others to develop contingency theories of decision-making which try to match decisions and behaviors to situations, rather than trying to specify one best way to respond to all situations. Finding a satisfactory alternative to a decision, rather than an optimal alternative, is imperfect but more efficient. "Most human decision-making, whether individual or organizational, is concerned with the discovery and selection of satisfactory alternatives; only in exceptional cases is it concerned with the discovery and selection of optimal alternatives."[33]

Another way to describe decision-making is as a learning process in which each decision experience contributes to the next. Organizations exist in an uncertain and unpredictable environment, they must maintain a viable coalition of members, and they suffer from limitations on the amount and correctness of the information available to them. Therefore, Cyert and March argued that an adaptive rational system of decision making will be used by people in organizations.

Adaptive rationality theory contends that decisions are based on an exhaustive list of environmental variables organized into a set of rational concepts. Decisions will adapt to their irrational environment because they are:(1) quasi-resolutions of conflict rather than a consistent effort to manage conflicts; (2) avoiding uncertainty rather than confronting and attempting to control it; (3) problematic searches responding to stimuli for a solution rather than possibility explorations;

(4) organizational learning experiences for acceptable behavior rather than deliberate, anticipatory moves to control the environment.[34]

Building on the work of Simon, March, and Cyert, Thompson argued that decisions are made in organizations by individuals under societal norms of rationality. He contended that organizations, ". . . do nothing except as individual members within them act."[35] Each person is a unique individual. Each has a different heredity, experiences, behavior patterns, and attitudes. The individual is brought up and exists within a social culture which prescribes or proscribes some form of action.

Within a given society the culture predetermines large areas of behavior so administration can take these for granted. Beyond these, managers create internal work environments where employees can exercise discretion and judgment. Individuals will act in the way that seems best to meet their aspirations, standards, knowledge, and beliefs about cause/effect relationships in their world, within the recognized constraints of the organization. Thompson's argument is especially cogent for multinational organizations. Decisions concerning one organization are made in different contexts and cultures. The societal norms of rationality will not be the same in all the locations where decisions are made. Thus Thompson set forth a matrix to organize different types of decisions, and he suggested four strategies classifying decisions.

Preferences regarding possible outcome

		Certainty	Uncertainty
Beliefs about cause/effect relationships	Certainty	Computational Strategy	Compromise Strategy
	Uncertainty	Judgmental Strategy	Inspirational Strategy

Figure 1: Thompson's Decision Matrix

Thompson describes his decision matrix this way:

> . . . where there is certainty regarding both causation and outcome performance, we will refer to the judgmental strategy for decision making. Where the situation is reversed and there is certainty regarding cause/effect but uncertainty regarding outcome preferences, the issue can be regarded as calling for a compromise strategy for decision making. Finally, where there is uncertainty on both dimensions, we will speak of the inspirational strategy for decision making, if indeed any decision is forthcoming.[36]

Important, responsive, strategic decisions always involve uncertainty and require some form of rationality. The management process is an overall concept guiding the total direction and control of the whole organization in its societal context. Complex, purposive organizations are natural systems subject to rationality norms ". . . and the significant phenomena of administration arise precisely because of the inconsistencies of that duality."[37] Natural systems should be self-sustaining, and administrators of both for-profit and non-profit organizations establish the rationality norms prevalent in their organization.

Maynard-Moody argues that non-profit organizations are value-rational organizations. Therefore, their corporate rationality is based on the common bond of their purpose (i.e., charitable, service, social, etc.). Thus, while economics may be one of the values shared by the members or employees of non-profit organizations, he contended it is not their primary value. Because these organizations will be value-rational, their decisions will be made to optimize their corporate purpose and its corresponding values, rather than to optimize the economic efficiency.

Earlier the analogy was used of information as the impulse transmitted through an organization. That comparison has been made often in the literature by cybernetics. Cybernetics compares the autonomic control system formed in living creatures by the brain and nervous system to the mechanical control system formed in an organization by the management information system.

Griesinger used the cybernetic paradigm to suggest ways that management information and decision support systems could be incorporated into strategic and operational management. These are achieved through preferred ways of functioning and recommendations for future actions which would steer an organization to its preferred mode of operation. Griesinger explained that feedback of results and reassessments of premises are at the heart of this adaptation process. Cybernetic rationality occurs when,

> A comparison between the state of nature as it is perceived (factual premises) and the decision maker's goals (value premises) reveals a gap that is the driving force in a cybernetic system. . . . A discrepancy between a goal and a perception motivates the individual to find a behavior to reduce the gap . . . the alternative is normally chosen that is believed most instrumental in achieving the person's goals.[38]

Ultimately, Griesinger argued that organizational rationality requires both organizationally rational choice and cybernetically rational action. Administrators steer and control an organization through both their decision choices and their implementing actions.

> Organizational decisions are termed rational if information representing events, beliefs, and aspirations converge to dominant representations that are reasonably veridical, shared, and accepted within the organization as the premises guiding organizational choice. The gap between the organizational goals and perceptions motivates the search for alternative courses of action each of which is evaluated based on shared beliefs (or demonstrable evidence) of cause and effect, and the alternative best able to meet organizational goals is chosen for implementation. . . . *For organizationally rational action* to follow, each step in the means-ends chain leading to implementation must be the product of an organizationally rational process. . . . True organizational rationality, then, includes not only rational choice but also rational implementation, which of necessity links the macro-behavior of the organization with the micro-behavior within it.[39]

In summary, rationality is a problematic search, based on information provided by a management control system which spans the organization's environmental boundaries. In the end, decisions are made at some sub-optimal level of rationality, influenced by the environmental norms of the individual and the society. These decisions drive the management process and allow an organization's members to learn from their experiences and adapt to changing conditions.

> Such learning from errors plays as great a role in the solution-process as in everyday life. While the simple realization, that something does not work, can lead only to some variation of the old method, the realization of why it does not work, the recognition of the ground of the conflict, results in a correspondingly definite variation which corrects the recognized defect.[40]

Evaluation research is one method non-profit organizations use to help determine "if" and "why" programs are or are not working. Evaluation research findings allow administrators to identify their rational choices, to modify their decisions, and to take corrective actions to reduce the gap between their desired and actual outcomes.

EVALUATION RESEARCH

Administrators are constantly making evaluative decisions of varying degrees of difficulty and consequence. Various evaluative forms and sources of information are used, but they all allow management to evaluate a program's performance. Evaluation research is one form of assessment used in non-profit organizations to determine service effort and accomplishment. Understanding the background, types, and uses of evaluation research will help clarify its role in both program management and organization administration. The alternative sources of data suggested for these efforts, introduces the possibilities for pluralistic evaluation methods which allow self-assessment and self-control.

Background

Evaluation research has long been used in education to assess the results of alternative teaching methods. Since the time of the New Deal, public policy programs have been the subject of social research to determine their benefits. During the 1950's evaluation studies became larger scale as post-World War II redevelopment programs came under study. Many international aid and development organizations were founded during this period. In the United States, President Lyndon Johnson's Great Society programs were also an impetus to more complex research studies.

Evaluation methodology also improved during this period with advances in research design, social survey techniques, and computer-assisted statistical analysis. Moreover, qualitative changes occurred. Evaluators incorporated policy development and program implementation into their field of study. They began to ask questions about policy intents and program goals, trying to link them with program results and impacts on their intended beneficiaries. Alternative ways of delivering the services were also subject of study. The value of evaluation research to management has continued to grow. Evaluation research is ". . . a political and managerial activity, an input into the complex mosaic from which emerge policy decisions and allocations for the planning, design, implementation, and continuance of programs to better the human condition.[41]

Types of Evaluation

Various categorizations of evaluation research are possible. Rossi *et al* classify evaluation studies into five groups which follow a program's life-cycle: (1) evaluation for program planning and development provides information that will enable the program to be designed using requisite knowledge of the program's goals, location, problem, and participants; (2) evaluation for program monitoring assesses whether or not a program's operations conform to the program design and delivers the goods or services specified; (3) evaluation for program impacts determines if a cause/effect relationship exists between a program's activities and outcomes and the magnitude of these changes; (4) evaluation for program efficiency estimates the benefits and costs for the program's outcomes; (5) comprehensive program evaluation is a macro-evaluation study incorporating all four types of evaluation analysis.[42]

Perkins also categorized evaluation research into five types which can each be conducted independently or which can be combined into a comprehensive program evaluation. These five types can be described as follows: (1) strategic evaluation identifies a social problem, need, or issue and formulates a policy to address it; (2) compliance evaluation operationalizes the policy through a legislative or organizational objective and designs a program plan and delivery system to fulfill the policy; (3) management evaluation focuses on the efficiency and effectiveness with which managers deploy resources; (4) intervention effect evaluations establish the relationship between activities and outcomes; (5) program impact evaluations study the actual attainment of legislative and policy goals through program outcomes.[43]

Perkin's conceptualization of evaluation research depicts a control function which is integrated into the program or project life cycle. His concept presents six decision links between these five types of evaluation and he argues that both the evaluation work and the subsequent decision affects the next phase of any project.

Stufflebeam *et al* also relate evaluation and decisions, but their concept goes further to show how evaluation permeates the environmental boundaries of a program and decisions recycle to affect subsequent actions. Euske describes this concept and its relationship to the management process further:

> Planning decisions are used to determine goals and are essentially based on the diagnosis of a particular situation. Structuring decisions determine the project design resulting from questions and objectives generated during planning decisions. Implementing decisions are made to control project operations. Finally, recycling decisions deal with reacting and making judgments in regards to project realignments and reallocations. . . . In each case the evaluation is concerned with analyzing the relationship between the actual and desired effects of decisions.[44]

Uses of Evaluation

The above typologies of evaluation clearly show that evaluation research is a feedback mechanism to aid decision-making. "The purpose of evaluation is to identify the strengths of program activities and outcomes so they can be reenforced or replicated, while at the same time identifying weaknesses so they can be minimized. . . . The utilization process, then, goes on to make decisions based on those judgments, and to take actions based on those decisions."[45]

While project managers use evaluation research to formulate and modify programs, corporate administrators and funding agencies use evaluation to formulate and modify policy decisions. Rossi *et al* argue that executive utilization, albeit different, is of paramount importance to evaluation research.

> The major impetus for rational policy making and program development are political and pragmatic, and it is the politician, the planner, and the foundation executive who exercise the leadership in the evaluation field. It is persons of power and influence, not academicians, who are the evaluation research lobby and who are responsible primarily for the widespread growth of the evaluation endeavor.

> . . . the general direction of activities in most countries and most human service fields is clear. Whatever the social value, the program goals, and the objectives of those in powerful positions, information on program efficiency, efficacy, and accountability are persuasive inputs to the elusive influence and decision-making processes that surround policy development and implementation . . . it is persons with aspirations to direct the course of social life and the rhythm of social change who stimulate the demand for evaluation research.[46]

The chain of decisions made by individuals throughout the life of a program forms and transforms both the program and the organization. At the program level, managers make these decisions continuously. At the administrative and policy levels, managers make these decisions periodically. In order for evaluation information to affect the corporate management process and to be considered a potential "service effort and accomplishment" measure for external accounting information it must first be timely and relevant for these internal decision makers. Timeliness would indicate that the information must be incorporated systematically and routinely into the management control system. Relevance would suggest it must be contextually compatible and consider alternative sources of data.

Alternative Sources of Data

While administrators make decisions which affect programs based on evaluation information, evaluators make decisions on how to measure and value program outcomes. In this way, evaluation acts as a surrogate market in non-profit organizations.

In for-profit organizations, accountants measure and value inputs (based on historical market prices) while the market (customers acting collectively) measures and values outputs. The difference between these two is profit. In human services institutions, accountants can still measure inputs, but the "customers" of these institutions are an ill-defined group who do not act collectively. Evaluation researchers are asked to appraise the effects, or benefits, derived from the goods and services provided by programs. The role of valuation is to relate the program inputs, transformation process, and program outputs.

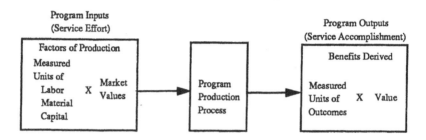

Figure 2: Role of Valuation in Human Service Programs

The scientific research method used by the social scientist in evaluation research aims for statistically valid and reliable data to determine cause/effect relations of program activities to outcomes. Unfortunately, these approaches often require a great deal of time, so the results often lag behind the program implementation. They are therefore not available to influence the management decision process and thereby help to form the project. Further, the statistical results support the evaluators' findings but their relevance to others has been questioned.

Patton suggested "a paradigm of choices" which allows evaluators to use more pragmatic forms of validity.[47] He contended that evaluation does not have to use scientific research designs and quantitative data for validity and reliability. The logical framework of scientific evaluation research is a useful analytic tool, but, he argued, one methodology is not appropriate to all programs.

Guba compared alternative paradigms and developed a naturalistic methodology for evaluation research. He contended that which paradigm is most useful depends upon the characteristics of the program to be studied. ". . . some questions can be better understood within a physiological framework and thus call for a scientific paradigm, but others are more properly understood as mental manifestations and therefore require a naturalistic paradigm."[48] Determining which evaluation approach is appropriate to a particular study is then incumbent on the evaluator and/or the management that commissioned the work.

If the value of evaluation research lies in its ability to span the boundary between an organization's internal and external environment while identifying and measuring qualitative characteristics of the enterprise and its operations, then a pluralistic approach to evaluation would imply that there is more than one kind of ultimate reality. Members of diverse ethnic, racial, religious or social groups could represent their special interests, traditions, cultures, values, and beliefs with a collective effort. Pluralistic evaluation approaches would allow more stakeholders in human service programs to value program outputs and determine the effects of program outcomes. Using the alternative sources of data suggested for these analyses introduces the possibilities for participative evaluation methods which allow self-assessment and self-control in decentralized operations.

SELF-CONTROL

The management literature on control has been influenced greatly by psychology and sociology. While economic incentives for control were accepted for many years, after World War II, the human relations schools introduced democratic and individual forms of control. The overriding issue in self-control is a search for managerial methods "to tap the unrealized potential present in their human resources."[49] Pluralistic evaluation approaches try to tap the human resources available to non-profit organizations for self-control in diverse operating locations as well as for management control of the aggregate groups.

Management by Integration and
Self-Control

McGregor argued that "control involves the selection of means which are appropriate to the nature of the phenomena with which we are concerned" (e.g. selective adaptation to human nature rather than expecting human nature to conform to organizational wishes).[50] As organizations have become more sensitive to human values, they have allowed employees to exercise self control through a positive, conscious, ethical code of social responsibility towards all constituencies. The creation of conditions such that the constituents of the organization can achieve their own goals best by directing their efforts towards the success of the enterprise is what McGregor called the integration principle of the Theory Y.

> Perfect integration of organizational requirements and individual goals and needs is, of course, not a realistic objective. In adopting this principle, we seek that degree of integration in which the individual can achieve his goal best by directing his efforts towards the success of the organization. 'Best' means that this alternative will be more attractive than the many others available to him: indifference, irresponsibility, minimal compliance, hostility, sabotage. It means that he will continuously be encouraged to develop and utilize voluntarily his capacities, his knowledge, his skills, his ingenuity in ways which contribute to the success of the enterprise.
>
> . . . people will exercise self-direction and self-control in the achievement of organizational objectives to the degree that they are committed to those objectives. If that commitment is small, only a slight degree of self-direction and self-control will be likely, and a substantial amount of external influence will be necessary. If it is large, many conventional external controls will be relatively superfluous, and to some extent, self-defeating. Managerial policies and practices materially affect this degree of commitment.[51]

Integration of organizational and individual goals is an active process of mutual involvement by all constituents in the determination of objectives through instruction and exploration which allows both subordinates and superiors to be committed to their plans. McGregor contended that acceptance of responsibility for the plans, for self-direction, and for self-control are correlated with commitment to the objectives. Detailed plans for specific actions within a particular time frame constitute a basis for individuals to evaluate their own accomplishments at the end of the time period.

According to McGregor, the effective use of participation (in all management functions and to conduct program evaluations) is a consequence of an administrative point of view which includes confidence in the potentialities of subordinates, awareness of management's dependency downward, and a desire to create opportunities for people to influence decisions effecting them. Further, he suggests that participation is a major form of satisfaction for both the supervisor and subordinates: ". . . there is a greater sense of independence and of achieving some control over one's destiny. Finally, there are the satisfactions that come by way of recognition from peers and supervisors for having made a worth-while contribution to the solution of an organizational problem."[52]

Integrating the organization's goals with the various constituencies' goals in an environment of self-control is a strategy for managing people. It forces management to examine its assumptions about people and the productive process of their enterprise. The tools for operationalizing any managerial philosophy are attitudes and beliefs about people developed into policies and practices which reflect manifestations of these beliefs.

Pluralistic evaluation approaches allow non-profit organizations to integrate their objectives with the objectives of their constituencies, when all parties participate effectively in the evaluation process. Tactics of specific action plans must be worked out in light of the circumstances present at each operation location. Mary Parker Follett called this the law of the situation and the authority of the facts. She recognized that the decisions which are best for the organization are dictated by all the facts being taken into account and objectively appraised in the circumstances. Here everyone agrees to take their orders from the situation, thus depersonalizing orders. Management's job is ". . . not how to get people to obey orders, but how to devise methods by which we can best discover the order integral to a particular situation. . . . (then people) should exercise the authority of the situation."[53]

System 4: The Participative Group

Building on these concepts that plans must be worked out in light of circumstances, situations, and facts, Likert advocated System 4 type management: the participative group. He proposed that for any organization the results which it achieves are equal to the quality of the decisions people make multiplied by their motivation to implement the decision. Likert argued, "Adequate measurement coupled with participation in decision-making provide an organization with a two-fold advantage: (1) better decisions, based on more accurate information, and (2) greater motivation to implement these decisions."[54]

Likert developed an extensive participative group management system. He argued that there are consistent, dependable, and marked relationships among causal, intervening, and end-result variables which profoundly alter the management control process. Therefore, the central task of management is building and maintaining a highly effective interaction-influence system between the organization's external and internal constituencies and environments.

Thus, the most important function of management is facilitating a human organization through which all work is accomplished. In such an interaction-influence environment,

> The primary purpose of measurement in System 4 organizations is to provide managers and non-supervisory employees with information to help them guide their own decisions and behaviors. These data aid the members of the organization to accomplish both the specific goals they have set for themselves and the broad objectives they have helped to set for the organization. Measurement of all three kinds of variables are eagerly sought when they provide valuable information to help guide decisions and actions and are not used punitively by supervisors. All members of the organization want the data and clearly recognize the necessity for the measurements to be accurate. There are strong motivational forces among members to do all they can to assure that the data are accurate and correctly reflect conditions and developments in the organization when the measurements are used for self-guidance.[55]

Argyris confirmed this perception of measurement and the use of feedback information for self-control.

> As trust increases . . . controls will change to instruments of opportunity for increased self responsibility and psychological success. Information will be collected to guide the individual in achieving the work. The information collected 'on' an individual will be collected 'by' him and evaluated by him, and he will take the appropriate actions.[56]

Pluralistic forms of evaluation allow the stakeholders affected by, or whose community will be effected by, a program or project to participate in measuring and assessing its efforts and accomplishment. Participatory evaluation is a special case of pluralistic evaluation which allows all project participants to form a participative group to design and use their program's evaluation plan. Applying the writings of McGregor, Follett, Likert, and Argyris to participatory evaluation suggests policies, procedures, and practices which integrate the individual and the sponsoring organization's objectives for performance and control by measuring and reporting on both internal and external variables. The collecting and reporting of information is carried out by the participants themselves in decentralized operating locations.

Decentralization

Organizational structures are designed to facilitate the organization's performance. Decentralization was developed by DuPont and refined by General Motors in the 1920's, to manage their operationally diverse and geographically dispersed organizations. It promotes self-control and facilitates the interaction of competing and complementary work groups. Drucker cites five main reasons why decentralization has emerged "as the dominant structural principle" of modern enterprises. (1) It focuses the vision and efforts of managers directly on business performance and business results; (2) the danger is lessened of self-deception by concentrating on the old and easy rather than on the new and coming; (3) the manager of a unit knows better than anyone else how he (she) is doing, and needs no one to tell him (her), hence the number of people or units under one manager can be expanded to a much wider span of managerial responsibility; (4) responsibility units are a training and testing grounds for tomorrow's top managers; (5) the organization can test a person's capacity to manage the whole business responsibility.[57]

Decentralization structures an organization for self-control by limiting the inter-dependence of sub-systems in complex organizations and by diluting the internal power structure of competing groups. It focuses each manager's attention on the results of his (her) unit and their contribution to the collective good.

In this structure, central administration coordinates unity and harmony by "reserving general welfare clauses" for decisions that affect the business as a whole, its long-term welfare, and the right to override individual units' decisions. Finally, all the decentralized units adhere to common principles, aims, and beliefs: "the unity of purpose and beliefs that makes a community with common citizenship is strengthened by diversity in practice."[58]

Decentralization allows local units to scan their own external environment and balance parochial demands with corporate objectives. As organizations become more geographically dispersed and a world economy establishes market conditions, this flexibility will become more essential. Autonomy of operations, however, also brings with it responsibility for performance and results. Management by objectives facilitates the corporate enterprise's unity of direction and is only possible in conditions of self-control.

Philosophy of Management By Objectives and Self-Control

Drucker first introduced management by objectives and self-control in 1955.[59] He argued that the natural tendency of enterprises is not to organize for overall performance, but rather, to organize geographically by specialization of duty, or in a hierarchy, all of which tend to insulate people from one another. He called for an enterprise to build a true team and weld individual exertions into a common effort producing the desired results by having each first line manager take responsibility for themselves, their unit, and for the corporate whole. Thus he argued, even in cutting stone, workers would realize that they are also building a cathedral.

> An effective management must direct the vision and efforts of all managers towards a common goal. It must ensure that the individual manager understands what results are demanded of him. It must ensure that the superior understands

what to expect of each of his subordinate managers. It must motivate each manager to maximum efforts in the right direction. And while encouraging high standards of workmanship, it must make them (the workmanship standards) the means to the end of business performance rather than ends in themselves.[60]

Each person's objectives should be clearly spelled out and state what performance their unit will produce, what contribution this individual will make to others and to the unit, and what contribution the unit and others will make to this individual. The emphasis is on teamwork and team results achieved through interrelated, individual efforts.

Each manager along the management control decision chain has responsibility to set the objectives of their unit themselves, in collaboration with and with corroboration from, his superiors and subordinates. Both long-range and short-range considerations should be included, as well as objectives set and performance measures established in a variety of key result areas (e.g., operations, product development, and service delivery). Drucker says, ". . . every manager should responsibly participate in the development of the objectives of the higher units of which he is a part. To 'give him a sense of participation' (to use a pet phrase from the 'human relations' jargon) is not enough. Being a manager demands the assumption of genuine responsibility."[61] Responsibility requires each person to commit themselves to these objectives with a "positive act of assent."

The philosophy of management by objectives and self-control is the abiding ethics of participatory evaluation. Each project participant must know and understand the ultimate goal or "business" of this project and of the sponsoring organization. They determine what is expected of them in their project and why; they decide together what their performance will be measured against and how. In turn, each participant sub-group is expected to think through what their units' objectives are and participate actively and responsibly in defining them. Then higher level management can know what to expect of each program or project and can make exacting demands focused on performance, not personality or persuasion. Care is taken to give support which rewards correct behaviors, emphasizes correct results, and directs people's actions toward performance for the common good of the project.

The measurements required for self-control are simple and well suited to the operations of multinational non-profit organizations. Drucker suggested: (1) that in addition to knowing goals, a manager needs to have clear and common measurements in all key areas of a business, (2) these measures need not be rigidly quantitative nor exact but simple and rational, (3) they have to be relevant to the situation and direct attention and effort to performance, (4) they should be reliable to the extent that their margin of error is acknowledged, understood, and compensated, (5) they should be easily understood. They should also provide the entire project with aggregate measures of their common performance. These should be gathered, summarized, and reported.

Thus it is possible for project participants to control their own performance and for project constituents to control their own program. Drucker argued that "self-control means stronger motivation: a desire to do the best rather than just enough to get by. It means higher performance goals and broader vision."[62] Objective and goals are the basis of the project participants' ability to direct themselves and their work; being governed by group objectives and goals set collectively requires management by self-control rather than management by dominational control.

Drucker contended that management by objectives and self-control requires self-discipline and forces people to make high demands on themselves. It is not permissive nor freedom from constraint. In fact, Maslow argued that it will demand too much of people. Drucker noted,

> Maslow pointed out that the demand for responsibility and achievement may well go far beyond what any but the strong and healthy can take. He sharply criticized me and McGregor for 'inhumanity' to the weak, the vulnerable, the damaged, who are unable to take on the responsibility and self-discipline which Theory Y demands. Even the strong and healthy, Maslow concluded, need the security of order and direction; and the weak need protection against the burden of responsibility.[63]

Maslow argued that it is not enough to remove the restraint, structure, security, and certainty of a Theory X approach to management. A need is created for command and penalties to be substituted by self-direction and self-control to take corrective actions. McGregor assumed all people want to be adults; Maslow countered that not all people act as adults, and self-control is a stern taskmaster and makes demands not all people can meet. Correspondingly, Drucker assumed all people want to be responsible, want to contribute, want to achieve, and will act as they are expected to act. These assumptions are especially applicable to the young educated people who will be tomorrow's managers in organizations operating in both the first and third world. These contentions were echoed by Naisbitt in *Megatrends*:

> When social scientists, management consultants and public-opinion experts speak about the 'new breed of employees,' the new motivational theories, the new entitlements and rights attitudes, what they are really describing are the values of the demographic cohort that exploded on college campuses in the late 1960's and 1970's. Now they have gone to work. . . . Now workers are better educated, more self-confident about governing themselves (in politics and at work). . . . [64]

Drucker acknowledged that in the intervening years since he introduced management by objectives it has been widely used as a slogan, often reduced to a gimmick, sold as a technique, or policy. He believes that it is much more.

> What the business enterprise needs is a principle of management that will give full scope to individual strength and responsibility, as well as common direction to vision and effort, establish team work, and harmonize the goals of the individual with the commonweal. Management by objectives and self-control makes the commonweal the aim of every manager. It substitutes for control from outside the stricter, more exacting, and more effective control from inside. It motivates the manager to action, not because somebody tells him to do something or talks him into doing it, but because the objective task demands it. He acts not because somebody wants him to but because he himself decides that he has to—he acts, in other words, as a free man.

> I do not use the word philosophy lightly; . . . But management by objectives and self-control can properly be called a philosophy of management. It rests on a concept of the job of management. It rests on an analysis of the specific needs of the management group and the obstacles it faces. It

rests on a concept of human action, behavior, and motivation. Finally it applies to every manager, whatever his level and function, and to any organization whether large or small. It insures performance by converting objective needs into personal goals. And this is genuine freedom.[65]

In summary, the philosophy of management by objectives and self-control affirms the rights of the individual and exacts responsibility. It supports the views that organizations are open systems where people must be aware of both its internal and external environment in order for it to adapt, perform, survive, and grow. It acknowledges that people will make decisions at some sub-optimum level, but they will be rational decisions given the information at the person's disposal. It also requires new tools of management and changes in traditional management thinking and practices.

From this philosophy, several constraints are implied for management information and control systems: (1) they cannot be used to prompt moral actions, because only employees can decide what should be done and how it can "properly" be accomplished; (2) they cannot be substituted for individual judgment, but they must identify the non-routine event that does not fit the normal pattern and requires special handling and individual decision; (3) they must require facts, data, reports, and procedures which are beneficial for the person who provides them, for meeting their needs in achieving results for performance. Evaluation research information is equally accountable to these standards and constraints. Participatory evaluation is a new management tool which incorporates the principles of self-control with open systems theory.

Participatory Evaluation

The use of participation in program evaluation has been very limited, but is emerging. Bryk examined recent experiences with two highly publicized programs. The Cities-in-Schools program and Jesse Jackson's Push/Excel program both developed pluralistic evaluation processes which involved various program audiences—community leaders, school administrators, and government officials—in their evaluations.[66] In education programs, evaluation specialists have also suggested using ". . . an interactive mode (of evaluation) which allows the emergence of a common conceptualization of the educational program among all involved parties and fosters a consensus of program needs, design, implementation, and evaluation."[67]

In third world countries implementing agencies, as well as supporting agencies, are designing evaluation methods for self-control. Evaluation is viewed as a continual process in which all interested parties interact to review alternative viewpoints, reconcile differences of opinion, resolve conflict, and establish common, measurable objectives. The Indian Social Institute in New Delhi reported using a stakeholder evaluation method in a housing program.

> We desire an evaluation process and method which will promote social justice, increase self reliance, and enable 'grassroots' people to be the primary agents of their own change and development. Only complete participation among community people, personnel of the implementing agency, representatives of the supporting agency, and an outside evaluator acting as a facilitator, has been found to create a proper sense of social consciousness about, and commitment to, community development.[68]

These efforts to involve interested parties in program evaluation use an evaluation consultant to oversee the evaluation process. Stakeholder' experiences and opinions are systematically assessed through use of various means designed by an evaluation specialist. However, the program recipients do not design and carry out the program evaluation themselves; rather, they are conduits for the evaluation specialist to gather information and assessments.

The American Council of Voluntary Agencies for Foreign Service confirmed the need for the evaluation process to "go beyond the experimental, quantitatively oriented research designs . . . to develop low cost, small scale, highly participatory, internally organized approaches."[69] The council contended that projects will be more effective if community members are actively involved in all phases of the evaluation process. Further, they contended that participatory evaluation develops human resources, because community members gain skills for self-reliance when evaluation is viewed as a dialogue between two coworkers about a project. Information comes out of and is fed into a community decision process directed towards action, while it is also systematically integrated into the management cycle of programming, budgeting, and decision making.[70]

A common need stressed by programs which involve various audiences in the evaluation process was a way to incorporate these participatory evaluation findings into the formal management decision system of the program, of the administering agency, and of the sponsoring organization. After developing a comprehensive impact assessment effort that includes citizen involvement the Nuclear Regulatory Agency noted, "If we are serious about making social costs more than a trivial consideration in selecting the appropriate course for technological development, then we must improve the basis for their (citizens) input into the planning process."[71] The Urban League suggested that "Program evaluation feedback can be most effective when it is regularly and consciously sought, structured into the administrative decision process, and accompanied by a set of incentives to encourage program changes based on the feedback received."[72]

Since the mid-1970's, Canada has had extensive public participation in evaluating its government programs. In 1979, Sewell and Phillips conducted a study of 22 programs using stakeholder evaluation methods. As Figure 3 demonstrates, a high degree of citizen involvement corresponds with a high degree of equity where all potential opinions and values are heard. However, the efficiency of evaluation is reduced. Participation requires high costs in time, personnel, and other resources required to reach a decision. The trade-off is very important and expensive.

Sewell and Phillips identified eight needs to improve the efficiency, while maintaining the effectiveness, of the participatory evaluation process: (1) an autonomous evaluation system to independently assess the public's assertions; (2) an ongoing evaluation process built into the program reporting scheme for continuous assessment; (3) a basis to ensure all participants' inclusion; (4) a means to legitimately resolve all parties' concerns; (5) a method to institutionalize public participation into the formal decision-making process; (6) genuine one-on-one communication between program personnel and the citizenry in workshops, on task forces, and through information programs; (7) the administering agency to remain flexible, open to new ideas, new issues, new public groups, new procedures, and be receptive to innovation and change; (8) a working environment which allows participants to challenge the existing order.[73]

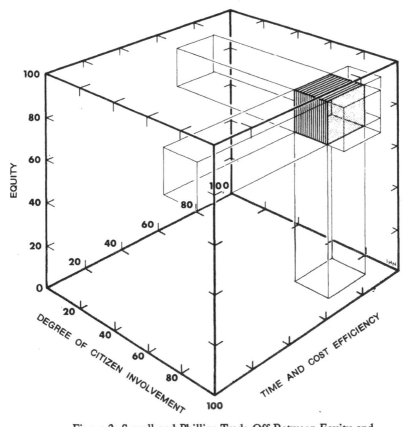

Figure 3: Sewell and Phillips Trade-Off Between Equity and
Efficiency by Degree of Citizen Involvement.

These needs were identified in a developed country with high
education and awareness levels in its population. But the same concerns
are applicable to any institution which uses participatory evaluation. The
information must be relevant, timely, and systematically incorporated
into the management decision process. Routinely incorporating
participatory evaluation findings into the management information
system presents possibilities for far-reaching changes in the management
process.

MANAGEMENT PROCESS

For the purpose of this study, the management process directs an open-system enterprise which is sensitive to its total environment, through an information feedback system to facilitate decision making for planning, programming, resource allocation, measurement, and control. Anthony's earliest work on planning and control systems proposed a decision framework which continues to be the basis for expanding and developing the management process.

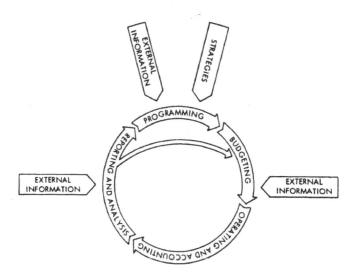

Figure 4:   Anthony and Dearden's Phases of Management Control.

Anthony identified three major decision categories for the management process:

> Strategic planning is the process of deciding on objectives of the organization, on changes in these objectives, on the resources used to attain these objectives, and on the policies that are to govern the acquisition, use, and disposal of these resources.

> Management control is the process by which managers assure that resources are obtained and used efficiently in the accomplishment of the organization's objectives.

> Operation control is the process of assuring that specific tasks are carried out effectively and efficiently.[74]

Strategic planning forms the critical, long-range, comprehensive, integrated plans and policies that determine or change the character or direction of the organization. Strategic planning decisions affect the physical, financial, behavioral, and organizational framework within which operations are carried out.

The management control process is carried on within the guidelines established by strategic planning and is intended to make possible the achievement of planned objectives. The process involves making decisions about what to do in the future within the constraints prescribed by the strategic policies and guidelines. These two decision processes shade into one another because there are important interactions between them. These transcend the boundaries between the internal and external environment.

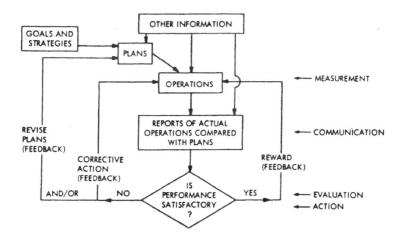

Figure 5: Anthony and Dearden's Control Process

Management control also relates to current operations. Objectives, policies, organizational structure, product lines or program orientation, physical facility locations, capacity, leadership climate, and other long-range parameters are all decided in the strategic planning process. The management control process communicates these throughout the organization, stimulates operations, and provides feedback to top management on the progress being made towards achieving objectives. Operational control focuses on individual tasks, decisions, performance measurements, and aggregating the results.

For all three controls, the management information system provides information while the management process is a chain of interrelated decisions which propel the organization. Decisions operationalize the ideas based on values and facts. Anthony and Dearden do not discuss where evaluation research fits into their general management process model, but Ritchie places evaluation research in the strategic level of management activity. He suggests that evaluation research be used in the execution and control stages of a program.[75]

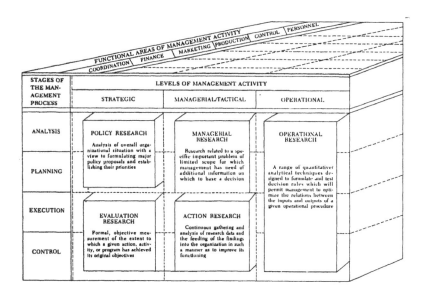

Figure 6: Ritchie's Classification of Research Methodologies According to Three Dimensions of the Management Process.

Evaluation writers agree with this use of evaluation research. However they see evaluation used in other phases of programs as well. Several management and accounting writers have expanded the Anthony framework for the various management functions. Their perceptions of evaluation research provide insight into why empirical research is needed on evaluation research and the management process.

Planning

Dermer develope a process model for multi-cycle planning and control. He contended that "planning is the process of narrowing the range of alternative behaviors through a series of problem-solving cycles until a single set of actions can be specified."[76]

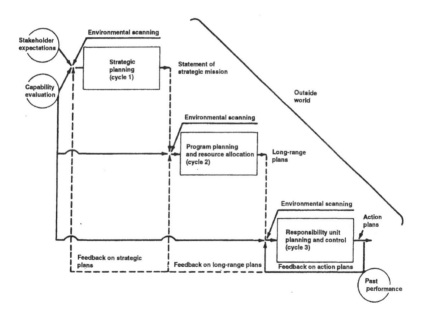

Figure 7: Dermer's Three-Cycle Planning and Control Process.

The model involves three cycles, each with its own problem solving steps: (1) strategic planning for designing, intelligence gathering, and formulation of a mission statement; (2) program planning and resource allocation for developing new program activities, conducting program evaluation on potential projects, allocating resources, and specifying long-range plans; (3) responsibility unit planning and control for designing, implementing, evaluating, and revising the operations of individual programs. The schematic presentation of these cycles shows how each interaction is an open system process which, through a series of decisions, transforms organizational objectives into specific action plans.

Feedback and evaluation occur at each stage, but the evaluative devices and criteria presented by Dermer are financial (e.g., payback, benefit-cost ratio, internal rate of return), statistical (e.g., Monte Carlo simulation and sensitivity analysis) or systemic (e.g., systems audits which incorporate organizational and operational considerations). The correspondence is easy to see between program evaluation models based on the project life-cycle and the planning control process. However, the management planning and control process presented by Dermer does not incorporate the performance results and impact assessment of evaluation research.

Programming

Maciariello introduced cybernetics into the management control process. He developed a self-regulating management control process formed around the management information system and governed by individuals' decisions. Building on the work of Anthony and of Bower, Maciariello expanded their concepts into a management control process for diverse activities and at all levels of the organization.

In describing how decentralized operations and diverse activities are linked together through the management control process, Maciariello stated,

> To summarize, the control process paradigm includes the essential elements of planning (goals), decision making (behavioral choice), and control (comparator-feedback). It operates within the control structure (i.e., a hierarchy of control paradigms) and has as its purpose the continuous attainment of organizational goals and objectives. Responsibility centers are linked to one another by their control processes in a hierarchical structure of control

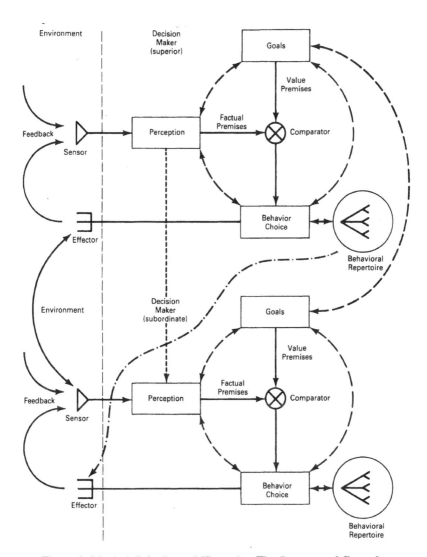

Figure 8: Maciariello's Control Hierarchy: The Structure of Control.

according to reporting relationships. In this manner, each organizational sub-unit is linked to the whole by myriad interlacing relationships. . . . The cybernetic model of the control process is an information processing model. . . . The

> cybernetic paradigm and the control hierarchy lead us to
> conclude that . . . each part (of the organization) is concerned
> with assuming that its human, physical, and technological
> resources are used in achieving its goals and objectives. In
> other words, each is concerned with management control.[77]

By superimposing the cybernetic model onto the management
control process, Maciariello also designed an open system process
which provides feedback and requires evaluative decisions at each stage
in the control hierarchy. The specific measurement and evaluation
devices discussed to assess program performance are also financial and
economic in nature. The type of evaluative feedback information
presented in the evaluation research models has not been incorporated
in the Maciariello control process.

Budgeting

Hopwood described a management process in which the
information generated by the system is used for two purposes: financial
reporting and performance review. His research was limited to the
budgeting process, but he generalized his findings to the entire
management control process. He conducted clinical research and
observed the contexts in which performance measures are used. He
examined how budget figures are established and how reports
comparing budget to actual performance are used for review, evaluation,
and reward. He found three different styles of evaluation which were
associated with widespread differences in managerial behavior,
managerial attitudes, and the leadership climate of the organization.

Hopwood's study of budgets enriched our understanding of the
effective use of imperfect evaluation procedures in the management
process by suggesting that what is measured and how the information
is used is more important to the management process than the
measurement techniques which are used. In fact, Hopwood cautioned
that measurement of managerial performance will never be perfect nor
precise. However, despite imperfect measurement techniques for project
or program attributes, the procedure of measuring for evaluation is
valuable.

Hopwood contended that ambiguous situations will always occur
between the organization's purpose, employees' personal goals, the

behaviors measured by a management system, and the rewards received by employees. He portrays these relationships in a general measurement-reward process model.

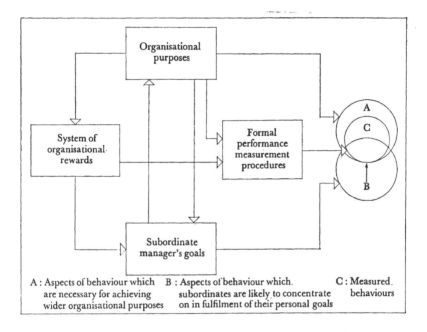

A : Aspects of behaviour which   B : Aspects of behaviour which.   C : Measured.
   are necessary for achieving   subordinates are likely to concentrate   behaviours
   wider organisational purposes   on in fulfilment of their personal goals

Figure 9: Hopwood's Measurement-Reward Process
with Imperfect Measurement.

The most effective management control process would maximize the common area on the venn diagram (ABC). Since the performance measurement process and the reward system encourage concern and attention to what is measured, selecting the proper attributes for measurement is critical to integrating individual and organizational objectives.

> . . . consideration need to be given to changing some aspects of accounting systems and in doing this, there is a real need for a view of accounting which sees it as a part of a much more complex process for influencing behavior in

> organizations. Accounting systems for performance measurement represent only one means of control and their final effectiveness is dependent upon how they interact with the other approaches to the control problem.[78]

Hopwood concluded that not taking an integrated view to the management process causes it to fail to achieve its full potential. Management information and control systems design requires an analysis and assessment of those organizational and environmental factors which influence total effectiveness. Adaptive, flexible management systems are needed to organize and control complex activities.[79] Hopwood proposed a pluralistic view of control, which only implicitly encompasses techniques such as evaluation research.

Control

Tannenbaum developed a synergistic idea of control in modern, complex organizations. He studied control in various types of organizations—business enterprises, voluntary organizations, and trade unions—by asking participants their judgments on questionnaire items dealing with the amount of influence or control exercised by various groups in their organization. He then plotted the average scores as an organizational index to measure control.

Tannenbaum's graphic presentation shows the relative hierarchical differences in influence and the total amount of control at work in an organization.

> The assumption of a variable amount of control in organizations represents, we believe, an assumption of basic theoretical and practical importance. Theoretically, this assumption opens up a number of possibilities that would not otherwise be apparent. Consequently, it allows us to resolve what might otherwise appear to be opposing and irreconcilable arguments concerning the implications of control in organizations. . . . Assumptions about control in organizations also have practical consequences, because organizational leaders who hold these assumptions are likely to act on the basis of them. The practical importance of these assumptions is compounded by the fact that the choice of assumptions may lead to self-fulfilling prophecies.[80]

Tannenbaum found that the total amount of control can expand and contract. The distribution of control can change; when it does, the relative patterns of control at different hierarchical levels may also change, as an intended or unintended effect. Thus, program controls

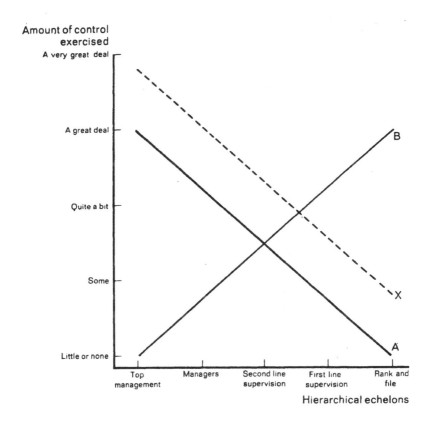

Figure 10: Tannenbaum's Control Graph

designed to decentralize influence over decision making can increase the influence of lower echelons in the organization while maintaining, increasing, or decreasing the influence of higher levels of the organization. Overall organizational performance is enhanced as control is increased, coordinated, and becomes complementary.

Tannenbaum concluded that effectiveness was more closely associated to the total amount of control rather than the distribution or pattern of control. This expansion of control may occur in two ways. First, it may come from external expansion of power into the organization's environment consistent with open systems theory. Secondly, it may come through an organization's structural conditions, if they expedite interaction and influence among members consistent with the philosophy of self-control. Here, motivational conditions increase interest by members of the organization in exercising control and a great amenability by members to be controlled for the collective good. Tannenbaum suggested various reasons and conditions which may account for the expansion of control. These include exchange of resources from a sense of justice, participation to expand partial inclusion, orderliness through control to increase negative entropy, and complete connection between the networks for voluntary self-control. He argued, however, that total effectiveness will be increased as total control increases.

In discussing open-system theory, Tannenbaum quotes Burnes and Stalker. Their work on the network system of control contends that the traditional bureaucratic organizational structure, based on the military or church model, will not work in modern organizations.

> The effectiveness of control in this type of organization derives more from the member's deep involvement and presumed community of interest with the rest of the working organization in the survival and growth of the firm . . . (rather than) from a contractual relationship between himself and a non-personal corporation. . . . The network system of control and the involvement of members in their organizational roles implies a highly integrated system . . . which is more flexible, or adaptable . . . members respond and adjust mutually and integratively to change.[81]

In discussing the control-enhancing characteristics of participation, Tannenbaum quotes March and Simon to support his contention of synergistic control,

> Where there is participation, alternatives are suggested in a setting that permits the organizational hierarchy to control (at least in part) what is evoked. 'Participative management' can be viewed as a device for permitting management to

> participate more fully in the making of decisions as well as a
> means for expanding the influence of lower echelons in the
> organization[82]

A concerted, holistic response by the enterprise would require high levels of information, knowledge, and control. The various constituencies of these organizations have latent capabilities, talents, and knowledge about the environment which are not utilized. Participative evaluation could tap these human resources and expand total control in the organization through indigenous assessments. Self-control or participative small-group control requires a high degree of trust, sharing of mutual values and vision, decentralized authority, individual responsibility, and willingness to take action. These are the "adult" characteristics described by Drucker for management by objectives and self-control.

Tannenbaum's findings confirm Drucker's contention that decentralized self-control is indeed more control than hierarchical, central control. They lead to the conclusions that, if total organizational effectiveness improves with increased control, and self-control maximizes the total amount of control, then some form of pluralistic, democratic, collective, participative self-control is theoretically best as well as socially appealing. The upper limit of self-control is a Pareto-optimality: that point at which one worker's exercise of control does not reduce the total control, or infringe on another person's rights and freedom to exercise self-control. The management control system is the collective action mechanism organizations use to maximize total control, while coordinating individual control, for the commonweal.

Tannenbaum's work suggests organizational effectiveness would be improved by a participative evaluation process which was integrated into the management control process of non-profit enterprises. However the management control literature does not explicitly incorporate evaluation research as a common feedback element, even in the literature on non-profit organizations where evaluation research is used most often.

Management Control Process in Non-Profit Organizations

Anthony and Herzlinger developed a management control model for non-profit organizations. They contended that, "the basic control concepts are the same in both profit-oriented and non-profit organizations, but that because of the special characteristics of non-profit organization, the application of these concepts differ in some important respects."[83]

Their goal was to design a management control system which measures both inputs and outputs. Inputs are usually expressed in monetary terms, then assigned to a program and responsibility center. They concluded that, unfortunately, ". . . outputs can be measured only if the goods and services produced can be expressed in quantitative terms, either as revenues or some physical quantities. . . . (nevertheless) Although outputs may not be measured, or may not even be measurable, it is a fact that every organization unit has outputs; that is, it does something."[84]

In order to use efficiency and effectiveness ratios as relative indices of performance, some alternative means to measure and value output needs to be developed.This has been the role of evaluation research in non-profit organizations. Anthony and Herzlinger suggest that evaluation for control actually occurs in two processes.

One is the regular, routine, recurring monitoring process which management uses to keep informed on current activities. This flow of quantitative and qualitative information is typical of the monthly management reports. In Maciariello's model, management analyzes these data using various comparator techniques to identify discrepancies between planned and actual outcomes.

Second is an evaluation to see what the organization has done. This type of evaluation differs from the monitoring process in four principal respects: (1) the evaluation process occurs at irregular, infrequent intervals; (2) the evaluation of a given activity or program is much more thorough; (3) the evaluation is usually conducted by someone other than the operating manager's line superior; (4) the techniques of analysis are different.[85]

Considering these differences, two types of evaluation research are discussed by Anthony and Herzlinger. Operations evaluation focuses on the organization's efficiency in their delivery process. Program evaluation focuses on the organization's effectiveness in achieving results. Outside evaluators are strongly advocated for both of these studies.

> An operations evaluation requires a knowledge of the management process, of principles of human behavior and of efficient work methods and other techniques. These principles and techniques are similar for most types of organizations. By contrast, the program evaluator should be knowledgeable about the specific type of program being evaluated. An expert in education is not likely to make a sound assessment of a health care program.[86]

Similar themes emerged in the evaluation literature, with slightly different names and classifications. According to these writers, evaluation research is an external, surrogate market used to measure and value outputs.

Conversly, Ramanathan developed what he called a behavioral approach to the management control process for non-profit organizations. His model places evaluation research in the programming function similar to Rossi's Program Planning Evaluation and Perkins' Strategic Evaluations. Although he did not discuss evaluation research specifically, he discussed at length the need for control surrogates to measure and value inputs and outputs. Many of the surrogates he suggested are the types used by evaluation researchers (e.g., number of cases completed per month and increase in life earnings of program beneficiaries). His reporting and evaluation process, however, involves financial and managerial performance assessments (e.g., budgeted to actual spending analysis and actual to performance-norm comparisons) without specific emphasis or attention on service accomplishment or impact analysis.

In these management control models, evaluation research is not incorporated into the management process nor explicitly discussed as a control technique. In the Anthony and Herzlinger model for non-profit organizations it is a non-routine, external element done periodically (every 3-5 years) in order for management (presumably at some top level) to direct a strategic or management policy. The management literature on self-control would indicate this is, theoretically, an inefficient solution.

Total control could be increased and organizational effectiveness improved by routinely incorporating a participatory form of evaluation research into the formal management control process of a multinational organization. Once a participatory evaluation process was effectively functioning in a non-profit organization, then its potential as a service effort and accomplishment measure could be determined. Initially, however, empirical research could enrich general understanding of how participatory evaluation research is established, how evaluation data is gathered, and how evaluation findings are used in a multinational non-profit organization.

RESEARCH QUESTIONS

The purpose of this study was to determine how participatory evaluation affects the management control process of a multinational non-profit organization. This review of the literature revealed that many organizations have used pluralistic evaluation methods, but that an evaluation specialist had been involved in the processes to oversee and facilitate the efforts. The evaluation process described in this study does not use an evaluation specialist; the skillful practitioner is an organizational staff member who facilitates the efforts of community members to carry out the evaluation process.

Pluralistic evaluation models allow organizations to interact with their environment and with various stakeholders. These models and their evaluation processes are manifestations of the philosophy of management by objectives and self-control. Participatory evaluation was designed to open a multinational non-profit organization's complex and geographically dispersed operations to its total environment, thereby serving the needs of both the external and internal users for operating information.

Three research questions emerged from this literature review. These questions are ordinally related; each question must, therefore, be answered affirmatively before the examination of the next question is meaningful. The logic of these questions is presented in Figure 11. The decision tree shows that if any of the questions is answered negatively, then the analysis should stop until the function in question is operating properly. Further analysis is meaningless until the prior condition is met. The first three questions were examined in this dissertation to begin initial analysis of participatory evaluation as a service effort and accomplishment element in accounting information.

Research Question 1

CAN MEMBERS OF A HOST COMMUNITY DESIGN AND USE THEIR OWN PROJECT EVALUATION PLAN?

This question was asked to determine if the participatory evaluation process was functioning; and if so, whether it was producing an open-system environment as well as requisite operating information for assessment. An open-system environment would be created by the participatory evaluation process if the organization was interacting with its external environment for planning and resource allocation. Requisite operating information would be provided by the process if the various stakeholders could evaluate and control the project through a mutual decision process. If the evaluation process is not functioning and producing its desired attributes, then the process should be refined until it function properly. Only when the process is functioning effectively can evaluation information, findings, and reports be available for management reporting.

Research Question 2

CAN EVALUATION FINDINGS BE INCORPORATED INTO THE FORMAL MANAGEMENT CONTROL SYSTEM OF A MULTINATIONAL, NON-PROFIT ORGANIZATION?

This question was asked to determine if the formal management control system of a multinational non-profit organization is capable of incorporating indigenous evaluation reports. The analysis for this question would seek to ascertain if adequate information was provided to assess project effectiveness and to make the decisions necessary for managerial control. Providing adequate information to assess project effectiveness would be achieved if routine evaluation reports are being produced, distributed, and used. These reports should articulate with other management information and reports on the project, thereby

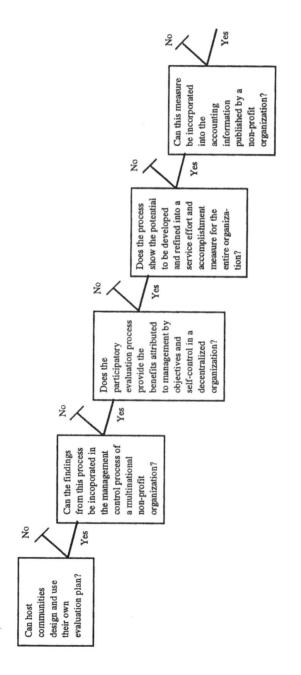

Figure 11: Decision Tree Logic-Research Questions

allowing users to assess the project's effectiveness and to make decisions concerning the project.

If the management information system is not capable of incorporating these reports into the feedback mechanism, then the system should be modified to accommodate these reports or alternatively, the evaluation reports should be adapted to the systems specifications. For only when the reporting system is compiling and recycling evaluation information can the full benefits of management by objectives and self-control be present.

Research Question 3

DOES THE PARTICIPATORY EVALUATION PROCESS PROVIDE THE BENEFITS ATTRIBUTED TO MANAGEMENT BY OBJECTIVES AND SELF-CONTROL IN A DECENTRALIZED ORGANIZATION?

This question was asked to determine if the participatory evaluation process displayed the characteristics suggested by the management literature for self-control.Three characteristics should be present if self-control is indeed occurring. The people closest to the project should be performing the evaluation tasks. Information, responsibility, decision power, and control should all be enhanced for the project participants. Finally, the process should allow them to assess project outcomes relative to their goals and to determine if resources are used most efficiently in achieving these goals.

These characteristics will be analyzed to examine how participatory evaluation research affects the management control process. All three research questions will form the analytical basis for assessing the utility of participatory evaluation and how it affects the management control process in Chapter VI.

SUMMARY

This chapter has attempted to synthesize the concepts of popular and modern management thinking with evaluation research and the management process into a new orientation for management of non-profit multinational organizations.Open-systems theory is important because participatory evaluation is an information feedback mechanism which allows organizations to be aware of their environments and take corrective actions when necessary. Central to open-systems theory is the importance of feedback, decisions, and control. Rationality theory assumes that these decisions will be made at some sub-optimum level of bounded reality, incorporating a decision maker's personal, cultural, and corporate values; correspondingly, it is expected that people will learn from their decisions.

Evaluation research is one tool available for improving accountability. Pluralistic evaluation methods allow for self-control and many of the corresponding benefits attributed to participation, decentralization, and the management by objectives philosophy.

Finally, this chapter reviewed the management process: the origins of this work, the dominant models which have been developed, and the difference in perception on incorporating evaluation research into the management process. Evaluation researchers see their work as pervasive while management researchers virtually ignore the process in their writings.

Open-systems theory and rationality theory justify incorporating evaluation research into the management process. The philosophy of management by objectives and self-control justifies incorporating participative evaluation research. The need to selectively adapt management practices to multinational non-profit organizations justifies exploring further participatory evaluation research in cross-cultural settings. Therefore, this dissertation sought to determine how participatory evaluation functions when it is introduced into the management control system of a multinational non-profit organization, and how it affects the management control process in that organization to determine if self-control is occurring.

NOTES

18. Fortune Magazine, May 13, 1985, p. 20.

19. Tom Peters and Nancy Austin, *Passion For Excellence*, (New York, New York: Random House, 1985).

20. John Naisbitt, *Megatrends*, (New York, New York: Warner Books, 1984), p,. xxii-xxiii.

21. World Bank *"1983 World Development Report,"* (Oxford, England: Oxford University Press, July 1984), p. 41.

22. Peter F. Drucker, *The Changing World of the Executive*. (New York, New York: Times Books, 1984), p. xvii.

23. Ibid., p. 253.

24. William F. Christopher. *Management For the 1980's*, (Englewood Cliffs, New Jersey: Prentice-Hall, Inc., 1980), p. 11-14.

25. Ludwig von Bertalanffy, Carl G. Hempel, Robert E. Bass, and Hans Jonas, "General Systems Theory: A New Approach to Unity in Science," *Human Biology* XXIII. (Dec. 1951), p. 303.

26. Kenneth E. Boulding, "General Systems Theory—The Skeleton of Science," Management Science, April 1956, p. 201.

27. Daniel Katz and Robert L. Kahn, *The Social Psychology of Organizations*, (New York, New York: John Wiley & Sons, Inc, 1964) Chapter 2.

28. Ibid, p. 25.

29. Ibid, p. 25.

30. Ibid, Chapter 2.

31. Herbert A. Simon, "Theories of Decision-making in Economics and Behavior Science," *American Economic Review*, (June, 1959), p. 269.

32. Herbert A. Simon, *Administrative Behavior*, (New York, New York: Macmillian Publishers, 1957), p. 75.

33. James G. March and Herbert A. Simon, *Organizations*, (New York, New York: John Wiley, 1958), p. 141.

34. Richard M. Cyert and James G. March, *A Behavioral Theory of the Firm*, (Englewood Cliffs, New Jersey: Prentice Hall, 1963).

35. James D. Thompson, *Organizations In Action*, (New York, New York: McGraw-Hill, 1967), p. 99.

36. Ibid., pp. 134-135.

37. Ibid., p. 144.

38. Donald W. Griesinger, "Management Theory: A Cybernetic Perspective," Unpublished Working Paper, (GMC-8601), January, 1986, p. 4.

39. Ibid., pp. 38-39.

40. K. Duncker, "On Problem Solving," *Psychological Monographs*, (1945), p. 14.

41. Ibid., pp. 26-27.

42. Peter H.Rossi, Howard E. Freeman, Sonia R. Wright, *Evaluation A Systematic Approach*, (Beverly Hills, California: Sage Publications, 1979), pp. 32-46.

43. D.N.T. Perkins, "Evaluating Social Interventions: A Conceptual Schema," Evaluation Quarterly, Vol. I (November 1977), p. 645.

44. Kenneth J. Euske, "Management Control: Planning, Control, Measurement, and Evaluation," (Reading, Massachusetts: Addison-Wesley Publishing Company, 1984), p. 66-67.

45. *Evaluation Sourcebook* (New York: American Council of Voluntary Agencies for Foreign Service), 1983, p. 137.

46. Rossi et al, pp. 25-29.

47. Michael Q. Patton, *Qualitative Evaluation Methods*, (Beverly Hills, California: Sage Publications), 1980.

48. Egon G. Guba and Yvonna S. Lincoln, *Effective Evaluation*, (San Francisco, California: Jossey-Bass Publishers), 1982, p. 82.

49. Douglas McGregor, *The Human Side of Enterprise*, (New York, New York: McGraw-Hill Book Company, Inc., 1960), p. 4.

50. Ibid., p. 9.

51. Ibid., pp. 55-56.

52. Ibid., p. 131.

53. H. C. Metcalf and L. Urwick, (Eds.) *Dynamic Administration: the Collected works of Mary Parker Follett* (New York, New York: Harper, Row, and Co., 1940), p. 42.

54. Rensis Likert, *New Patterns of Management* (New York, New York: McGraw Hill Book Company, Inc., 1961) p. 212.

55. Rensis Likert, *The Human Organization: Its Management and Values*, (New York, New York: McGraw Hill Book Company, 1967), pp. 134-135.

56. Chris Argyris, *Integrating the Individual and the Organization*, (New York, New York: John Wiley & Sons Inc., 1964), p. 275.

57. Peter F. Drucker, *The Practice of Management*, William Heinemann Ltd: London, England 1955), pp. 252-255.

58. *Ibid.*, p. 271.

59. Ibid., Chapter 2.

60. Ibid., p. 156.

61. Ibid., p. 156.

62. Ibid., p. 161.

63. Peter F. Drucker, *Management*, (New York, New York: Harper and Row, Publishers, 1973), p. 233.

64. Naisbitt, pp. 204-205.

65. Drucker, (1973), p.442.

66. Anthony S. Bryk, *Stakeholder Based Evaluations*, (San Francisco, California: Jossey-Bass Inc., Publishers, Ca., 1983), Chapters 2 and 3.

67. Ibid., p. 3.

68. Indian Social Institute, *Evaluation*, (New Delhi, India: 1983) p. 49.

69. American Council of Voluntary Agencies for Foreign Service, (1983), p. 3.

70. Ibid., Chapter 3.

71. Edward J. Soderstrum, *Social Impact Assessments* (New York, New York: Praeger Publishers, 1981), p. 103.

72. Harold Wolman, "The Determinants of Program Success and Failure," *Journal of Public Policy*, (1982), p. 462.

73. W. R. Derrick Sewell and Susan D. Phillips, "Models for the Evaluation of Public Participation Programs," *Natural Resources Journal*, April 1979, pp. 356-358.

74. Robert N. Anthony, *Planning and Control Systems*, (Boston, Massechusetts: Division of Research, Graduate School of Business Administration, Harvard University, 1965), pp. 16-18.

75. J. R. Brent Ritchie, "Roles of Research in the Management Process," MSU Business Topics, Summer 1976, pp. 13-22.

76. Jerry Dermer, *Management Planning and Control Systems*, (Homewood, Illinois: Richard D.Irwin, Inc., 1977), p. 58.

77. Joseph A. Maciariello, *Management Control Systems*, (Englewood Cliffs, New Jersey: Prentice-Hall, Inc, 1984), pp. 14-17.

78. Anthony Hopwood, *Accounting and Human Behavior*, (Devon, Great Britain: Accountancy Age Books, 1974), pp. 116-117.

79. Ibid., pp. 190-191.

80. Arnold S. Tannenbaum, *Control In Organizations*, (New York, New York: McGraw Hill Book Company, 1968), p. 12-14.

81. Ibid., p. 21.
82. Ibid., p. 20.
83. Robert N. Anthony and Regina E. Herzlinger, *Management Control in Non-profit Organizations*, (Homewood, Illinois: Richard D. Irwin, Inc., 1975), p. 2.
84. Ibid., pp. 5 & 13.
85. Ibid., p. 511.
86. Ibid., p. 529.

CHAPTER III

Research Methodology

Some major points of the literature review in Chapter II can be summarized to explain the choice of topic and methodology for this dissertation. In the management control process, evaluation takes many forms, one of which is evaluation research. Since the management control process and the evaluation process parallel one another, an efficient management control system should serve both needs. Evaluators use data uniquely to analyze operating performance, results, and impacts; while managers, generally, use data to compare expected and actual financial results as a basis for their operating decisions. Furthermore the management literature asserts that self-control results in congruence of individual and organizational goals, thereby, improving performance. Moreover, project or program evaluation in multinational organizations presents unique circumstances of being geographically dispersed, functionally diverse, and culturally contextual.

Therefore, the research for this dissertation was an empirical field study of a situation in which both the management control process functions and the evaluation process functions could be influenced. Its aim was to describe how useful participatory evaluation research is at the operating level and how effective it is in the formal control process.

The purpose of this chapter is to describe the research methodology and research techniques that were used in conducting the study. Topics included are divided as follows: (1) general analysis, (2) the organization, (3) participatory evaluation, (4) research design, (5) research observation, (6) research instrument construction (7) data collection, (8) data analysis, (9) summary of the research methodology, (10) summary.

GENERAL ANALYSIS

Robert Kaplan, speaking in 1984 on "The Role for Empirical Research in Management Accounting," argued that observation and description must be the starting points for scientific research. He suggested that they are also the building blocks upon which accounting theory formulation, causality, and hypothesis testing rest. He stated,

> Cost accounting and management control procedures function in complex organizational settings. Any empirical research method would need to capture this complexity. Field research methods . . . provide an opportunity to study management accounting systems in their organizational context.[87]

Fritz Roethlisberger helped pioneer field-based management research while working on the Hawthorne studies. In his autobiography, *The Elusive Phenomena*, he formulates scientific inquiry for management into "The Knowledge of Enterprise." In describing his principle of complementarily and relating knowledge of an enterprise to action, Roethlisberger stated,

> The elusive point I am making is that the relationship between knowledge and action in the social sciences is an intrinsic relation, such that the two cannot be easily separated. . . . A principle of complementarity as a way of conceptualizing social reality helps to clarify the role and skill of administration at empirical levels. . . . It is not easy to grasp the nature of an administrator's role and skill, for they escape our traditional ways of thinking. The difficulty resides in the fact that both have to do with maintaining relationships between incommensurables (A-relations: social interpersonal relationships; and B-relations: abstract, extrinsic relationships between groups or entities). . . . The clinical knowledge that we need will be developed in the form of case descriptions of relatively stable patterns or syndromes of behavior. . . . We need more of the kind of knowledge represented by these (kinds of) findings to guide decisions and actions of proactive

> managers. Even when we have it, their decisions, not being
> sanctioned by general propositions at high levels of
> abstraction, will be importantly characterized by skill and such
> personal qualities such as judgment, commitment, awareness
> of their own and others' feelings, and authenticity. Clinical
> knowledge will help validate the conditions and directions
> within which such qualities operate usefully.[88]

Roethlisberger's conceptualization for the development of knowledge outlines the logic used in this dissertation.

Inductive logic develops knowledge by observing a phenomena and ordering its characteristics systematically. People begin to improve their relationship with their surroundings when skillful practitioners, who understand the phenomena with which they are dealing, learn to manipulate characteristics to their own advantage.

With skilled practitioners already present in organizations, management scientists can enter and, using clinical research methods, attempt to develop systematic knowledge of the phenomena and of the means used by the practitioner. In describing how an accounting researcher might apply these concepts to the management control process, Kaplan claims:

> . . . a fortunate researcher may become involved with an
> organization which, for its own reasons, undertakes a major
> change in its measurement and reporting system. Which such
> an occurrence, the researcher would then be in a position to
> document the impact of the change. [89]

Such are the circumstances of this research. A multinational, non-profit organization introduced participatory evaluation into it management process worldwide. The research strategy used involved a program of field-based research incorporating questionnaire surveys based on the following descriptions of the organization and of the intervention.

THE ORGANIZATION—INTEGRATING DIVERSE ACTIVITIES IN DISPERSED LOCATIONS

The literature search argued that multinational non-profit organizations are complex entities in which geographic, cultural, product, program, and functional specialization need to be considered by management in organizing the enterprise's activities. The purpose of this section is to show the complexity and diversity of a multinational non-profit organization which provides human services and in which a participatory evaluation process was introduced.

The Enterprise

World Humanitarian Aid (WHA)[90], a pseudonym see footnote, is typical, in many respects, of modern organizational giants. It is a compound of many national organizations operating in both the first and third world. It redistributes wealth gathered in the developed world to communities in under developed countries through a myriad of programs and projects. To accomplish the many tasks involved in conducting such an enterprise efficiently, its human and physical resources are organized to provide specialized functions for the kinds of activity in which it is engaged in each country in which it operates.

Looking at an entity of this complexity from the top down can be an overpowering experience. More insight into its management process can be gained by looking at the tasks it is organized to achieve and the specialized functions it has created to accomplish these tasks.

Funding

WHA is a private, non-profit organization. Its funding comes from individual donors, corporate or foundation donors, and grants from other agencies. The enterprise has an enormous demand for unrestricted funds and it is organized to solicit these funds on a consistent long-term basis.

For economy, efficiency, and local control, five autonomous national organizations are located in major countries and continents of the developed world solely for the purpose of fund raising by marketing the philosophy of WHA's development work. Each unit is a decentralized responsibility center with its own Board of Directors who establish strategic priorities and commit funds to the international operations. Each organization's staff conducts various marketing and finance functions such as solicitations, campaign drives, billings, collection, and reporting, as well as internal operations management.

International Operations

The primary business of WHA is human resource development. The international operations support relief, rehabilitation, and development projects in cooperation with local partner agencies in individual third-world countries. The support can be in the form of direct funding for activities or professional assistance for specialized functions. Project specialists oversee funding support while functional specialists contribute operational support. Both must be organized and coordinated to keep the national units operating effectively.

Within each national unit there are many human service processes operating concurrently. For example, a single office in an African country may be engaged in famine relief activities, in rehabilitation and relocation activities, and holistic development activities in an area not directly affected by the draught. One process responds in an emergency to meet immediate needs to save lives; the other process begins neo-development and re-establishes a stable environment; while the third process builds socio-economic infrastructure for human development. Thus within one responsibility unit, different kinds of program and project skills are required. Moreover, the same processes are carried out at sub-offices throughout these individual countries and at other national locations throughout the world. Knowledge about these processes and their outcomes must be shared between specialists, among specialties, and across national boundaries.

Central Administration

In a decentralized operation certain administrative tasks must be coordinated for the commonweal of the enterprise. These functions are also subject to economies of scale in terms of supervision, training, planning, and information flow across functional lines. The chosen size of the international headquarters suggests that top levels of management, higher echelons of basic functional management, and the corporate specialized functions (e.g., strategic planning) are best housed in a single location where rapid and recurrent personal communication occurs across all areas of specialization.

To show the relationship of the functions discussed, an abstract version of the enterprise's organizational chart is presented in Figure 12. The chart attempts to show graphically how specialized functions interrelate. The chart indicates the extreme degree of diversification at WHA. When this is extended to offices in thirty-three countries around the world, the enormity and divergence of functions performs in dispersed geographic locations is evident.

This enterprise is organized on the classic hierarchical model of the church and military using vice presidents to create operationally decentralized responsibility units instead of autonomous entities as suggested by decentralization. Tracing the technical support and finance activities shows the interrelationship between project funding support and project functional support. There is a corporate vice- president for technical support who directs research and the staff functions for field operations. There is a Director of Field Development for central administrative tasks of policy research, planning coordination, and evaluation. In addition, there are three regional vice-presidents, one for Asia, Latin America, and Africa. They are served by a Director of Field Services Support systems for design and implementation of project reporting and information systems. They oversee the National offices in their region of the world.

Operating Locations

Projects are located entirely in the undeveloped world. However, corporate economies of scale can be achieved in funding-distribution and functional-labor specialization when an enterprise is organized to take advantage of these similar tasks performed in different locations. For example, national offices are established in twenty-eight countries, with field offices and sub-offices serving specific geographic areas. National employees, who have philosophies of human development congruent with WHA's philosophy, are used almost exclusively. These large numbers of local contact points between WHA and its diverse operating locations are the best example of organizing to take advantage of diversity.

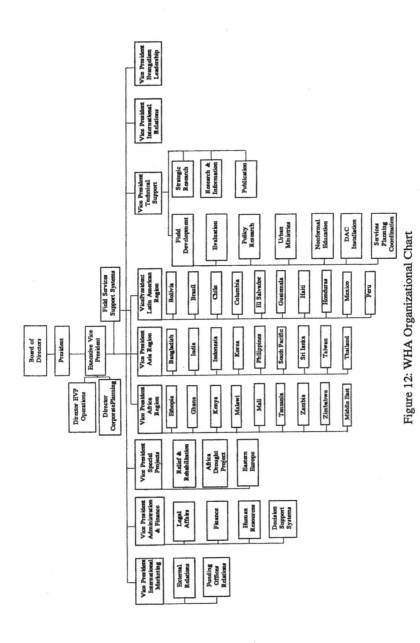

Figure 12: WHA Organizational Chart

National Offices Administration

Each of the twenty-eight national offices has its own Director and full complement of staff. Each country has an operations administrator who directs the activities of the Project Specialists, the first line staff members who work with partner agencies in conducting development projects, whether they are receiving financial and/or functional support. Further, the operations administrator directs the activities of the functional specialist who provide in-kind support to projects. In all, a form of administration for operations is defined at six levels or more above the first-line project specialist who actually interacts with the project participants.

In finance, the line of administration moves down from the Vice-President of Finance and Administration, through the Finance Department to the field operation's controller, who reports to the National Office Director. In each country a finance administrator directs the activities of the accountants, who distribute funds directly to projects. There is no formal coordination between funding and project operations, except as observed and noted by each Project Specialist acting independently.

Output

The entire human development process has human services as its output. The most common form of output is funding, which must be properly allocated, dispersed, and utilized by the partner agency with no direct operational function conducted by WHA. The second most common (and increasing) form of output is direct establishment of services (such as health-care, nutrition, education, revolving loans) through the operating assistance of a development specialist working in a project.

Extraordinary output would be massive feeding programs now occurring in Africa, relocation activities conducted in Cambodia and Thailand since the Vietnam War, or the redevelopment projects undertaken in Bangladesh. Delivery of services, whether funding or operations, must be scheduled, costs controlled, accountability assured, capacity planned, and new activities developed in a systematic manner to meet on-going project needs and emergency demands. Further, these outputs must be measured and valued by the evaluation process for effective control decisions to be made by various people.

Populations Affected

The people involved in, working with, and affected by WHA services are segmented into several groupings, any one of which may participate with another group. WHA projects are confined to one type of operation at a time which incorporates various activities for and by the people involved. For example, a first-line project specialist working in a specific geographic area may work with ten partner agencies, each conducting their own development project. Oversight responsibility for the project is granted to a project committee; while administrative and operational responsibility rests with a project director and project staff. Functional specialists are involved on either a permanent or itinerate basis. The local community members directly involved in the project both participate in the project operations and receive the benefits of the project intervention. Community members not directly involved in the project and WHA administrative staff are secondarily affected by project operations.

Project characteristics and the evaluation-control function need to be designed to meet the related operating needs of each segmented group at each location. Therefore, project plans, program activities, budgets, evaluation assessments and reports must serve the people directly and indirectly involved in the project. However, operating economies and strategic considerations make it useful for WHA to organize itself internationally in order to best serve the needs of many individual projects in diverse locations.

The Process of Human Resource Development

Stepping back from the details of the enterprise and considering what major forces shape the management task in the human resources development process, one stands out: andragogy. Andragogy is a method of teaching and learning which incorporates the total environment, experience, and development of the teacher and the student in the educational process. Pedagogy comes from the Greek root word *paed or ped*, meaning child or childhood. Therefore, pedagogy is a formal educational method designed for children. Andragogy comes from the Greek root word *andr* meaning adult or a human being with developed strengths. Therefore, andragogy is a non-formal educational method designed for teaching adults, which incorporates their life-long experiences. Adult education programs use non-formal teaching techniques. In management, Knowles related andragogy to organizational development programs which capitalize on the employees' formal education, professional development, and life experiences through a series of mutual causation situations that produce a learning process. [91] In these situations the employees, working with the facilitator, work together to produce the final outcome or effect.

The human development process is one in which people must grow in spirit, knowledge, and talent. Human services organizations are constructive responses to ambiguous social problems. The management process and it various functions must all facilitate, encourage, and appreciate that growth. Keeping these needs in mind, it is possible to begin to understand the complex learning process that provides context to the participatory evaluation process designed by WHA.

Conclusions on the Organization

WHA is a multinational non-profit organization which redistributes wealth from developed societies to people in developing societies. Their primary activity is funding projects which are operated by partner agencies in the local community. These projects carry out traditional development activities such as education, health, nutrition, and training for holistic human development.

In this case study, human development was identified as an andragogical process where adult people learn from their experiences; they modify all aspects of their being—physical, intellectual, emotional, social, and spiritual—from what they learn and what they experience. The management processes of enterprises engaged in human development activities should, therefore, provide opportunities for project participants to learn from all components of the project—it administration as well as its programs and activities.

At the risk of belaboring the point, the traditional concepts of task specialization and administrative integration for coordination reach very refined manifestations in the multinational organization. No one human being can be aware of and oversee such a large, complex enterprise.

No mechanical, paper-based reporting system can provide information on a timely enough basis to be useful for rational decision making. Sophisticated management systems and management skills are required for effective administration.

A systems management approach is needed which allows communication and coordination to occur throughout the world. Specialists in one country must be able to exchange information with other specialists wherever they are working. National administrators must have ready access to a complete flow of project or program information including funding appropriations, spending patterns, target dates, task objectives or quotas, and subsequent changes in all project details. The international administrators must have ready access to aggregate information on the same patterns as well as corporate strategic information.

This need for large amounts of detailed and aggregate information available at dispersed geographic locations must be kept in mind throughout the description of the evaluation and control process. The process must be designed to serve the andragogical needs of individual projects for their participants, and yet at the same time, the administrative needs of a large, complex organization.

PARTICIPATORY EVALUATION—PEOPLE LEARNING FROM THEIR OWN EXPERIENCES

Understanding the nature and specific activities of the participatory evaluation process is also essential if the research findings are to be relevant to new generalizations on evaluation research and management control. Describing in more detail the process studied will help explain how it allows project participants to measure, value, and assess the outcome of their project.

Evaluation at WHA involves the process by which objectives, goals, and activities of the many development projects are established, monitored, and reported by the recipient community members to the management hierarchy. The time horizon for each project evaluation is the five-year anticipated life-span of a project. The "evaluation-plan" referred to by staff and management, would be described as closer to an annual plan according to the usual conception of the budget-planning spectrum. The evaluation plan is to be designed at the project's inception; the process is also being introduced, however, to projects currently in-progress as well.

Management Process Model for
Development Projects at WHA

The project life-cycle provides a helpful structure for describing the management and evaluation processes for a development project.

Conception: A project is conceived when someone or some group identifies a need, desires to do something about it, has a germane idea, or identifies an issue or service where people can help one another. A local partner agency agrees to become involved and sponsor the project. The partner agency contacts the community to see if they are interested in having a project. The partner agency and members of the local community meet together informally to discuss the problem or needs and to commit themselves to the project. They identify resources and talents available in the community. Realizing that they do not have adequate resources, talents, abilities, or funds, they approach WHA to provide funding or operational support.

WHA's Initial Involvement: The project specialist visits the proposed project site and decides whether or not to complete a project checklist, workbook, and funding proposal. This is a critical operating decision for WHA because, in the several years of this research, few project proposals were ever formally denied by the higher level management. Thus project acceptance or rejection, virtually, took place at this point.

The project specialist prepares a standard checklist assessing this community's conditions, completes a standard project workbook describing the community's needs and resources, and then, together with community members and the partner agency, drafts a funding proposal for a new project. The project proposal contains the plans, goals, activities, target dates, budget, evaluation plan, base line measures and an evaluation monitoring device to track project operations. Thus, evaluation is considered in the negotiation and design phase of a project.

The project negotiation brings together the partner agency, project committee, community members, project director, project staff, and WHA project specialist in considering whether to accept or reject a project and in formulating the project content. All six of these parties are jointly responsible for the decisions about the project content and form.

Initial Evaluation Activities: The participatory evaluation process developed by WHA stimulates and facilitates project participants' assessments and evaluations of their own environment. Using non-formal education techniques, the project specialist helps the community members describe, investigate, and analyze their present conditions. In describing their community, participants may make a list, draw a picture, or sketch a map of their town to show current relationships of dwellings, roads, paths, walls, gardens, community gathering places, and other features. After describing the physical relationships of their community, the participants decide what additional information they need to investigate further the needs, problems, and resources available in their area. They obtain this information by directly asking their friends and neighbors specific questions (e.g.: number of family members, ages, health problems, water supply; some open-ended questions are also asked.)

Next the community members, partner agency, project committee, director, staff, and WHA project specialist analyze the results of their investigation, in light of their own description, and together decide their project's purpose, objectives, measurable goals, tasks and activities to accomplish these goals, indicators to measure changes in these goals, and a monitoring device to record project activities. If further current measuring is necessary, they also complete baseline measurements for these indicators. This group considers alternative spending levels to fund their project and prepares a budget. All of these steps relate to the management process. Deciding on indicators, designing a monitoring device, and taking baseline measures are, however, usually considered more evaluation specific while the other functions are usually considered more management specific.

Implementation and Monitoring of the Project: A formal project proposal, specifying the project content decided on by this group, is then prepared and submitted to WHA for approval. The majority of information generated by this process is stored at the project site and at the project specialist's home office. The formal proposal and subsequent operating information remain in the National Office files. The custodial accounting system contains only financial information.

Once the project is approved, implementation of the activities and programs is carried out by the partner agency, project committee, director, staff, community members and any functional specialists providing in-kind support. To monitor the project's activity, the project specialist makes monthly project visits to assess performance and complete progress-to-date reports. On this visit, several forms of examination occur: financial records are reviewed; the project operations are observed; discussions are held with various project participants; and, the evaluation monitoring devices are used.

Assessment and Evaluation: Through dialogue and discussion, the project specialist facilitates the review and validation of project outcomes. Community members report their progress in various program activities, and the group discusses these outcomes. Then, together, the project participants reach a consensus on how well they are doing currently and what their next month's plan-of-action should be. Subsequently, monthly, quarterly, and annual reports are filed on project operations and spending. No routine evaluation report is filed; however, project specialists prepare a case by case written report detailing the community's progress in implementing its project.

By realizing the outcomes of their actions, community members can learn from their experiences, decide to maintain or modify their activities as appropriate, and continue on into the next phase of their project. Correspondingly, WHA employees also use the information provided by the evaluation process when deciding to continue or modify their activities, especially funding and in-kind support.

Conclusions: The management process model described for development project evaluation at WHA shows evaluation research functions being incorporated into each phase of the management process by community members. A total picture of the model and the corresponding evaluation functions is presented in Figure 13. The matching of management process phases and participatory evaluation functions makes the preceding description more precise. However, it does not indicate that all these phases and functions should be performed in this particular order when using participatory evaluation. The model does not prescribe what a project specialist should do; rather, it depicts a pattern of what is going on between participatory evaluation and the management process. Awareness of the pattern should facilitate understanding the research results presented in Chapters IV and V.

The planning, needs assessment, and problem identification phase of the project is largely a technical process leading to project formation. The programming, deciding on goals and objectives, and selecting activities phase of the project is largely a behavioral and social process leading to project content. The implementation and evaluation control

CONTROL MANAGEMENT PHASE	HOW COMMUNITY MEMBERS PARTICIPATE FOR EVALUATION
Planning	Describe, investigate, analyze their environment. Identify needs or problems. Decide how need(s) or problem(s) can be alleviated.
Programming	Decide which activities to undertake. Establish measurable goals for these activities. Decide on indicators to measure outcomes for these goals. Design a monitoring device to record these outcomes. Take baseline measures for current status of indicator.
Budgeting	Consider how much money is needed to fund these activities. Decide how much to spend.
Implementation	Carry-out the activities of the project. Record their outcomes in/on the monitoring device.
Evaluation/Control	Compare actual outcomes to anticipated outcomes established in the goals. Decide to maintain or modify activities.

Figure 13: The Participatory Evaluation Process
and Management Control Phases

phases of the project combine technical and behavioral processes; they generate the project's outcomes while being created and conducted in the cultural context of the community. All of these functions are adult learning experiences contributing to human resource development; but each is only slightly affected by the higher echelons of the multinational organization. How well prepared the project specialist is to introduce and facilitate the participatory evaluations process is, therefore, critical to its installation and continued functioning.

Evaluation Training

The evaluation literature review identified various pluralistic evaluation models and several organizations which had used stakeholder evaluation methods. In these instances, however, an evaluation specialist had been involved in the process to oversee and guide the efforts. WHA's evaluation process does not use a person technically trained in evaluation. Rather, their own national staff member facilitates the community through the evaluation process and represents WHA's interest in the project. To prepare the national staff for this task, an evaluation training program was designed to teach the staff the technical evaluation skills and non-formal education methods necessary for program evaluation.

The training consists of two workshops held in the host country and conducted in the native language. The first workshop lasts eight days and presents the description, investigation, analysis, goal setting, indicator selection, and baseline measurement skills required for needs assessment and project design. A second workshop is held six months later. It lasts five days and presents the monitoring, reporting, assessing, and project activities assessment skills needed to maintain or modify the project's content.

Each workshop is limited to twenty participants, and the employee mix is balanced between first line operating staff (project specialists), technical support staff, and administrators. Each participant agrees to use the participatory evaluation techniques and skills learned at the workshop shop in at least one project in which they are working.

Summary of the Participatory Evaluation Process

The participatory evaluation process designed and developed by WHA allows all people affected by a project to assist in designing and using the evaluation plan for that project. The evaluation process combines technical evaluation skills and non-formal education methods into a process to measure, value, and assess project outcomes. The process allows project participants to experience and learn from predicting and setting their own goals, measuring their outcome, comparing their results to their predictions, and evaluating the difference to decide if they should maintain their course of action or change their plans. These evaluations of project performance are then used directly by the project participants to control their project activities; they are also used indirectly by the management and staff of WHA to control their corporate activities. Thus the participatory evaluation at WHA is intended to create experiences for project participants to learn the basic elements of decision making, to create indigenous assessments of program efforts and accomplishments, and to create an open-system environment for management by objectives and self-control in a decentralized organization.

RESEARCH DESIGN

The purpose of this dissertation was to study how participatory evaluation affects the management control process of a multinational non-profit organization. Comparing the evaluation literature and the management control process literature revealed a difference in perception on incorporating evaluation findings into the regular and routine management reporting system. Evaluation writers emphasized the importance of having their findings used by management in the decision process. Yet the dominant management control process models emphasize financial evaluative assessments rather than operational evaluative assessments.

Therefore, evaluation research findings may have been excluded from routine management reporting and assessment processes, as the evaluation writers assert only because managers and system designers have not consciously considered the benefits of including these findings in the systematic data collection and control decision processes. Alternatively, evaluation research findings may have been excluded from routine management reporting and assessments processes for two other reasons: (1) because the evaluation research findings do not lend themselves to being routinely and systematically collected and used in the control process, or (2) because management control systems are not capable of compiling and conveying these alternative forms of qualitative and quantitative data. Both of these questions were considered in this research as prerequisite conditions to determining how participatory evaluation affects the management control process of a multinational non-profit organization.

Adapting Roethlisberger's knowledge enterprise model to this research problem, clinical knowledge should be acquired by observing and describing the organization, its processes, and its international and procedural relationships. The beginnings of analytical knowledge should be presented in the form of elementary measurements which define concepts and variables. An integrated, programmatic mode of research design was most suitable for documenting the knowledge and skills of administrator's using the participatory evaluation process.

John Buckley, *et al*, in their monograph for the National Associations of Accountants on research methodology and business decisions, specified observation and experience as the operative criteria for empiricism. Opinion research can capture people's impressions about themselves, their environments, and their responses to changing conditions. Buckley, *et al*, contended that perceptions differ from reality. Thus, asking people's opinion about a phenomena can be the starting point in describing and measuring its characteristics; but empirical research should also explore how the persons behaved when using the means or phenomena and where they found it useful.[92]

Emory points out that experience surveys can ask persons their ideas, opinions, or perception on which are the important issues or aspects of a means or a phenomena.

> Seldom is more than a fraction of the existing knowledge in any field put into writing. Thus, we will profit by seeking information from persons experienced in the area of study. Such persons can help us secure an insight into relationships between variables. To get an accurate picture of the current situation we need to solicit the views of those believed to know what is going on.[93]

Eugene Stone, in his book *Research Methods in Organizational Behavior*, discussed alternative empirical research strategies. He contended that alternative research strategies should be integrated into the research design after considering eight dimensions of the research problem. He argued that, ". . . the nature of the problem being dealt with should be the major determinant of the strategy used by the researcher."[94]

A field study using survey questionnaires is well suited to the unique nature of participatory evaluation in a multinational non-profit organization for several reasons:

1. The research is ex-post facto, no independent variables were manipulated by the researcher.
2. The system studied was intact and naturally occurring in the organization.

Rated Dimension	Laboratory Experiment	Simulation	Field Experiment	Field Study	Sample Survey	Case Study
COST:						
Initial "Set-up"	M	L-H	M-H	M-H	H	L-H
Marginal Cost per subject	L	L-H	M	M	L-M	L-H
VARIABLES:						
Strength of Independent						
Variables	L	L-M	M	H	H	H
Range of Variables	L	M	M	H	H	L-H
Potential to Manipulate						
Independent Variables	H	M-H	M	N	N	N
CONTROL:						
Potential for Testing						
Causal Hypotheses	H	M-H	M	L	L	N
Potential for Study to						
Change Researcher	L	L	M	M	L	H
Potential for Controlling						
Confounding Variables	H	M-H	L-M	L	L	N
ARTIFACTS:						
Potential for Experimenter						
Expectancy Effects	H	M	M-H	M	L	H
Potential for Demand						
Characteristics	H	M	M-H	M	L	H
Potential for Evaluation						
Apprehension	H	M-H	M-H	M	L	H
SETTING:						
Naturalness of Setting	L	M-H	H	H	H	H
Degree to which Behavior						
is Setting-Dependent	H	L-M	H	H	L	H
GENERALIZABILTIY:						
Applicability of Study's						
Results to Different						
Populations	L-H	L-H	L	L	H	N

N-None L-Low M-Moderate H-High

Figure 14: Stone's Comparison of Empirical Research Strategies

3. The focus of this research was to describe how the management control process was affected by this technique.
4. The researcher's intrusion on the process needed to be minimal;
5. The variables needed to be systematically measured.
6. Data needed to be collected directly from the organization's employees.
7. Respondents needed to provide the data in their natural geographic setting.
8. Responses from the employees are assumed to be largely unaffected by the various work settings in which they were elicited.
9. The costs of visiting all these sites (in both time and money) was prohibitive, while not substantially contributing to the reliability of the data.

Based on Stone's criteria comparison for empirical research strategies (See Figure 14), an integrated research design using case study descriptions and field studies incorporating questionnaire surveys would enhance internal validity and allow for generalizing the findings to other similar organizations.[95]

RESEARCH OBSERVATIONS

The observations and document reviews used in this study were done over a five year period. Initial contact with the organization and study of the process began in November of 1980. Routine observations of the organization and the evaluation process began in the Spring of 1981 and continued throughout the study. During development and design of the process and of the training program, on-site visits were conducted to document and note maxims, philosophies, purposes, policies, goals, objectives, and procedures which were set forth together. During introduction, training, and initial implementation of the process, organizational source documents describing and assessing the process were reviewed to identify critical issues. After the process was functioning, a systematic documentation of the components was compiled to assemble and classify attributes. Throughout the study, management review and reflection proceedings were also observed to identify patterns of response.

RESEARCH INSTRUMENT CONSTRUCTION

Two questionnaires were designed for this research. Both were based on the literature review and prevailing issues raised by the organization's staff in internal memos, management reports, and interviews. Guba suggested that critical issues would emerge from an iterative process of interviewing, reviewing source documents, and noting the number of times a common theme was discussed.[96]

One questionnaire asked the employee's expectations from participatory evaluations. The other questionnaire asked the employees using participatory evaluation about their experiences. Both questionnaires were initially administered to an English-speaking National office staff to ensure clarity of content and that the time required to complete them was within the desired limit. Both questionnaires were translated into native languages when possible. Translation validity was checked by having each questionnaire retranslated back into English by a different translator. (See Appendix A).

Expectations Questionnaire

In order to determine how people in the organization expected to use evaluation research information in their work, this questionnaire was designed to ask them their expectations from program evaluations. This questionnaire contained open-ended and directed questions on evaluation issues and evaluation reports as well as personnel data.

The directed questions and the primary definitional characteristics of evaluation research which they addressed were:

1. Purpose: How should evaluations be defined?
2. Goals: Why should evaluations be conducted?
3. Supervision: Who should manage the evaluations?
4. Technical Workers: Who should do the technical evaluation work?
5. Protocol: How should requests for help be channeled in the organization?
6. Assistants: Who should provide support or assistance?

7. Critical Issues: What are the important issues to understand when doing technical evaluation work in development organizations?
8. Beneficiaries: Who should benefit from evaluation findings?
9. Distributions: How should findings be reported and shared?
10. Uses: How would employees use evaluation reports in their work?

Each question was followed by a list of replies developed from internal documents and the literature review. The employees were asked to respond to each item listed on a high to low rating scale (i.e.: agree/disagree, important/unimportant, desirable/undesirable).

In order to analyze the data by region of the world, country, job position, education level, and length of service to the organization, the questionnaire asked ten demographic questions: (1) Name (optional), (2) Office, (3) Job Title, (4) Name of projects, (5) Length of time with these projects, (6) Length of time with the organization, (7) Sex, (8) Age Group, (9) Educational Attainment, (10) Location where education was received.

Demographic data allowed the replies to be grouped by various classifications. Results of the study could then be analyzed to ascertain if different classifications responded differently. For example, did different levels within the hierarchy or different geographic locations respond differently to the same issues? The methodology of analyzing these data is presented later in this chapter and the results are presented in Chapter IV.

Experience Questionnaire

What an organization's employees expect from a new management tool provides the benchmark from which to judge performance. Information on how the tool is actually working is also needed. This questionnaire was designed to ask the staff, those who had been trained to use participatory evaluation methods and who were subsequently implementing these methods in at least one project, about their experiences. This questionnaire contained open-ended and directed questions on implementing the participatory evaluation methods and on the behavioral responses of project participants to the process. Personnel data was used to do demographic analysis on these responses as well.

The methodology of analyzing these data is presented later in this chapter and the results are presented in Chapter V.

Implementations of Participatory Evaluation Methods: How well a management tool functions to accomplish its desired task is an important prerequisite to determining how it effects other functions in the management control process. These questions on implementation followed the order of evaluation procedures taught to the organization's employees for the participatory evaluation methodology. The evaluation functions included were.

1. Needs assessment,
2. Designing the project,
3. Organizing the project,
4. Taking baseline measurements,
5. Preparing the project proposal forms,
6. Assessing the project's performance,
7. Reporting the evaluation findings.

Each question was followed by a list of replies developed from internal documents and the literature review. The employees were asked to respond to each item listed on a high to low rating scale (i.e.: helpful/hindered). Respondents were asked their perception of how helpful all groups involved in the project found the evaluation methods to be.

Behavioral Responses to Participatory Evaluation: The value of a management tool lies not only in how well it works to accomplish the task, but also how well (or poorly) it is received by the people who must use it. These questions addressed the behavioral issues involved in management by objectives and self-control, value-rationality theory, and open-systems theory. The behavioral issues included were:

1. Group dynamics,
2. Communications,
3. Relationship towards the project,
4. Interpersonal relationships,
5. Values,
6. Responsibility,
7. Decision making,

8. Power structure,
9. Control.

Each question contained a list of replies developed from internal documents and the literature review. The employees were asked to respond to each item listed on a high to low rating scale (i.e.: helpful/hindered, agree/disagree). Respondents were asked their perceptions of how other groups involved in the project felt about the evaluation process.

Rationale For Construction of These Questionnaires

Field studies using questionnaire surveys have several strengths and weaknesses. The necessity to balance these carefully in cross-cultural management research is critical. Field studies seek to examine management systems operating in their natural setting. Respondents are individual employees working within the subject organization. The researcher relies on the respondents to give self-reported findings on their experiences, perceptions, or opinions.

The strength of the results and findings in representing the phenomena under study is greater than can be obtained from a surrogate respondent group in a laboratory; however, the strength of the variables lies in their description and identification of phenomena, not in their determination of causality.

In a field study, the researcher has no control over independent or dependent variables (participatory evaluation methods and management control functions in this case) nor over the confounding variables (behavioral responses to the process; political, cultural, or economic conditions). Thus, empirical propositions or hypotheses may be suggested from the findings and causal or interviewing variable may be implied, but further influences would be difficult to justify. Moreover, using a one-time questionnaire establishes a cross-sectional time study, but does not allow for a longitudinal study, which could help justify further inferences.

However, the realism of field studies allows an indepth assessment of very complex issues. Unfortunately, complexity requires a large number of variable and very long questionnaires. The questionnaires were designed to be relevant to the organization and phenomena being studies. Even with a large number of questions and possible responses, standardized reply methods can force people to subscribe to statements they do not fully endorse or understand. The use of internal documents to formulate the questions and identifying the replies was intended to overcome this problem, and, thereby allow the questions to be better indicators of the characteristics being studied and each reply to be a better indicant of the parameters underlying those characteristics.

In cross-cultural research, the research instrument must also be as unobtrusive as possible to encourage objective responses. Decreased willingness of people to respond to surveys, or to respond candidly, because of suspicion, fear, or a felt need to respond "as management wants" is especially acute in this type of research. Low response rates can be expected even when management willingly supports the research and guarantees anonymity. Therefore, the questions chosen for inclusion in the questionnaires had to represent the general phenomena, be written to be organizationally specific, and to encourage responses from a very wide audience.

DATA COLLECTION

Collecting data from a geographically dispersed subject population required carefully planned logistics. Prior approval of all effected administrators had to be obtained. Subject employees for each office had to be identified. Finally, the questionnaires had to be distributed and collected.

Administrative Approvals

The questionnaires were designed and initially drafted during the summer and fall of 1983. In January of 1984, they were drafted in their final form. In February and March of 1984, executive administrators reviewed them and gave approval for their distribution. The questionnaires were then translated.

In June, all National Office Directors were contacted by the Director of Evaluation, requesting their permission to involve the staff from their office in the study. By July, all offices had agreed to participate in the study and the questionnaires were distributed to predetermined employees.

Identification of Subject Employees

Employees were selected to participate in the research based on their job position. Since the research was studying a management tool which affected both operations and financial administration, all employees with decision-making responsibility were invited to participate in completing the expectations questionnaire. Only those employees who had been trained in the participatory evaluation methodology, and would subsequently be using the techniques in at least one project, were asked to complete the experience questionnaire.

The expectations questionnaire sought to identify how people at WHA thought the participation process should function. It was prepared to gather information from all persons involved in the decision process concerning projects at WHA. In the national offices this group included employees in administration, finance, direct project operations, indirection staff operations, and evaluation/training. At the international headquarters this group included members of the Board of Directors, executive management, finance, operation, and the support staff. All of these persons make decisions about WHA projects and may directly or indirectly need to know and/or use the evaluation findings produced from the participatory evaluation process.

The experience questionnaire sought to examine how the participatory evaluation process was working in the various projects where it was being introduced. It was written to gather data from all persons who had been trained at the participatory evaluation workshops. Each of these trainees had agreed to use the participatory evaluation process and its specific techniques in at least one project in which they were working. This group only included employees from the national offices; they represented administration, direct and indirect operations staff, and the evaluation/training department.

Distribution of the Questionnaires

The questionnaires and a sample cover memo were mailed by international courier to each National Office Director. The questionnaires were given to staff members with a cover memo from their own National Director, endorsing the study and requesting that they complete the questionnaire. The purpose of the questionnaire and the research was clearly stated and statements were made which gave further reassurances of respondent confidentiality.

A follow up memo was sent out by the National Director in five days thanking the people who had already responded and requesting the remaining staff members to reply. All questionnaires were returned to the National Office Director in a sealed envelope. Then the questionnaires were sent directly to the researcher by international courier.

After two months, all National Office Directors whose offices had not responded, were contacted by the Director of Evaluation and asked to have their staff complete the questionnaires. After four months, the executive administrators offered to contact every National Office administrator again. But further pressure from "top administration" to complete the forms could have biased the results so significantly that the findings would not have contributed to the study. Therefore the effort to collect questionnaires stopped six months after they were initially mailed.

DATA ANALYSIS

Themes having saliency for respondents who have a common employer are likely to be salient for other similar organizations, and their employees. Thus, in spite of the limitations cited earlier, a contribution can be made to the accounting literature on service effort and accomplishment measures as well as to the general literature on multinational management and control processes in non-profit organizations by identifying and describing the characteristics of participatory evaluation in one multinational non-profit organization. These characteristics will allow initial analysis of evaluation research as a possible service accomplishment element for financial reporting.

In this section a description of the approaches used to analyze the data will be presented. The open-ended questions could not be analyzed due to the difficulty of translating the many languages represented. The quantitative analysis was performed using the Statistical Package for the Social Sciences (SPSS).[97] Descriptive statistics were used for the various replies to the directed questions and confidence intervals were then constructed for the directed questions. F-tests were used to analyze the replies from various respondent groups using the personnel data.

Descriptive Statistics

Descriptive statistics is a process to reduce the large volume of numerical information produced by a research study into more manageable and meaningful dimensions. The mean-value (or average) indicates the central tendency of the responses. The standard deviation measures how widely the responses disperse around the central value.

Descriptive analysis provides a profile of characteristics and are especially useful when the distribution of variables representing the phenomena is uncertain or yet to be determined. Therefore, when management has no idea how helpful a new management tool is, the average rating of helpfulness by a sample or specific population of their employees is an important first indication of utility. Such one-dimensional analysis also provides a benchmark from which future strategies can be directed and future changes can be measured.

Confidence Intervals

Often researchers state that their results are/are not statistically significant if they do/do not reach the .05 or .01 level of significance. Such findings use a decision rule to accept or reject a preconceived hypothesis about the population. Exploratory research to examine and describe a new phenomena does not lend itself to quality control rules of accepting or rejecting characteristics. Rather variables must be examined and classified or categorized with some degree of confidence. Confidence has been described as ". . . the faith which one is willing to place in a statement that an interval established by a sampling process actually contains or bounds a parameter of interest." [98]

Following the logic of Roethlisberger's Knowledge Enterprise, science and research are concerned with finding the theoretical relations. Therefore, a particular functional relationship is studied either because it is interesting in its own right or because it helps discover or clarify a theory. The functional relations studied in management often seek to discover correlations between management variables and/or differences in central tendency between differently applied management techniques. Thus management research results are usually reported in some form of correlation co-efficients (e.g.: factor analysis, multiple regression) or differences between means (e.g.: multiple analysis of variance).

Another approach is to construct confidence intervals and state precise probability values of research outcomes. Kerlinger explained it this way,

> The basic idea is that, instead of categorically rejecting hypotheses if the .05 grade is not made, we say that probability is .95 that the unknown value falls between .30 and .50. Now, if the obtained empirical proportion is, say, .60, then this is evidence for the correctness of the investigator's substantive hypothesis, or in null hypothesis language, the null hypothesis is rejected.[99]

Walker and Lev described confidence intervals more simply,

> A statistic with the desirable qualities of unbiasedness and consistency provides an estimate of the parameter which may be assumed to be numerically close to that parameter. An estimate of a parameter which is often more satisfactory is one that uses two statistics, unequal in value, which jointly provide an interval estimate of the parameter. The parameter is stated as lying between these statistics in much the same way that one might say "I'm fully confident John's age is between 25 and 30."[100]

This research seeks to identify what the definitional characteristics of participatory evaluation are and to estimate its usefulness in fulfilling evaluation procedures. The parameters it establishes will then be compared to determine how the evaluation process affects the management control process for this multinational organization. The use of confidence intervals to classify estimated values when the sample size is small has also been addressed.

> It is not always necessary to use a large N, and there are ways of telling when enough data has been gathered to have faith in statistical estimates. Most of the statistics which are used (means, variances, correlations and others) have known distributions, and, from these, confidence intervals can be derived for particular estimates. For example, if the estimate of a correlation is .50, a confidence interval can be set for the inclusion of the "true" value. It might be found in this way that the probability is .99 that the "true" value is at least as high as .30. Technically, it would be more correct to say that

the probability is .99, that the range from .30 to 1.00 covers the parameter. This would supply a great deal more information than to reject the null hypothesis only. . . . (confidence methods) tell the experimenter how much faith he can place in his estimates, and they indicate how much the N needs to be increased to raise the precision of estimates by particular amounts.[101]

Walker and Lev explain that confidence intervals for very small samples are only approximately correct because of the discontinuities that are created from using a small number of observations. However, when the number of observations become larger, the binomial probability distribution becomes smoother because there are more points to plot and less discrepancy between them. As the size of the sample increases to approach the size of the population, then the confidence interval narrows—even to a mere line.[102]

For a given sample size, such as occurs in this research, the confidence interval would be wider if less confidence can be placed in the interval; and conversely, the confidence interval narrows as more probability can be attached to each number in the interval. Mehrens and Ebel go on to state more definitively, "A clear understanding of the degree of the approximation involved in any actual case can again be obtained by the use of confidence intervals."[103] Narrow confidence intervals indicate less approximation.

While the concept of probability is best used in reasoning research problems from a known population to a random sample, the concept of confidence is best used in reasoning research problems from an observed sample to its unknown population. Rozeboom argued that descriptive research reports using confidence intervals to segregate variables are not biased by any apriori hypothesis or inclinations; rather they make ". . . an impartial simultaneous evaluation of all the alternatives under consideration."[104] He contends that confidence intervals not only are quantitative assessments of hypothesis probabilities, but also and the most effective way to eliminate the total likelihood of error, not just Type I or Type II error.

To discover which characteristics and parameters are of most importance to the participatory evaluation process and to the management control process, confidence intervals were constructed for each questionnaire and its respective sample size. Any response items with mean-value scores falling within one interval would be inferred as significantly different from response items falling in another interval. Therefore any items with mean-value scores which caused them to be grouped in the first category would be inferred as being more favorable to the participatory evaluation characteristic examined in that question; response items with mean-value scores falling in lower intervals would be inferred as less favorable to the characteristics in question.

The purpose of these intervals was to determine if the spread between mean-value scores of response items representing similar evaluation characteristics was statistically significant. Sorting response items on a questionnaire into categories based on confidence is a useful way to examine, categorize, and explain observed organizational phenomena. The confidence interval derivations for both the expectation questionnaire and the experience questionnaire are presented and explained in Appendix B.

Finally, the research questions will be analyzed by comparing the expectations from participation evaluation with the experiences using participatory evaluation to examine the three research questions posed in Chapter II. These analytical methods were selected for use in this research study because the statistical analyses used must serve the research issues involved (i.e.: observing samples and making influences about the population) and the utility assessments must examine the research questions investigated (i.e.: unknown effects on the management control process).

SUMMARY OF THE RESEARCH METHODOLOGY

Applying the logic of Roethlisberger's "The Knowledge Enterprise" for scientific inquiry to this research, the study begins to identify what the definitional characteristics of participatory evaluation are and to estimate their usefulness in fulfilling evaluation research procedures. These conditions are then compared to determine how they affect the management control process of a multinational non-profit organization. Figure 15 presents the research model used to discover these initial findings on participatory evaluation.

Roethlisberger summarizes the products generally expected from each level of enterprise as follows,

> Each level of knowledge has its own kinds of products and findings. Knowledge of acquaintance at the level of skill

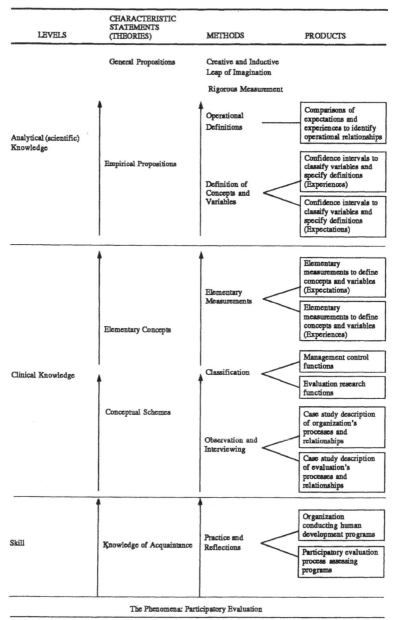

The Phenomena: Participatory Evaluation

* For the development of knowledge, read from the bottom up; for the practice of knowledge, read from the top down.

Figure 15: Research Model Based on
Roethlisberger's Knowledge Enterprise

results in simple how-to-do-it statements of aphorisms about the phenomena. The products at the clinical level are descriptive cases about the phenomena. The products at the level of elementary concepts are statements such as x is the function of y; x is dependent on y; x has a consequence for y; or x correlates with y. The products at the level of empirical propositions and statements to the effect that x varies with y in such and such a fashion under certain given conditions (e.g., Boyle's law). At the level of general propositions, the products are sets of statements that include general propositions from which, under certain stated conditions, empirical propositions can be deduced (e.g., Newton's law of motion). At this level, scientific theory and explanation have been achieved.[105]

This research seeks only to propose elementary concepts and operational definitions through exploration, descriptions, and elementary measurements presented in the case study and empirical data analysis. Initial operational definitions describing the functional relationships of participatory evaluations and their relationship to self-control in the management process would serve as a foundation for future research to specify empirical propositions of cause-effect relationships between evaluation research and accounting information. Only then could general propositions for an interdisciplinary theory on evaluation research and management control be developed and any effects on external reporting in non-profit organizations be tested.

SUMMARY

The purpose of this chapter was to describe the research methodology and research techniques used in conducting the study. The objectives of this study were to identify how participatory evaluation affects the management control process of a multinational non-profit organization. To accomplish this object, an integrated research strategy was chosen as the appropriate methodology. Two case study descriptions of the organization and its evaluation process were conducted. Two self-administered questionnaires were constructed based on internal documents and the literature reviews to provide empirical findings for analysis.

The research approach taken was exploration, descriptions and identification of inferred key variables. The exploration and descriptions were accomplished by descriptive statistical analysis. Confidence interval construction was used to classify and identify key variables. The three research questions were analyzed by comparing organizational expectations with experiences. Finally, empirical propositions for operational relationships were specified.

This chapter has focused on the details of the methodology followed in this research. Presentation and discussion of the questionnaire results and their analysis is presented in the following chapters. The study's findings on the research questions are presented in Chapter VI. The empirical propositions are stated in Chapter VII.

NOTES

87. Robert S. Kaplan, "The Role of Empirical Research in Management Accounting," (Unpublished remarks) July 1984.

88. Fritz J. Roethlisberger, *The Elusive Phenomena* (Cambridge, Massachusetts: Harvard University Press, 1977), pp. 466-472.

89. Kaplan, p. 30.

90. WHA is a pseudonym given to the actual organization studied in this research. They were guaranteed anonymity as a condition for agreeing to be the subject for this dissertation.

91. Malcom S. Knowles, "Human Resources Development in OD," *Public Administration Review*, March/April 1974. pp. 115-123.

92. John W. Buckley, Marlene H. Buckley, and Hung-Fu Chiang, *Research Methodology and Business Decisions*, (New York, New York: National Association of Accountants and The Society of Industrial Accountants of Canada, 1976), p. 35-40.

93. C. William Emory, *Business Research Methods*, (Homewood, Illinois: Richard D. Irwin, Inc. , 1976).

94. Eugene F. Stone, *Research Methods in Organizational Behavior*, (Glenview, Illinois: Scott, Foresman and Company, 1978), p. 139.

95. Ibid, p. 116, 128-135.

96. Guba, Chapter 4.

97. Norman H. Nie, Dale H. Bent, and C. Hadlai Hull, Statistical Package for the Social Sciences, (New York, New York: McGraw-Hill, 1970).

98. Robert E. Chandler, "The Statistical Concept of Confidence and Significance," *Psychological Bulletin*, Vol. 54, 1957, p. 429.

99. Fred N. Kerlinger, *Foundation of Behavioral Research*, (New York, New York: Holt, Rinehart and Winston, Inc., 1973), p. 170.

100. Helen M. Walker and Joseph Lev, *Statistical Inference*, (New York, New York: Holt, Rinehart and Winston,1953), p. 52.

101. Jim Nunnally, "The Place of Statistics in Psychology," *Educational and Psychological Measurement*, Vol. 20, 1960, pp. 646-647.

102. Walker and Lev, p. 54-55.

103. William A. Mehrens and Robert L. Ebel, *Principles of Educational and Psychological Measurement*, (Chicago, Illinois: Rand McNally and Co., 1967), p. 196.

104. William W. Rozeboom, "Fallacy of the Null-Hypothesis Test," *Psychological Bulletin*, Vol. 57, 1960, p.426.

105. Roethlisberger, p. 392.

CHAPTER IV

Findings of Expectations Questionnaire

As part of this field study research, empirical data were collected from the employees of WHA asking them what characteristics would constitute an ideal participatory evaluation process for their organization. How the questionnaire was developed is discussed in Chapter III and the questionnaire is presented in Appendix A. This section will display and discuss the results of the expectations questionnaire administered to WHA employees and report the results of the statistical analysis also outlined in Chapter III. The general format of this chapter will follow the evaluation characteristics outlined in the questionnaire and will have four sections: (1) data collection, (2) personnel data, (3) characteristics of the ideal participatory evaluation process at WHA, and (4) a summary of the expectations questionnaire findings.

DATA COLLECTION

The data analyzed in this study were collected from employees of WHA during July, August and September, 1984. A self-administered questionnaire was distributed to designated employees in each national office, a total of 760 people. The overall response rate was 42%. Table 1 presents the responses by individual offices.

TABLE 1

SURVEY RESPONDENTS
EXPECTATIONS QUESTIONNAIRE

	Number of Employees Surveyed	Number of Respondents	% of Total Respondents
AFRICA			
Regional Office	15	0	0
Ethiopia	13	7	2
Ghana	18	8	2
Kenya	26	12	4
Malawi	10	0	0
Mali	4	0	0
Tanzania	8	0	0
Zambia	10	0	0
Zimbabwe	15	0	0
Middle East	5	5	1
ASIA			
Regional Office	9	3	1
Bangladesh	18	14	4
India	42	37	12
Indonesia	39	0	0
Korea	13	11	3
Philippines	85	56	18
South Pacific	21	11	3
Sri Lanka	19	5	3
Taiwan	23	1	1
Thailand	49	43	13
LATIN AMERICA			
Regional Office	16	0	0
Bolivia	10	0	0
Brazil	66	0	0
Chile	15	15	5
Columbia	34	0	0
Ecuador	21	5	2
El Salvador	26	23	7
Guatemala	21	17	5
Haiti	20	17	5
Honduras	21	1	1
Mexico	19	1	1
Peru	11	4	1
EASTERN EUROPE	1	0	0
INTERNATIONAL HEADQUARTERS	37	24	7
	760	320	100

Response Rate   42%

When offices responded at all, the response rate was generally very high. Low response rates occurred where a national office itself did not participate in the study. Prior agreement to participate did not insure a response. Translations were provided in Spanish, Thai, and Portuguese. Translations being provided did not seem to effect the response rate either. Some countries which were given translated questionnaires did not respond, while other countries which had to translate the questionnaires, did so, and had a high response rate. The drought and famine in Africa during the months of this study, along with the difficulty of translation, probably explain the low response rates there.

PERSONNEL DATA

The last section of the questionnaire was developed to gather specific demographic data regarding the respondents. The questions asked in this section are discussed in Chapter III and are presented in Appendix A. The purpose of these questions was to determine the general characteristics of the respondents.

A question on job title was asked to identify organizational level so comparisons could be made between sub-groups by the hierarchical echelon. Since the organization generally uses the same job titles throughout the world, job titles could be classified into five groups. Administrators were defined as those persons having general oversight responsibility of one or more work sub-groups, without any direct operating responsibilities. Finance staff was defined as those employees working within the Administration and Finance function. Direct operating staff was defined as those employees working in projects or having immediate oversight responsibility for first line project workers. Support staff was defined as employees who provide indirect assistance to the project workers. Evaluation and training staff was defined as those employees who are responsible for the evaluation and training programs in their own national office, but who also provide only indirect assistance to the project workers. The number of respondents for these groups is outlined in Table 2.

TABLE 2

SURVEY RESPONDENTS CLASSIFIED
BY JOB POSITION

	Number of Respondents	% of Total Respondents
Administration	52	16
Finance	25	8
Direct Operations	173	54
Support Staff	22	7
Evaluation & Training	26	8
Missing	22	7
	320	100

The response patterns and composition of these respondents is important to note. Of the twenty-one national offices which participated, only four National Office Directors responded. From the International headquarters only one administrator of Vice President or higher level responded, while all the Board of Directors members responded. This may have occurred for several reasons, but it is important to note that even though top management would agree to the research effort in concept, they did not respond to the survey. Therefore, they did not participate in forming the substance of the ideal evaluation process determined by this research. Moreover, eleven other National Office Directors agreed to have their employees participate and then did not respond.

The choice not to respond, and thereby not contribute to the development of an internally generated evaluation process, should be considered as it reflects on the organization's, and its employees', attitude toward participation. These response patterns indicate that top management did not actively support a participative process when invited to do so. Further, the remaining results depicting the ideal or expected evaluation process at WHA, must be considered as reflecting lower management and the staff's opinion, not top management's ideas on evaluation.

Questions on years in current position and years with WHA were asked to determine length of service and experience with the organization. The mean number of years with the organization was 5.0 years; but the median years (or middle number of years) with the organization was 3.0 years and the standard deviation was 4.7 years. In total, the distribution of years worked for the organization and in their current position was skewed towards the low end. Table 3 presents the respondents' years of experience with WHA.

TABLE 3

RESPONDENTS' YEARS OF EXPERIENCE WITH WHA

	Years in Current Position		Years Service with WHA	
Years	Respondents	%	Respondents	%
1	98	31.0	57	18.0
2	80	25.0	49	15.0
3	40	13.0	37	12.0
4	27	8.0	28	9.0
5	6	1.7	26	8.0
6	11	3.0	19	6.0
7	1	.3	10	3.0
8	—	—	11	3.0
9	—	—	8	3.0
10	—	—	11	3.0
11	—	—	10	3.0
12	—	—	1	.3
13	—	—	1	.3
15	—	—	2	.6
17	—	—	3	.9
21	—	—	2	.6
22	—	—	2	.6
23	—	—	1	.3
26	—	—	1	.3
31	—	—	1	.3
Missing	57	18.0	40	13.0
	320	100.0	320	100.0

Most respondents have ten years of total experience or less and have been in their current position an average of two years. After two years, however, the staff members should be able to identify and articulate their expectations of and ideas on a participatory evaluation process for WHA projects.

The age, sex and educational attainment profile of this population is young adult, well educated, and contains a substantial proportion of both male and female respondents. Two hundred and one males responded (63%) and 82 females responded (26%), with 37 respondents not indicating their sex. The age range under thirty-five had 170 respondents (53%), while 96 respondents (30%) were between the ages of 36 and 50 years, 22 respondents (7%) were between the ages of 51 and 65 years, and 32 respondents (10%) declined to give their age. Of the respondents, 251 (78%), reported having a university level education and the other 69 (22%), reported a secondary education level.

The educational attainment level and location of education received were asked to determine if level and location of education affected a person's perception on participation (i.e., would people educated in the west reflect western values more than their peers who were educated nationally). Unfortunately, the education locations reported were primarily national and too many missing values were received to provide valid inferences on effect of education. Fifty-seven percent of the respondents from Africa reported being educated in Africa; 65% of the respondents from Asia reported being educated in Asia; and 66% of the respondents from Latin America reported being educated in Latin America. The reported education locations are presented in Table 4.

TABLE 4

LOCATION OF RESPONDENTS' EDUCATION

	Number of Respondents	% of Total Respondents
Africa	17	5
Asia	117	37
Latin America	55	17
West	49	15
Missing	82	26
	320	100

The demographic profile provided by these data indicates that the respondent group consisted of young adults, nationals, well educated, at an early stage in their career, a good proportion of males and females, and primarily representing the operating staff of WHA. The evaluation characteristics they identified as desirable should be viewed in light of these demographics. The normative ideas of this group may not represent the ideas of the third world communities in which they work nor the older administrators for whom they work. However, they are representative of the dominant emerging population of workers identified in the literature search as the employee group that management and organizational systems must accommodate.

CHARACTERISTICS OF THE IDEAL PARTICIPATORY EVALUATION PROCESS AT WHA

The questionnaire on the ideal participatory evaluation processes expected by WHA employees was developed to provide a conditional requirement "benchmark" from which to compare the employees' experiences with participatory evaluation.

The directed questions asked in this questionnaire each represented one evaluation characteristic of interest. Each question was followed by a list of replies, representing issues raised in the internal documents of WHA or the literature review. Each reply was rated by the respondent on a four, five or six-point rating scale—high (very desirable 4.0) to low (not desirable 1.0).

Descriptive statistics were prepared on each response item. Confidence intervals of size .30 were constructed for each definitional characteristic, and used to classify response items into groups according to their mean-value scores. The purpose of these intervals was to determine if the spread between mean-value scores of response items representing similar evaluation characteristics was statistically significant. The confidence intervals presented compare different response items within one question in order to sort and classify items representing various evaluation components, functions, and characteristics. These findings are displayed for each characteristic by showing the individual response item name, number of respondents, standard deviations, and mean-value score segregated into groups by their statistical significance. The confidence interval derivation is presented in Appendix B.

The format of this section follows the ten primary definitional characteristics of evaluation research which are: (1) Purpose—how should evaluation research be defined? (2) Goals—why should evaluation research be conducted? (3) Beneficiaries—who should benefit from evaluation findings? (4) Uses—how would employees use evaluation reports in their work? (5) Critical Issues—what are the important issues to understand when doing evaluation work in development organizations? (6) Supervision—who should manage the evaluations? (7) Technical Workers—who should do the technical evaluation work? (8) Protocol—how should requests for help be channeled in the organization? (9) Assistants—who should provide support or assistance? (10) Distribution—how should findings be reported and shared?

Purpose

To determine the views held by WHA employees on what the purpose of participatory evaluation research should be at WHA, question 1 asked to what degree they agreed/disagreed with each response in a list of possible definitions for evaluation research in WHA. Respondents rated the response items from strongly agree (4.0) to strongly disagree (1.0). Using the confidence interval size of .30, response items could be divided into three groups based on the level of their mean-value scores. These findings are displayed in Table 5.

The nine response items examined to determine the purpose of participatory evaluation at WHA were all identified by the review of internal WHA documents. Their range of mean-value scores was 3.35 to 2.43. Four response items were inferred as the most significant characteristics for the purpose of participatory evaluation because their mean values were between 3.35 and 3.05.

By combining them, the definition of evaluation research which respondents favored is to have the community people involved in the project continuously aware of project results by measuring changes caused by the project. These response items would indicate the statement of purpose for participatory evaluation at WHA to be routine, periodic self-assessment of project performance by the indigenous population.

Examining all nine response items' mean-value scores by an F-test analysis with the personnel data revealed only one statistically significant difference between the job position categories on a variable in the least favorable group of responses (i.e., the lowest interval). Seven statistically significant differences were found by an F-test analysis between respondents from the four geographic regions.

TABLE 5

AGREEMENT WITH THE
PURPOSES OF EVALUATION AT WHA

*To what extent do you agree or disagree with each of the
following definitions for evaluation at WHA?*

Response Items	N	SD	$\bar{X}$ 3.35- 3.05	$\bar{X}$ 3.04- 2.74	$\bar{X}$ 2.73- 2.43
Periodic measuring of impacts or changes caused by project results	314	.61	3.35		
Continuous awareness of project results and outcomes	313	.66	3.24		
Community examination of project performance	310	.81	3.13		
Self-examination by people involved in project	310	.81	3.07		
Regular checking up on project performance	313	.73		2.82	
Routine assessment of project performance	307	.79			2.72
Management examination of projects	310	.75			2.66
Regular checking-up on peoples' performance	312	.81			2.63
Management examination of peoples performance	306	.82			2.43

Note: Range of replies from strongly agree (4.0) to strongly disagree (1.0).

For variables in the most favorable group of response items ($\bar{X}$=3.35 to 3.05), the F-test analysis by geographic region ($F_{(3,319)}$=2.16, P<.05) revealed that: (1) the international headquarters respondents' mean value for the response item "continuous awareness of project results and outcomes" was lower than the other geographic regions

(F=4.14); (2) the Africa region respondents' mean value for the response item "community examination of project performance" was higher than the other geographic regions (F=3.14); (3) the Latin America region respondents' mean value for "self examination by people involved in the project" was higher than the other regions (F=3.14). These findings show the operating staff's strong commitment to indigenous evaluation. The International Office respondents seem to feel that continuous assessment is not as important, or perhaps even impossible.

For the five response items in the second and third groups, the international headquarters respondents' mean values were lower on three of these items than the respondents' in geographic areas where the operations occur. This finding suggests that the headquarters' staff does not view evaluation similarly to the other regions' employees. They do not view it as summatively; for them it is not to review the cumulative outcomes, effects, or progress made at the end of a project and then to express a conclusion about the project efforts or accomplishments. Nor do they view it as punitively, it is not to judge performance and impose discipline for control. Rather, they view evaluation as more constructive and formative in the project operations than the respondents from the national offices.

Further, the F-test analysis by geographic region ($F_{(3,319)}$=2.60, $P<.05$) also revealed that the respondents from Latin America scored the response item "routine assessment of project performance" lower than the respondents from the other geographic areas. This finding would indicate that offices in Latin America would prefer non-routine assessments.

Overall the Pearson product moment correlations were very low between the variable "routine assessment of project performance" with the variables "self-examination by people involved in project" (.05) and "community examination of project performance" (.06). Thus, people responded differently to these options, indicating some general difference in viewpoint between routine assessment and indigenous assessments. The indigenous characteristic is rated higher (more desirable) than routine assessments, and authoritarian characteristics are rated the least desirable definition of evaluation at WHA.

The purpose of project evaluation in WHA can be defined as allowing community people who are involved to be continuously aware of project results by measuring changes caused by the project. The goals for evaluation are specified even more clearly, and they correlate closely with this purpose.

Goals

To discover the views held by WHA employees on what the goals for evaluation research ought to be, question 2 asked respondents to rate various reasons why WHA needs to conduct project evaluations. By understanding the critical reasons why WHA should conduct evaluation research in projects, the goals of evaluation can be formulated to fulfill these important needs. Response items were rated from very important (4.0) to not important (1.0). Using the confidence interval size of .30, response items were divided into four groups based on the level of their mean-value scores. The findings are displayed in Table 6.

The range of mean-value scores for the twelve response items examined to discover the reasons why evaluation was needed in WHA projects was 3.65 to 2.65. These items represent issues raised in both WHA internal documents and the literature. The four items in the group with highest mean-value scores (between 3.65 and 3.35) were judged to be the most significant reasons why project evaluation is needed.

Therefore, the most important reasons respondents gave for why evaluation research is needed at WHA were to learn lessons from project experiences and to' determine impacts resulting from project activities. Further, these variables would indicate that an evaluation process needs to continuously assess the project's performance and provide information needed for making decisions about the project's outcomes.

The two variables classified in the first group are evaluation research specific in nature. They indicate important reasons commonly given for evaluation research, and they are reasons which can easily be translated into goals for an evaluation process. Two reasons for evaluation which related to WHA corporate goals were also classified in the first group of reasons for evaluation. Therefore, WHA corporate goals (e.g.: effective management activities, building community self-reliance), were primary issues.

Examining the response items' mean values with the personnel data by an F-test where $F_{(4,319)}=2.37$, $P<.05$, only revealed two statistically significant differences between the job position categories on all the response items. One item came from the first group of most important

TABLE 6

IMPORTANCE OF THE
GOALS FOR EVALUATION AT WHA

*How important do you think each of the following reasons
is for evaluating WHA development projects?*

Response Items	N	SD	$\bar{X}$ 3.65-3.35	$\bar{X}$ 3.34-3.04	$\bar{X}$ 3.03-2.73	$\bar{X}$ 2.72-2.42
Needed to learn lessons from project activities and results	317	.60	3.65			
Needed to determine the impacts resulting from project activities	314	.61	3.61			
Making decisions about project outcomes	313	.73	3.50			
Continuous assessment of project performance	306	.73	3.48			
Developing self-reliance skills in the community	308	.88	3.36			
Help integrate the management activities in projects (planning, setting goals, selecting activities, budgeting, etc.)	310	.81	3.35			
For accountability	308	.83		3.26		
To focus management's attention on the project's outcome and results	314	.84		3.19		
To identify projects not meeting our expectations	307	1.07			2.85	
For credibility in the international development community	302	1.04			2.81	
To identify exceptional projects	305	.98				2.65

Note: Range of replies from very important (4.0) to not important (1.0).

reasons for evaluation. The support staff respondents' mean value for the variable "continuous assessment of project performance" was lower than the other job position categories (F=3.86).

Three statistically significant differences were found between the geographic regions. An F-test where $F_{(3,319)}$=2.60, P<.05, revealed that the international headquarter respondents' mean values were lower for the three variables: "making decisions about project outcomes" (F=3.38), "continuous assessment of project performance" (F=20.67), and "help integrate the management activities in projects (planning, setting goals, selecting activities, budgeting, etc.)" (F=17.08). It is important to note that the respondents from the national offices, where the development occurs, see goals for participatory evaluations not seen by the respondents from the international headquarters. They expect it to help them make decisions about the project outcomes. They assigned continuous assessment an average value of 3.61 with a standard deviation of .66, while the respondents from international headquarters assigned it an average value of 2.41 with a standard deviation of .91. These differences in viewpoint show that the national office staffs expect more from the evaluation process than the International Office staff.

Further, the national offices respondents' mean value score for integrating management tasks was 3.45, while the International Office respondents' mean value was 2.29. This difference in viewpoint indicates the national office employees expect evaluation to articulate with the other management control process functions and the home office staff does not see that as being so important.

Generally, the variables identified as important reasons why evaluations should be conducted in WHA projects pertained to the evaluation research function. The primary goals were: (1) to learn lessons from project activities and results, (2) to determine the impacts resulting from project activities, (3) to provide information for making decisions about project outcomes, (4) to continuously assess the project's performance, (5) to develop self-reliance skills in the community, and (6) to help integrate management activities in projects. The higher level expectations between the national offices' respondents and the International Office's respondents is important to note in establishing the goals for evaluation research. Identifying the people who should benefit from evaluation findings is a way to define the group towards whom those goals are directed.

Beneficiaries

Identifying and ranking who should benefit from evaluation findings helps establish the audience and customer for the products of evaluation research. To ascertain the people who are the customers for project evaluations, question 9 asked who should benefit from development project evaluation's results, findings, conclusions, and reports. Response items were rated from most benefit (4.0) to least benefit (1.0). Using the confidence interval size of .30, response items were categorized into four groups by the level of their mean value scores. The classifications are displayed in Table 7.

The twenty response items examined in this question represented the entire WHA organizational structure and hierarchy plus external constituents identified as important to the evaluation process in WHA documents and the literature search. The range of mean-value scores was 3.59 to 2.61. The group with the highest scores, judged to be those who should benefit most from evaluation reports, included seven beneficiaries.

The grouping of response items shows a striking and clear pattern of division of beneficiaries by their geographic relationship to the project. When asked to rate who should benefit from evaluation reports, the respondents grouped participants directly involved in the project in the first group to benefit most, with the exception of the evaluation coordinator. The Evaluation Coordinator in the National Office is the transition position between the people directly involved with the project and the national office staff. Positions at the National Office indirectly involved in the project were grouped to benefit second, with the Evaluation Department at the International Office as the transition position to the remaining groups. The third and fourth groups classified other positions from the regional and International Offices.

Examining the response items mean values with the personnel data by an F-test analysis where $F_{(3,319)}=2.60$, $P<.05$, revealed nine statistically significant differences by geographic location. Respondents in Africa expected the entire community to benefit more from participatory evaluation than the respondents from other regions ($F=4.65$). The other eight differences represented respondents from the international headquarters reporting lower mean values than respondents from other regions.

TABLE 7

MOST IMPORTANT
BENEFICIARIES OF EVALUATION AT WHA

*To what extent do you think each of the following
should benefit from project evaluations?*

Response Items	N	SD	$\overline{X}$ 3.59- 3.29	$\overline{X}$ 3.28- 2.98	$\overline{X}$ 2.97- 2.67	$\overline{X}$ 2.66- 2.36
Involved community	314	.70	3.59			
Project Specialist	310	.66	3.55			
Project Committee	309	.74	3.54			
Project Staff	313	.65	3.53			
Project Director	312	.68	3.53			
Evaluation Coordinator	296	.76	3.38			
Partner Agency	305	.77	3.37			
Operations Coordinator	301	.80		3.27		
Suboffice/DAC Staff	278	.88		3.27		
Entire Community	303	.93		3.25		
National Office Director	301	.86		3.21		
International Office Evaluation Department	290	.93		3.05		
Regional Office/Desk	296	.97			2.85	
Field Development Division	289	.96			2.81	
Agency Donors	273	.99			2.78	
Administrative Coordinator	286	.93			2.77	
Support Offices	278	.97			2.71	
Individual Donors	287	1.03			2.67	
Vice President Technical Support	280	.99				2.63
Systems Audit	281	1.00				2.61

Note: Range of replies from most benefit (4.0) to least benefit (1.0).

Most notably, international headquarters respondents' mean scores indicated they had much lower expectations for the National Sub-offices and Development Activities Centers (DAC) to benefit from evaluation findings than the national offices' respondents. Here again, those working closest to the projects expected the local people to benefit more ($\overline{X}$=3.24, SD=.63) from the evaluation findings than the International Office staff ($\overline{X}$=2.48, SD=.68).

Generally, the people expected to benefit from evaluation findings were clustered into geographical and hierarchical groups. The people directly involved in the projects were expected to benefit most; the National Evaluations Coordinator and the International Evaluations Department were identified as the transition positions into their respective offices. This pattern holds in other characteristics as well. Who should benefit from the evaluation reports relates directly to how people anticipate using evaluation reports.

Uses

To learn how evaluation reports would be used in WHA, question II.2 asked respondents when they now use or think they would use evaluation reports. Knowing when people expect to use the evaluation reports would help determine both the evaluation process components and the contents of evaluation reports (the components must supply the information needed for the report contents). Response items were rated from always (4.0) never (1.0). Using the confidence interval size .30, two groups of response items emerged for the range of mean value scores. These classifications are displayed in Table 8.

Eleven response items were examined to learn the intended uses of evaluation reports at WHA, representing uses suggested by both internal documents and the literature. Their range of mean-value scores was 3.39 to 2.78. The six uses identified in the first group were inferred as being the most frequently intended uses of evaluation reports and, therefore, the most important.

The primary uses of evaluation reports identified by the respondents correspond with the purpose and goals of evaluation research identified earlier. Further, the first six uses identified also relate to current operating procedures at WHA. Presently, projects are assessed monthly by the project specialist and an activities report is filed. Milestone/Plan of Action reports are the routine operating reports currently used in the reporting system. Thus evaluation reports are anticipated to be used in connection with established operating procedures and documents internal to the project. Using evaluation reports in management control decision making and in conjunction with other evaluative techniques (e.g.: internal audits, systems audit, etc.) are secondary or unanticipated uses as shown by their low mean-value scores and subsequent classification.

TABLE 8

USES OF EVALUATION REPORTS AT WHA

I expect to use evaluation reports when:

Response Items	N	SD	X̄ 3.39-3.09	X̄ 3.08-2.78
Assessing project performance	237	.80	3.39	
Reviewing milestone/plan of action reports	258	.83	3.36	
Reviewing project appropriateness/conformity to our annual goals and/or 5-year plan	254	.87	3.25	
Before deciding on continued funding	243	.87	3.21	
Before deciding on new funding	246	.94	3.15	
Before deciding to stop funding	243	.99	3.11	
Reviewing budget reports	253	.93		3.03
Before deciding on capital funding	234	.95		2.97
Before returning files for additional explanation	234	.89		2.89
Before preparing internal audit reports	218	1.02		2.78

Note: Range of replies from always (4.0) to never (1.0).

Examining the data for uses of evaluation findings reveals several differences in these responses worthy of noting. First, the number of respondents is lower. Second, the standard deviations are generally a little higher than on responses to other questions. Not as many people know how they expect to use the evaluation reports as have expectations for the other evaluation characteristics. Designing the participatory evaluation process is more difficult when people are less certain about how they will use the reports and information.

Finally, the F-test on personnel data by geographic location ($F_{(3,319)}=2.60$, $P<.05$), reveals a statistically significant difference on every variable. The International Office respondents had generally lower mean scores than the national offices respondents; most notably the variables, "reviewing milestone reports" (F=10.38) and "reviewing budget reports" (F=17.09). Perhaps their lower ratings on anticipated uses of evaluation reports occurs because they do not do this type of work at the International Office; or perhaps, it occurs because they do not view project evaluation as integrating these tasks. However, home office viewpoints have a way of transmitting themselves to national office employees. Therefore, how to effectively integrate evaluation reports into the decision process and management function is uncertain.

Critical Issues

On the other hand, the respondents show strong agreement and strong feelings on the background knowledge that evaluators must bring to their work. Establishing the essential background knowledge useful for participatory evaluation can provide the conceptual orientation for the technical work. Since non-profit organizations are value-rational, identifying and understanding what knowledge they consider critical for proper evaluation of a program is essential to its success. To ascertain what issues were important for persons doing development project evaluations at WHA to understand, question 5 asked respondents to rate six frequently cited issues identified from the internal documents' review. Response items were rated from very important (4.0) to not important (1.0). Using the confidence interval size of .30, two categories were determined, and they are presented in Table 9.

TABLE 9

CRITICAL ISSUES FOR EVALUATION AT WHA

To what extent do you think it is important that the people doing the technical work of evaluation should:

Response Items	N	SD	$\bar{X}$ 3.86- 3.56	$\bar{X}$ 3.55- 3.25
Understand the evaluation process	317	.42	3.86	
Understand WHA mission	316	.59	3.78	
Understand development projects	315	.49	3.77	
Understand the individual community	315	.58	3.77	
Understand the technical requirements of evaluation	316	.56	3.69	
Understand WHA management requirements	308	.84		3.41

Note: Range of replies from very important (4.0) to not important (1.0).

Especially interesting to note is the strong agreement on these issues. They have high mean-value scores (on a scale of 4.0 to 1.0), low standard deviations, and a total mean-value score range of 3.86 to 3.41, indicating most respondents agreed with these issues. Therefore, people doing evaluation work at WHA need to understand five key issues almost simultaneously and with equal significance. They need to understand: the evaluation process, WHA corporate purpose, development work, the locality, and technical evaluation requirements. Identifying the importance of these critical issues indicates why participatory evaluation is being used at WHA and more generally, when participatory evaluation is a useful management tool.

Since no one person can completely understand all these issues, a group approach to evaluation is needed. WHA has chosen to teach its staff the evaluation process and participatory techniques for evaluation research which enable them to work with the community. Potentially, this approach embodies the five most critical issues for evaluation at WHA. The staff understand and concur with WHA's corporate purpose; also they are national, professional development workers, familiar with the cultural context. Theoretically, the participatory evaluation process allows all project participants—community people, project committee, partner agency, and the project specialist—to help design the evaluation plan for their project. These critical issues provide the operative ethics for project evaluation at WHA.

The F-test on personnel data by location ($F_{(3,319)}$=2.60, P>.05), revealed three statistically significant differences in mean-value scores between the international headquarter's respondents and the respondents from the national offices. The International Office staff rated the variables "understanding WHA management requirements" (F=9.83) and "understand the technical requirement of evaluation" (F=4.47) lower than the other respondents. This indicates they are willing to accept the lower technical sophistication of indigenous evaluation. These findings continue to be of interest because they demonstrate the consistently lower expectations home office employees have for evaluation research generally, and more specifically, for the evaluation process to serve the other management functions. These expectations are much lower than those of the national offices' respondents.

Policy versus Operational Characteristics

These first five evaluation characteristics depict the policy characteristics of evaluation in WHA. They have addressed the issues of purpose, goals, audience, usage, and operative ethics. The next five questions examine the operational characteristics of evaluation at WHA. They address the issues of who should manage, perform, and provide support for the technical work of evaluation, how requests for help should be directed, and how reports on evaluation findings should be distributed. Policy issues define the content of the participatory evaluation process; operational issues specify the structure of the participatory evaluation process.

Supervision

To identify who should manage and have oversight responsibility for the evaluation process in each project, question 3 asked how desirable it would be to have the positions listed manage the evaluation of development projects. The person or persons assigned responsibility for the evaluation process must be acceptable to both the persons directly involved in the project and the persons indirectly involved, especially WHA administrators who are accountable to all the stakeholders. Response items were rated from very desirable (4.0) to not desirable (1.0). Using the confidence interval size of .30, four categories emerged and the response items classified in them are displayed in Table 10.

The nineteen response items examined in this question again represent the entire WHA organizational structure and hierarchy plus external constituents identified as possible administrators of the evaluation process in WHA documents and in the literature. Their range of mean-value scores was 3.44 to 2.21. The highest score category included six potential managers. However, only one person or group can be responsible for administering the evaluation process. Therefore further examination and consideration of the response items is necessary. Two general patterns are apparent: the grouping of response items clustered groups of the potential managers by their geographic and their functional relationship to the project.

Presently, WHA operating procedures specify that the project committee represent both WHA and the partner agency in assuming

TABLE 10

DESIRABLE PERSONS OR GROUPS TO
MANAGE THE EVALUATION PROCESS AT WHA

*How desirable are each of the following to manage
the evaluation of development projects?*

Response Items	N	SD	$\bar{X}$ 3.44-3.14	$\bar{X}$ 3.13-2.83	$\bar{X}$ 2.82-2.52	$\bar{X}$ 2.51-2.21
Project Committee	309	.79	3.44			
Project Specialist	307	.86	3.41			
Evaluation Coordinator	298	.92	3.39			
Community Members Involved in Project	312	.87	3.38			
Project Director	307	.96	3.22			
Project Staff	309	.89	3.14			
Partner Agency	302	.96		3.07		
Suboffice/DAC Center	264	.96		3.02		
Operations Coordinator	301	.96		2.99		
National Office Director	289	.11			2.71	
International Office Evaluation Department	284	1.08			2.69	
Entire Community	292	1.16			2.68	
Administrative Coordinator	287	1.04			2.57	
Regional Office/Desk	281	1.12				2.45
Systems Audit	265	1.09				2.43
Outside Consultant	272	1.00				2.42
Field Development Division	274	1.10				2.38
Support Offices	268	1.11				2.27
Vice President Technical Support	266	1.06				2.21

Note: Range of replies from very desirable (4.0) to not desirable (1.0).

general oversight responsibility for the project. Thus, in theory, they would be responsible for the evaluation process just as they are for the funding process, project activities, and the reporting process. In actuality, however, the project specialist is the WHA's representative in each project and is accountable for proper accounting and performance reporting procedures; therefore, they too share responsibility for the project's performance. The earlier findings of this research indicate that this division of duties will most likely occur with project evaluation as well.

The range of mean scores is very large, therefore requiring more intervals to classify all the responses. The lower confidence levels identify who should not manage the evaluation process, but the high standard deviations for these variables imply less certainty among the respondents as to who should not manage the process, than who should manage it.

For variables in the first category, the F-test by job position revealed one statistically significant difference when $F_{(4,319)}=2.37, P<.05$. The support staff respondents reported a lower mean value for the evaluation coordinator to manage the evaluation process in projects (F=3.37). Since these respondents are the support staff for other areas of specialty, perhaps they realize more clearly than the other groups the difficulty of having managerial responsibility for the task for which a person has coordination and support responsibility.

The F-test by location, where $F_{(3,319)}=2.60$, $P<.05$, revealed eight statistically significant differences in mean values, four of which were in the first category. The international headquarters' respondents reported lower mean values on three of the response items: Project Committee (F=4.37, X̄=3.10), Project Specialist (F=6.06, X̄=2.85), and community members involved in the project (F=4.81, X̄=2.96). On the response item Project Staff the regions were more divided (F=3.31); respondents from Africa (X̄=3.40) and Asia (X̄=3.25) rated this item higher while respondents from Latin America (X̄=2.97) and the International Office (X̄=2.85) rated it much lower. The person who should manage the participatory evaluation process in individual development projects is not clearly identified by these findings.

This research assumes that respondents rated the project committee first to manage the participatory evaluation process because, in their opinion, these are the best people to oversee the process. Perhaps one member of the committee would be charged with responsibility to coordinate the committee's indigenous evaluation activities. However, whether the respondents replied this way merely because this is the way other processes are currently managed at WHA, or because they thought the committee best suited to manage the evaluation process, cannot be determined.

Clearly, if management wants a different managerial relationship created within the evaluation process than is currently practiced in other management functions, then proper roles must be carefully considered, determined, and specified for each of these six potential managers identified in this research and any other major parties who are considered important to indigenous evaluation. Only one person or group can manage the process. Therefore, some definite working relationship must be arranged between those persons who will manage the process and those who will do the technical work of evaluation.

Technical Workers

To discover who should do the technical work of evaluation research, question 7 asked respondents who they thought were the best people to do the technical work of project evaluation (such as gathering data about the community, keeping records on the project's activities, confirming the changes in the community because of the project). For a truly indigenous evaluation process to be installed in projects and used in management reporting, the employees of an organization—management, technical staff and support staff—would have to agree to have the people immediately involved in the project do the technical work, and they would have to accept the findings. If all level of the organization do not agree that the community people are the most desirable persons to do the technical work of evaluations, then complete participation cannot occur. Response items were rated from very desirable (4.0) to not desirable (1.0). Using the confidence levels size of .30 to sort response items, five groups emerged for the range of mean-value scores. Table 11 presents the people and positions classified in these groups.

The twenty response items examined in this question represent the entire WHA organizational hierarchy and external constituents identified as possible stakeholders to participate in the evaluation process in both internal WHA documents and the literature. Their range of mean-value scores was 3.41 to 1.87. The wide range of mean values indicates the respondents could specify who they thought was more desirable and less desirable to do the technical evaluation work. The seven individuals and groups classified in the first category were inferred to be the most desirable people to do the technical wok of evaluation at WHA.

Again, the people closest to the project and those most equipped to monitor project activities systematically emerged as the dominant group. While there is no statistically significant difference between all of the persons classified in this group, an interesting pattern is apparent in their mean values, which shows a split structure in the first group that is not consistent with a participatory evaluation process. The project

TABLE 11

DESIRABLE PEOPLE TO DO THE TECHNICAL
WORK OF EVALUATION

*To what extent do you think each of the following people
are desirable to do the technical work of evaluation?*

Response Items	N	SD	$\bar{X}$ 3.41- 3.11	$\bar{X}$ 3.10- 2.80	$\bar{X}$ 2.79- 2.49	$\bar{X}$ 2.48- 2.18	$\bar{X}$ 2.17- 1.87
Project Committee	308	.75	3.41				
Project Staff	303	.78	3.36				
Project Director	304	.83	3.34				
Project Specialist	309	.86	3.32				
Evaluation Coordinator	294	.94	3.16				
Community Members Involved in the Project	311	1.00	3.15				
Community Leaders	307	.92	3.13				
Partner Agency	294	.86		3.00			
Suboffice/DAC Center	267	.95		2.99			
Operations Coordinator	295	.98			2.72		
International Office Evaluation Department	279	1.15				2.28	
Government Agencies	285	.97				2.28	
Entire Community	294	1.13				2.26	
National Office Director	285	1.08				2.25	
Administrative Coordinator	278	.99				2.25	
Outside Consultants	260	1.05					2.15
Systems Audit	259	1.08					2.06
Field Development Division	261	1.02					1.97
Regional Office/Desk	262	1.00					1.94
Vice President Technical Support	255	.99					1.87

Note: Range of replies from very desirable (4.0) to not desirable (1.0).

committee, staff, director, and specialist are all grouped together at the top of the category. The evaluation coordinator, community members involved in the project, and community leaders are grouped at the lower end of the interval. In general, the respondents did not view the community members as the best people to perform the technical work of evaluation. Yet the participatory evaluation process is designed for these people to conduct the needs assessment, monitor the project's activities, and assess the outcomes. This finding presents an incongruent perception between the WHA employees and the participatory evaluation process design.

No significant differences were found between the respondents analyzed by job position; sixteen were found by geographic location when $F_{(3,319)}=2.60$, $P<.05$. Six of the seven response items in the first category had statistically significant differences in their mean values analyzed by location of respondent. Respondents from Latin America and Africa rated the response items project committee ($F=8.68$), project specialist ($F=7.46$), and community leaders ($F=7.27$) higher than did the respondents from Asia and the International Office. Further, respondents from Asia gave the variable "community members involved in the project" a statistically lower mean value ($F=8.85$) than the respondents in the other geographic areas. Respondents from Africa rated the variable "Project Director" higher than respondents from other regions ($F=3.63$). International headquarters respondents gave "Evaluation Coordinator" a lower mean value than the other respondents ($F=3.31$).

These findings show generally strong agreement between Latin America and Africa respondents, but less agreement with respondents from Asia. The difference in Asia region's lower response score on community members and community leaders as the proper people to do the technical work of evaluation could be cultural. The two lower mean scores for project committee and project specialist could be due to a conflict of interest created if the project committee or the project specialist did the technical work and managed the evaluation process while having oversight responsibilities.

Properly, good internal control procedures would dictate that the group designated to manage the process should be removed from the possible groups to carry out the technical evaluation work. Even in this setting of under developed human resources, where technical competency can be a limiting condition, segregation of duties to improve reliability of the evaluation findings seems an important issue deserving of careful consideration.

More importantly, however, consideration should be given to the issue of who should do the technical work of evaluation in order for true stakeholder participation to occur and for the evaluation findings to be accepted as reliable. Further analysis using these findings to test the effects of participatory evaluation on the management control process should be viewed in light of these discontinuities.

Whoever is identified to do the technical work, they will need help, assistance, and support at various times. The next issues examined were how to request help from the organization and who should provide help when problems arise.

Protocol

To learn how requests for assistance in doing evaluation work should be properly channeled through the organizational hierarchy, question 4 asked respondents to whom they thought requests for help or assistance in meeting evaluation requirements should best be directed. Proper structuring of the chain of command and communication channels are imperative for the evaluation process to be accepted by the informal organizational environment and used in the formal organizational structure at the national offices. Response items were rated from very desirable (4.0) to not desirable (1.0). Using the confidence interval size of .30 to sort response items, five categories emerged. However, the mean values are so widely separated that only the first and last two categories contain response items. Table 12 presents all the categories and the four response items.

TABLE 12

DESIRABLE PLACE TO DIRECT
REQUESTS FOR HELP OR ASSISTANCE

			$\bar{X}$ 3.40- 3.10	$\bar{X}$ 3.09- 2.79	$\bar{X}$ 2.78- 2.48	$\bar{X}$ 2.47- 2.17	$\bar{X}$ 2.16- 1.86
It is most desirable that requests for help or assistance inmeeting evaluation requirements be directed to:							
Response Items	N	SD					
National Office	302	.82	3.40				
Suboffice/DAC Office	267	.97	3.33				
Regional Office/ Regional Desk	280	1.08				2.18	
International Office	277	1.13					1.96

Note: Range of replies from very desirable (4.0) to not desirable (1.0).

Requests for help should be directed to the National Office or the Suboffice/Development Activity Center (DAC) if one is established in the local area. Presently, national offices at WHA have the authority and responsibility to see that help is provided from various sources. DAC's are an emerging concept at WHA and may or may not have the authority to provide needed assistance. At the time of this study, WHA was experiencing a reorganization towards stronger decentralization to the national offices. That process was not yet complete. The regional offices were becoming administrative desks to coordinate and support the national offices' activities in the region, but not to perform activities for the national offices. The F-test analysis described below, where $F_{(3,319)}=260$, $P<.05$, reflected these changes.

In Asia and in some Latin America countries where the DAC concept was more fully developed, the respondents rated it as the proper place to request assistance ($F=8.90$). In Africa and in the other Latin American countries, where the concept was less developed, the respondents rated the National Office as the proper place to request help ($F=4.95$). The National Office was rated highest by the International Office respondents. Latin America was the last region to have the Regional Office converted to an administrative desk, and they rated the Regional Office higher than the other respondents ($F=11.28$). No significant differences were found for the first two variables by job position analysis.

These findings indicates that the employees feel the communication channels and operating procedures for requesting help in carrying out the participatory evaluation process should remain in the host country, National Office or Suboffice/DAC. From there, various sources of help and assistance are available.

Assistants

To identify who should provide assistance or help in doing the technical work of evaluation, question 6 asked respondents to what degree they thought particular positions in the community and the organization were desirable ones to provide support or assistance for meeting evaluation requirements. To design an effective participatory evaluation process, it is essential to recognize that certain positions in the project structure or the organizational hierarchy may be more acceptable or appropriate sources of help to the community and project participants as they design and use their evaluation plan. Response items were rated from very desirable (4.0) to not desirable (1.0). Using the confidence interval size .30, five groups emerged from the range of mean-value scores; they are displayed in Table 13.

TABLE 13

DESIRABLE PEOPLE TO PROVIDE ASSISTANCE IN
MEETING EVALUATION REQUIREMENTS

*To what extent do you think it is desirable for each of the following to
provide support or assistance for meeting evaluation requirements?*

Response Items	N	SD	$\bar{X}$ 3.58- 3.28	$\bar{X}$ 3.27- 2.97	$\bar{X}$ 2.96- 2.66	$\bar{X}$ 2.65- 2.35	$\bar{X}$ 2.34- 2.04
Project Committee	307	.64	3.58				
Community Members Involved in the Project	313	.68	3.58				
Project Specialist	308	.63	3.56				
Project Director	307	.65	3.55				
Community Leaders	309	.68	3.52				
Evaluation Coordinator	297	.67	3.51				
Project Staff	308	.70	3.45				
Operations Coordinator	294	.84		3.25			
Partner Agency	297	.80		3.22			
Suboffice/DAC Staff	265	.84		3.20			
Entire Community	304	1.00		3.00			
National Office Director	294	.98			2.96		
International Office Evaluation Department	276	1.05			2.80		
Administrative Coordinator	283	.98			2.67		
Systems Audit	264	1.06				2.52	
Outside Consultants	265	.97				2.48	
Regional Director/Desk	270	1.06				2.49	
Government Agencies	285	.90				2.47	
Field Development Division Vice President	267	1.04				2.46	
Technical Support	266	1.08					2.32
Support Offices	263	1.02					2.25

Note: Range of replies from very desirable (4.0) to not desirable (1.0).

Depending upon the nature of the evaluation need, several sources
of help are available. The twenty-one possible sources of assistance
examined in this question represented the entire WHA organizational
structure as well as external resources available to WHA. The range of
mean-value scores for these items was 3.58 to 2.25. Again, the people
directly involved in the project, in the community, and in evaluation
compose the primary support group. Interestingly, though, others with

similar expertise are ranked in much lower groups (e.g.: government agencies and outside consultants). Comments made earlier about internal control and segregation of duties are pertinent here as well.

Eight statistically significant differences were found in the analysis by geographic location where $F_{(3,319)}=2.60$, $P<.05$; two of them were in the first group of response items. Respondents from Africa and Latin America rated the project committee (F=3.74) and project specialist (F=7.37) higher than the respondents from Asia and the International Office. If the project committee has general oversight responsibility, while the community members involved in the project do the technical work of evaluations and the Project Specialist has reporting and accountability responsibilities for WHA, then getting help in meeting evaluation requirements from a source outside this directly involved group would increase reliability of the findings. Limited available human resources may constrain the sources of help, but the participatory evaluation process design should encourage and accommodate use of other sources, including outside specialists and experts.

Respondents in Africa and Asia scored the variable "government agencies" (F=8.61) higher than respondents from Latin America and the International Office, but only the respondents from Africa gave this local resource a high enough mean-value score for it to be considered an alternative source of help outside the project's participants. Perhaps the colonial history of Africa explains why this source of assistance is rated higher by these respondents.

The partner agency as a potential source of assistance received very mixed responses (F=5.30): Africa $\bar{X}=3.60$, Asia and International Office $\bar{X}=3.30$, Latin America $\bar{X}=2.90$. This difference can not be easily explained, nor are reasons why the partner agency is excluded from the primary sources of assistance readily apparent. In Asia and Latin America, again where the DAC concept is more fully developed, it was rated higher as a source of assistance than in Africa or the International Office (F=3.77).

Analyzing the data by job position where $F_{(4,319)}=2.37$, $P<.05$, revealed that, while no one rated government agencies very high, the Administration and Finance respondents and the operations staff rated them higher than the other groups (F=4.08). It is interesting to note, that the respondents from Evaluation and Training rated the Administrative Coordinator higher than the other groups (F=2.91, $\bar{X}=3.00$). This group may have special insights into a relationship not apparent to others.

Assistance could be a contextually adaptive operational characteristic—provided one way in one country and differently in another country. These mixed findings indicate that the choice of proper persons to provide assistance in the participatory evaluation process needs further consideration.

Distributions

To determine how evaluation findings should be shared at WHA, question 8 asked respondents how they thought the lessons learned in individual development project evaluations could best be shared with the entire WHA organization. In order to share evaluation information and lessons learned on a worldwide (or even on a nation-wide basis), some form of standardized reporting mechanism is necessary to accumulate and compile qualitative and quantitative data on projects and then transmit them to other locations. Response items were rated from very desirable (4.0) to not desirable (1.0). Using the confidence interval size of .30 to classify and sort response items, three categories were determined for the range of mean-value scores; Table 14 presents the findings.

The ten potential ways to distribute evaluation findings at WHA were all suggested in their internal documents; they do, however, also represent distribution means commonly suggested in the literature. The range of mean-value scores for these items was 3.37 to 2.53. When respondents were asked to rate possible ways which have been suggested to share evaluation information, an interesting paradox became apparent between the desirable policy characteristics for evaluation and the operational reality of evaluation research. Annual evaluation reports for each project and indepth evaluation reports dominate the first group. The idea of continuous awareness of project results is associated with monitoring project activities in the community, but for formal reporting, annual reports are rated higher than routine management reports on activities which are required monthly and quarterly. This seems like a reasonable difference since a period of time must pass before impacts or changes caused by the project can be measured, determined, and reported.

Reviewing the response item data from all the categories reveals a wide range of mean-value scores indicating what the respondents

TABLE 14

MOST DESIRABLE WAYS OF
REPORTING EVALUATION FINDINGS

*How desirable do you think each of the following is for sharing
lessons learned from individual development projects?*

Response Items	N	SD	$\overline{X}$ 3.37-3.07	$\overline{X}$ 3.06-2.76	$\overline{X}$ 2.75-2.45
Annual evaluation reports for each project	308	.85	3.37		
Worldwide WHA teams doing indepth evaluation reports	298	.86	3.26		
Annual evaluation reports for each region	302	.84	3.18		
Evaluation task forces	269	.89	3.15		
Informal discussion between staff	300	1.00		2.95	
Regional/National Office Directors' Conference Reports	292	.89		2.94	
Routine management reports	300	.94		2.91	
International Partnership Planning Meeting	274	.92			2.75
WHA International Board Meeting Reports	268	1.03			2.58
International Affairs Committee Meeting Reports	264	.97			2.53

Note: Range of replies from very desirable (4.0) to not desirable (1.0).

thought most and least desirable. Interestingly, as the next section of
this chapter will describe, the reports rated lowest were the primary
reports being used at the time of this study.

Examining the mean values by job position revealed no significant
differences between response items in the first category. Five

differences were found by the F-test analysis for the geographic locations where $F_{(3,319)}$=2.60, P<.05. In all cases, the international headquarters' respondents were lower than the other respondents, and three of these items were in the first category. The International Office staff rated annual evaluation reports for each project (F=5.57), for each region (F=3.89), and for Evaluation Task Forces (F=6.43) lower than other respondents; and conversely, they rated worldwide WHA teams doing indepth evaluation reports highest ($\overline{X}$=3.00) among the alternatives. This finding may imply that the international administrators do not believe that the greatest benefit would come from routine reports integrated into the management reporting system; or it may merely indicate that they do not see and use routine reports, and, therefore they believe the organization would benefit most from more conventional evaluation reports.

SUMMARY OF THE EXPECTATIONS QUESTIONNAIRE FINDINGS

The WHA employees responded with general agreement on the ideal evaluation process, especially on the policy characteristics. The homogeneity of these responses can be discussed several ways. First, the demographics of these respondents is very similar. They are young, well-educated, and have limited experience with this organization. Therefore they could tend to agree with each other due to their similar demographic characteristics. Second, WHA only hires employees who agree with their organizational philosophy and purpose. Thus, respondents could agree with one another because they share similar values and ethics. Third, WHA is a funding institution, hiring people and supporting development work, in countries where very few opportunities are available for employees. Therefore, employees might respond as they feel they are expected to respond, or as the organization hierarchy wants them to respond, in order to continue receiving funding. This latter explanation does not seem applicable to the expectations questionnaire because this part of the research was only asking what the respondents thought would be best and no direct project funding was involved.

Putting these together, the most appropriate way to view the general agreement in these findings is to acknowledge the philosophical agreement of these respondents, recognize that this respondent group primarily represents the operational staff and middle-level management, and note their demographic similarities. The general agreement and egalitarian nature of their responses is indeed interesting, especially in light of the literature review which identified this type of worker group emerging in the third world.

Table 15 summarizes the desirable policy and operational characteristics specified by WHA employees worldwide for a participatory evaluation process at WHA. Policy characteristics represent the conceptual framework of participatory evaluation in WHA (purpose, goals, beneficiaries, uses, and critical issues). The operating characteristics represent the procedures used to implement these concepts (supervision, technical workers, protocol, assistants, and distributions).

The main purpose of evaluation identified by WHA employees was to have the community people involved in the project continuously aware of project results, by measuring changes caused by the project. The most important goals for evaluation were to learn lessons from and to determine the impact resulting from project activities, by continuously assessing the project's performance and providing information needed for making decisions about the project's outcomes. The people who should benefit most from evaluation reports were the immediate project participants. How evaluation reports will be used is less certain than other policy concerns, but the four anticipated uses of evaluation reports were: assessing project performance, reviewing routine management reports, reviewing project appropriateness or conformity to National Office plans, and before making certain funding decisions. Critical issues for people doing evaluation work at WHA to understand were: the evaluation process, the organization's purpose, its work, and the indigenous location where this work occurs. These critical issues provide an operational ethic for the participatory evaluation process.

WHA employees' responses on the operational characteristics suggested that the people who should manage and do the technical evaluation work were those closest to the project. Support in meeting evaluation needs should be provided by several sources depending upon the location and nature of the need, but the best sources were still said to be people directly involved in the project or the community. Annual evaluation reports for each project were the most desirable way that evaluation information should be shared. Uncertainty about the uses of

TABLE 15

POLICY AND OPERATIONAL CHARACTERISTICS OF PARTICIPATORY EVALUATION

POLICY CHARACTERISTICS

PURPOSE	GOALS	BENEFICIARY	USES	CRITICAL ISSUES
Periodic measuring of impacts of changes caused by project results	Needed to learn lessons from project activities and results	Involved community	Assessing project performance	Understand the evaluation process
Continuous awareness of project results and outcomes	Needed to determine the impacts resulting from project activities	Project Specialist	Reviewing milestone or plan of action reports	Understand WHA's mission
Community examination by people involved in project	Making decisions about project outcomes	Project Committee	Reviewing project appropriateness/conformity to our annual goals and/or 5-year plan	Understand development projects
Self-examination by people involved in project	Continuous assessment of project performance	Project Staff	Before deciding on continued funding	Understand the individual community
	Developing self-reliance skills in the community	Project Director	Before deciding on deciding new funding	Understand the technical requirements of evaluation
	Help integrate the management activities in projects	Evaluation Coordinator		Understand WHA's management requirements
		Partner Agency		

OPERATIONAL CHARACTERISTICS

SUPERVISION	TECHNICAL WORKERS	PROTOCOL	ASSISTANTS	DISTRIBUTIONS
Project Committee	Project Committee	National Office	Project Committee	Annual evaluation reports for each project
Project Specialist	Project Staff	Suboffice/DAC Office	Community Members Involved in Project	Worldwide WHA teams doing indepth evaluation reports
Evaluation Coordinator	Project Director	International Office	Project Specialist	Annual Evaluation Reports for each Region
Community Members Involved in Project	Project Specialist		Project Director	Evaluation Task Forces
Project Director	Evaluation Coordinator		Community Leaders	
Project Staff	Community Members Involved in Project		Evaluation Coordinator	
	Community Leaders		Project Staff	

evaluation information signaled the difficulties identified by the field staff's experiences reported in the next chapter. The literature review found that policy characteristics are usually defined during strategic planning and operational characteristics are most often developed by staff managers in conjunction with line managers.

The full range of mean-value scores for all response items on the policy and operational characteristics are shown on bar graphs in Figure 16. While all the characteristics are well defined by confidence intervals, the policy characteristics appear better formulated than the operational characteristics due to their narrow ranges of total mean-value scores. For the operational characteristics, the respondents segregated replies more severely between what was and was not desirable. Correspondingly, the F-test analysis also revealed more diversity of opinion on the operational characteristics.

An issue often of concern in multinational operations, and especially of concern in human resource development organizations, is whether the recipient population and the people closest to the program work and project site are directly involved in their operations. Ever since the "ugly American syndrome" was recognized in the early 1960's, development organizations have emphasized the importance of indigenous populations being totally involved in program and project activities. A review of the responses for each characteristic that involved people by their geographic proximity to the project shows the local people are classified in the first category for all four characteristics in question. Table 16 shows that people at the local location level were classified first, as the most important persons for each definitional characteristic. The people at the national level were classified second, and people at the international level were classified last. Thus, the people associated with the evaluation process tend to follow the natural geographic and organizational progression leading from the project to the organizational hierarchy, as shown in Table 16. The evaluation coordinator is the transitional position between the local project and the national office.

Examining the empirical data on WHA's organizational expectations from participatory evaluations helps clarify the definitional characteristics of the process. These expectations will be used later in the study to assess the usefulness of participatory evaluation in creating an environment of self-control in this organization. However, the importance of participatory evaluation's dual role in the human

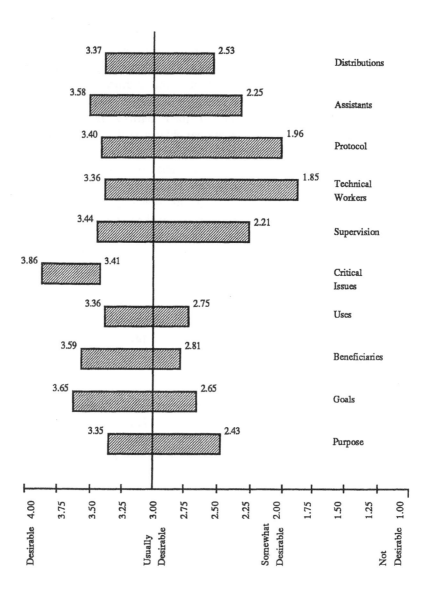

Figure 16: Range of Mean-Value Scores
Participatory Evaluation Characteristics

TABLE 16

SUMMARY OF PERSONS IDENTIFIED AS MOST IMPORTANT
TO THE EVALUATION CHARACTERISTICS BY THEIR GEOGRAPHIC LOCATION

Person / Location Level	Beneficiaries	Supervision	Technical Workers	Assistance
Local	Involved community Project Specialist Project Committee Project Staff Project Director Evaluation Coordinator Partner Agency	Project Committee Project Specialist Evaluation Coordinator Community Members Involved in the Project Project Director Project Staff	Project Committee Project Staff Project Director Project Specialist Evaluation Coordinator Community Members Involved in the Project Community Leaders	Project Committee Community Members Involved in the Project Project Specialist Project Director Community Leaders Evaluation Coordinator Project Staff
National	Operations Coordinator Suboffice/DAC Staff Entire Community National Office Director International Office Evaluation Department	Partner Agency Suboffice/DAC Center Operations Coordinator National Office Director International Office Evaluation Department Entire Community Administrative Coordinator	Partner Agency Suboffice/DAC Center Operations Coordinator International Office Evaluation Department Government Agencies Entire Community National Office Director Administrative Coordinator	Operations Coordinator Partner Agency Suboffice/DAC Staff Entire Community National Office Director International Office Evaluation Department Administrative Coordinator
International	Regional Office/Desk Field Development Division Agency Donors Administrative Coordinator Support Offices Individual Donors Vice President Technical Support Systems Audit	Regional Office/Desk Systems Audit Outside Consultant Field Development Division Support Offices Vice President Technical Support	Outside Consultants Systems Audit Field Development Division Regional Office/Desk Vice President Technical Support	Systems Audit Outside Consultants Regional Director/Desk Government Agencies Field Development Division Vice President Technical Support Support Office

development process to assess project outcomes and to teach the project participants how to make assessments for all decision making can not be over looked in developing operational definitions for the process and in building theories on control in non-profit organizations.

CHAPTER V

Findings of the Experience Questionnaire

As part of this field study research, the employees of WHA who had used the participatory evaluation process were asked about their experiences. The experience questionnaire was used to provide empirical data for initial measurement of participatory evaluation variables and in order to compare respondents' reported experiences with the organization's expectations from the evaluation process.

How the questionnaire was developed is discussed in Chapter III, and the questionnaire is presented in Appendix A. This chapter will display and discuss the results of the experience questionnaire using the statistical analysis also outlined in Chapter III. The chapter's general format will follow the outline provided by the questionnaire, examining the evaluation components, the behavioral aspects of participatory evaluation, and the respondents' conclusions about the process. This chapter has five sections: (1) data collection, (2) personnel data, (3) experiences with the participatory evaluation process, (4) summary of the experience with participatory evaluation, and (5) summary of the research findings.

DATA COLLECTION

The data analyzed in this study were collected from employees of WHA during July, August, and September, 1984. A self-administered questionnaire was given to all employees who had been trained to use the participatory evaluation process. All of these employees would have been included in the employees surveyed for the expectation questionnaire as well. However, due to the high number of anonymously returned questionnaires in both samples, the exact extent of the overlap between these two samples could not be determined. Most likely, the percentage of overlap is high since these respondents would have been very familiar with and interested in the participatory evaluation process.

The overall response rate was 74% for the experience questionnaire, and Table 17 presents the responses by individual national offices.

TABLE 17

SURVEY RESPONDENTS
EXPERIENCE QUESTIONNAIRE

	Number of Employees Surveyed	Number of Respondents	% of Total Respondents
AFRICA			
Kenya	13	6	9
Zimbabwe	7	0	—
ASIA			
Bangladesh	1	1	1
India	1	1	1
Korea	1	1	1
Philippines	17	14	19
South Pacific	1	1	1
Sri Lanka	1	1	1
Taiwan	1	1	1
Thailand	39	39	54
LATIN AMERICA			
Bolivia	5	0	—
Columbia	4	0	—
Ecuador	4	4	6
Peru	4	4	6
	99	73	100

Response Rate   74%

Similarly to the expectations questionnaire, when offices responded at all to the questionnaire, the response rate was very high. The low response rate from Africa may have been attributable to the short time lapse since they had received the evaluation training, to the difficulty of translating the questionnaire, or to the extreme drought conditions present in these countries during the time of this research.

In the Philippines, non-WHA employees, who were government guest workers in some WHA projects, had been trained in the workshop. They had since left their affiliation with WHA and could not be located for inclusion in the study. For Brazil and Colombia, the questionnaires were translated, but the offices did not respond. Thus training in the evaluation process, prior agreement to participate, and translation of questionnaires did not insure a response. The low number of responses will limit some of the statistical comparisons possible for this population.

The responses of people using the participatory evaluation process represent different time lengths of experience with the process. The descriptions of the participatory evaluation process given in Chapter III explains that WHA employees were given training in evaluation workshops on technical evaluation procedures and on participatory techniques to carry out these procedures. After attending the workshop, these WHA employees agreed to use the participatory evaluation process and techniques in at least one project. Table 18 displays when the evaluation training workshops were held; and thereby how long the project specialists would have been using the process.

Since these workshops were held in different geographic locations about six months apart, they create a time span of 18 months, 12 months, or 6 months between when the training was given and when this research was conducted. This is the nearest approximation to length of experience by employees using the process since no exact dates of implementation were maintained by the employees and reported in this study.

PERSONNEL DATA

The last section of the experience questionnaire was developed to gather specific demographic data regarding the respondents. The questions asked in this section are discussed in Chapter III and are presented in Appendix A. The purpose of these questions was to determine the general characteristics of the respondents.

TABLE 18

LENGTH OF TIME SINCE WORKSHOP TO
DATE OF STUDY REPORTED BY DATE AND LOCATION

		July-September 1984 Date of this Study
March 1983 Latin America Workshops Colombia Ecuador Peru		.... 18 months
	May/June 1983 Asia Workshops Bangladesh India Korea Philippines South Pacific Sri Lanka Taiwan Thailand	.... 12 months
	January 1984 Africa Workshops .... 6 months Kenya Zimbabwe	

A question on job title was asked to identify organizational levels so comparisons could be made between experiences of sub-groups within the organization. The same definitions were used to classify job positions as was used in the expectation questionnaire. The number of respondents for these groups is outlined in Table 19.

The questions on years in current position and years with WHA were asked to determine length of service and experience with the organization. The mean number of years with the organization was 4.5 years and the standard deviation was 2.9 years. The mean number of years in their current position was 2.3 years and the standard deviation was 1.2 year. In total, the distributions for years of experience are skewed to the left; they indicate these respondents have only worked a

TABLE 19

SURVEY RESPONDENTS CLASSIFIED
BY JOB POSITION

	Number of Respondents	% of Total Respondents
Administrators	7	10
Direct Operations	49	67
Support Staff	8	11
Evaluations & Training	3	4
Missing	6	8
	73	100

few years for WHA and in their current positions. Table 20 presents the respondents' years of experience with WHA.

While all these respondents had five years or less experience in their current positions, all but one of them had prior experience at WHA in another position. However, their perceptions of how the participatory evaluation process, methods and techniques worked, compared to other methods they are using, should be viewed with this limited time of experience always in mind.

The age, sex, and educational attainment profile of this population was young adult, well educated, and contained a substantial proportion of both male and female respondents. Fifty-two males responded (71%) and 18 females responded (25%), with three respondents not indicating their sex. The age range under 35 years had 51 respondents (70%), while 15 respondents (21%) were between the ages of 36 and 50 years, 4 respondents (6%) were between the ages of 51 and 65 years, and 3 respondents (4%) declined to give their age. Of the respondents, 49 reported having a university level education (67%), 23 reported having a secondary education (32%), and one respondent did not indicate a level of education.

The educational attainment level and location of education received was asked to determine if level and location of education affected a person's perceptions on their experiences using participation. Unfortunately, again the education locations reported were also primarily national for this population, and too many missing values were received to provide valid inferences on effect of education.

TABLE 20

RESPONDENTS' YEARS OF EXPERIENCE WITH WHA

	Years in Current Position		Years Service with WHA	
Years	Number of Respondents	%	Number of Respondents	%
1	22	31	1	1
2	19	25	15	22
3	18	25	19	25
4	7	10	10	14
5	4	5	9	14
6	—	—	4	5
7	—	—	2	3
8	—	—	3	4
9	—	—	4	5
11	—	—	1	1
17	—	—	1	1
Missing	3	4	4	5
	73	100	73	100

Thirty-three percent of the respondents from Africa reported being educated in Africa; 58% of the respondents from Asia reported being educated in Asia; and 88% of the respondents from Latin America reported being educated in Latin America. The reported education locations are presented in Table 21.

The demographic profile provided by this data indicates that the respondents are primarily young adults, nationals of the country in which their project is located, well educated, and at an early stage of their careers. Their experiences with the participatory evaluation process should be viewed in light of these demographics. Their experiences with, and perceptions of, the process are most likely relative to other projects in which they are working (rather than relative to years of experience with other processes and methods). However, they are adequately prepared to share their opinions, experiences, and perceptions in a research study.

TABLE 21

LOCATION OF RESPONDENTS' EDUCATION

	Number of Respondents	% of Total Respondents
Africa	2	3
Asia	34	47
Latin America	7	10
West	4	5
Missing	26	36
	73	100

EXPERIENCES WITH THE PARTICIPATORY EVALUATION PROCESS AT WHA

The questionnaire on the experiences of WHA employees using the participatory evaluation process was developed to gather empirical data on how the evaluation process is working. The findings of the experience questionnaire will be presented in this section of the chapter.

All of the questions and response items were based on issues raised in internal documents and or in the literature review. The first set of questions followed the general evaluation components or steps used in an evaluation research process. The second set of questions addressed the behavioral issues of participation as applied to evaluation research. The last set of questions summarized the respondents' conclusions on using the participatory evaluation process.

Each question asked in the questionnaire was followed by a list of response items representing various aspects of the issue raised by the question. Each item was rated by the respondent on a five-point rating scale from high (very helpful 5.0) to low (hindered 1.0) or had not experienced (0), and descriptive statistics were prepared on each, omitting the had not experienced (0) responses. Confidence intervals of size .30 were again used to classify response items based on their mean-value scores. The derivation of the confidence intervals is presented in Appendix B.

Evaluation Components

While specific techniques and skills may vary with different types of evaluation research models, similar evaluation components are used. The utility of participatory evaluation for each component was assessed in order to discover for which areas the process was more helpful and less helpful.

Needs Assessment: In order to assess changes occurring in a project setting, evaluators (whether they are outside evaluators or the indigenous community) must have some way of describing the project's initial environment, identifying what problem(s) the project addresses, and deciding how resources are being used to solve the problem(s). To determine how helpful the participatory evaluation process was for project participants to assess needs in their community, question 2 asked respondents to rate how helpful they perceived the techniques to be for various individuals or groups. Response items were rated from very helpful (5.0) to hindered (1.0). Four project participants were considered by the respondents—the project community members, the project committee members, the partner agency members, and the WHA staff workers themselves. Using the confidence interval size of .30, two classifications were determined for the range of mean-value scores. The findings are displayed in Table 22 in technical sequence.

The 36 response items examined represented nine general steps of needs assessment discussed in the literature and embodied in the participatory evaluation process and techniques developed by WHA. The range of mean-value scores for all 36 response items was 4.31 to 3.74. All nine steps were considered for the four project participant groups. In describing their environment and assessing the needs of their community, the respondents rated the participatory evaluation techniques and skills equally helpful for all the project participant groups, except the partner agency, although it certainly ranked high for that group as well. No particular patterns emerged for how helpful the process was to project participants for assessing particular project components (problems, talents, resources) nor for performing particular evaluation activities (recognizing, identifying, deciding).

The ratings given to five response items pertaining to needs assessment which appeared later in the questionnaire confirm these findings of question 2. Their total range of mean-value scores was from 4.38 to 3.59. The mean-value scores of two response items, which concern considering needs of all effected audiences and identifying more potentials, would be classified in the first category for the needs assessment items of question 2. The three other response items, which concerned mental assessments or judgments made by WHA employees and WHA required documentation, would not be classified within either of the categories for needs assessment; their mean-values were lower and would require a third category. Generally, however, these findings support the pattern of helpfulness reported for the participatory evaluation process in completing needs assessment. They also confirm later findings on the low compatibility of the participatory evaluation process and techniques with community decision making and completing required documents.

An F-test analysis by workshop was performed on all response items where $F_{(2,72)}=3.15$, $P<.05$. Of the 41 response items examined for their helpfulness to needs assessment, eight had statistically significant differences between their mean-values scores. For six of these, the six respondents from Africa, who had been trained in the methods six months before the study, rated them higher than the other respondents. This pattern continues throughout the findings; therefore, the responses from Africa will only be discussed when they deviate from that pattern.

The other two response items identified as different by the F-test analysis are of interest here. The respondents from Asia (12 months experience) rated the variable "identify possible ways to use talents and abilities in the project by the partner agency" higher ($F=3.36$) than the respondents from Latin America (18 months experience). The respondents from Latin America reported the variable "recognizing resources present in the community by the project committee" higher ($F=4.97$) than the respondents from Asia. These differences do not seem to be related to the different lengths of experience with the evaluation process; rather they may be cultural differences or differences in the ways in which the program is implemented. However, identifying which project participants are affected most in different components of these evaluation functions can increase management's ability to modify and adapt the process to alternative settings and circumstances.

Generally, the respondents rated the participatory evaluation process more helpful to the community members and the project committee than

TABLE 22

HELPFULNESS OF THE PARTICIPATORY EVALUATION PROCESS TO VARIOUS PROJECT PARTICIPANTS FOR NEEDS ASSESSMENT

In assessing the community's needs, how helpful were the participatory evaluation techniques for each of the individual or groups when considering the following:

Response Items	COMMUNITY				PROJECT COMMITTEE				WHA STAFF				PARTNER AGENCY			
	N	SD	$\bar{X}$ 4.31-4.01	$\bar{X}$ 4.00-3.70	N	SD	$\bar{X}$ 4.31-4.01	$\bar{X}$ 4.00-3.70	N	SD	$\bar{X}$ 4.31-4.01	$\bar{X}$ 4.00-3.70	N	SD	$\bar{X}$ 4.31-4.01	$\bar{X}$ 4.00-3.70
PROBLEMS																
Recognizing problems or needs of the community	71	.80	4.31		66	.82	4.06		67	.94	4.03		62	.89		3.74
Identifying possible ways the problems or needs could be corrected	71	.84	4.20		65	.81	4.09		69	.85	4.07		62	.91		3.77
Deciding on certain project activities to resolve the problems or needs	65	.80	4.20		63	.81	4.05		67	.93		3.84	62	.83		3.89
TALENTS AND ABILITIES																
Recognizing talents and abilities present in the community	68	.90		3.94	63	.81	4.08		69	.95	4.04		62	.88		3.67
Identify possible ways to use these talents and abilities in the project	69	.79		3.96	62	.74	4.02		68	.94	4.04		60	.76		3.78
Deciding on project activities to develop these talents and abilities	67	.92	4.00		61	.87	4.07		64	.87	4.03		59	.80		3.81

TABLE 22 (Continued)

HELPFULNESS OF THE PARTICIPATORY EVALUATION PROCESS
TO VARIOUS PROJECT PARTICIPANTS FOR NEEDS ASSESSMENT

In assessing the community's needs, how helpful were the participatory evaluation techniques for each of the individual or groups when considering the following:

Response Items	COMMUNITY			PROJECT COMMITTEE			WHA STAFF			PARTNER AGENCY		
	N	SD	$\bar{X}$ 4.31- 4.01	$\bar{X}$ 4.00- 3.70	N	SD	$\bar{X}$ 4.31- 4.01	$\bar{X}$ 4.00- 3.70	N	SD	$\bar{X}$ 4.31- 4.01	$\bar{X}$ 4.00- 3.70	N	SD	$\bar{X}$ 4.31- 4.01	$\bar{X}$ 4.00- 3.70

Response Items	N	SD	$\bar{X}$ 4.31-4.01	$\bar{X}$ 4.00-3.70	N	SD	$\bar{X}$ 4.31-4.01	$\bar{X}$ 4.00-3.70	N	SD	$\bar{X}$ 4.31-4.01	$\bar{X}$ 4.00-3.70	N	SD	$\bar{X}$ 4.31-4.01	$\bar{X}$ 4.00-3.70
RESOURCES AVAILABLE																
Recognizing, resources present in the community	70	.90	4.17		61	.81	4.18		68	.90	4.13		62	.85		3.97
Identify possible ways to use these resources in the project	70	.97	4.10		63	.92		3.98	68	.94	4.02		62	.93		3.84
Deciding on project activities which include these resources	69	.99	4.10		63	.91		3.95	69	1.05		3.90	61	.92		3.77

Note: Range of replies from helpful (5.0) to hindered (1.0).

to themselves or the partner agency. The confirming response items indicate that they found it less helpful in completing the reporting aspects of needs assessment.

Designing the Project and Evaluation Plans: To be useful, an evaluation plan must be designed to gather facts, figures, and illustrations which substantiate the changes that are occurring in the community due to the project. Further, for evaluation research to function as a control element, evaluation information for any program should articulate with other project documents so that the activities measured are the ones approved in the original project and subsequent modifications. Unanticipated results might also be discovered, but these are welcomed additions while agreed-to-plans are essential. Assuring usefulness of the evaluation information begins when the evaluation plan is designed to be congruent with the project plan.

To discover how helpful the participatory evaluation process was for project participants to design an evaluation plan for their project, question 3 asked respondents to rate how helpful they perceived the techniques to be for various individuals and groups in deciding on project programs. Response items were rated from very helpful (5.0) to hindered (1.0), and the same four project participant groups were considered by the respondents. The nine response items examined for designing the project and evaluation plans represent general steps discussed in the literature and embodied in the participatory evaluation process and techniques developed by WHA. The range of mean-value scores for all 36 items was 4.15 to 3.39. Using the confidence interval size of .30 to classify response items by their mean-value scores, three categories were derived. These findings are displayed in Table 23 in technical sequence.

For designing the project and evaluation plans, the respondents rated the participatory evaluation techniques and skills more helpful to the WHA staff member, the community, and the project committee, than to the Partner Agency. Later results show, however, that the respondents do not perceive that the Partner Agency feels ignored in the process, but the results support the idea that the process was designed to increase the community's self-reliance and decision-making skills, not the Partner Agency's.

Later in the questionnaire, respondents were asked to rate three other response items which pertain to the helpfulness of the participatory evaluation process when communities design their own project evaluation plans. The mean values for all three of these response items would be classified in the first, most helpful, category for designing these plans. Thus, they confirm the findings of question 3. Further, the low standard deviations on three items, (.47-.52) indicates that the respondents had stronger general agreement on them than they did to the initial questions on designing the project and evaluation plans.

These findings on the confirming items support the results on helpfulness in designing these plans. They indicate that the participatory evaluation process was helpful in developing a project plan which established project plans, goals, and program activities that utilize the resources available in the community and in designing an evaluation plan to document them. However, one interesting pattern to note is that selecting indicators to monitor activities was in the first, most helpful, category for all project participant groups. Then, deciding how to record these indicators was in the second, less helpful, category for the community, committee, and partner agency. Finally, developing a record-keeping device to use was in the third, least helpful, category for all groups.

The F-test analysis by workshops where $F_{(2,72)}=3.15$, $P<.05$, confirms and helps explain these problems. For the issue of selecting indicators to monitor activities, a significant difference between workshop groups was found for both the project committee (F=3.80) and the partner agency (F=8.03). Asia respondents (12 months experience) rated them higher ($\bar{X}=3.9$ and $\bar{X}=3.7$ respectively) than the Latin America respondents (18 months experience, $\bar{X}=3.0$ and $\bar{X}=2.3$ respectively).

For the issue of deciding how to record these indicators, a significant difference between workshop groups was again found for both the project committee (F=3.33) and the partner agency (F=5.30). Asia respondents rated them higher ($\bar{X}=3.7$ and $\bar{X}=3.4$ respectively) than Latin American respondents ($\bar{X}=3.0$ and $\bar{X}=2.0$). Again, Asia respondents rated the process more helpful in these steps than the Latin American respondents. These differences do not seem related to experience, but rather to culture or methods used in implementing the process in these locations with the project committee and the partner agency.

TABLE 23

HELPFULNESS OF THE PARTICIPATORY EVALUATION PROCESS TO VARIOUS PROJECT PARTICIPANTS FOR DESIGNING THE PROJECT AND EVALUATION PLANS

In assessing the community's needs, how helpful were the participatory evaluation techniques for each of the individuals or groups when considering the following:

Response Items	WHA STAFF				COMMUNITY				PROJECT COMMITTEE				PARTNER AGENCY				
	N	SD	$\bar{X}$ 4.15-3.85	$\bar{X}$ 3.84-3.54	N	SD	$\bar{X}$ 4.15-3.85	$\bar{X}$ 3.84-3.54	N	SD	$\bar{X}$ 4.15-3.85	$\bar{X}$ 3.84-3.54	N	SD	$\bar{X}$ 4.15-3.85	$\bar{X}$ 3.84-3.54	$\bar{X}$ 3.53-3.23
Considering the different activity levels that were possible for the task	67	1.00	3.97		62	.87	4.07		67	.93	4.09		63	1.00		3.79	
Selecting a reasonable objective for these activity levels	67	.75	4.05		69	.94	4.06		60	.81	4.08		62	.98		3.73	
Setting measurable goals for the project's activities	66	.85	4.15		68	.88	4.10		60	.87	4.08		60	.92	3.88		
Agreeing upon task quotas (or work levels) for people involved in the project	65	.86	3.91		64	.81	3.86		56	.81	3.88		57	.85		3.67	
Selecting indicators which we thought would best monitor these activities	61	.84	3.97		58	.95	3.93		52	.91	3.90		53	.88		3.66	

TABLE 23 (Continued)

HELPFULNESS OF THE PARTICIPATORY EVALUATION PROCESS TO VARIOUS PROJECT PARTICIPANTS FOR DESIGNING THE PROJECT AND EVALUATION PLANS

In assessing the community's needs, how helpful were the participatory evaluation techniques for each of the individuals or groups when considering the following:

Response Items	WHA STAFF				COMMUNITY				PROJECT COMMITTEE				PARTNER AGENCY				
	N	SD	$\bar{X}$ 4.15-3.85	$\bar{X}$ 3.84-3.54	N	SD	$\bar{X}$ 4.15-3.85	$\bar{X}$ 3.84-3.54	N	SD	$\bar{X}$ 4.15-3.85	$\bar{X}$ 3.84-3.54	N	SD	$\bar{X}$ 4.15-3.85	$\bar{X}$ 3.84-3.54	$\bar{X}$ 3.53-3.23
Deciding how to record these indicators	59	.88	3.92		57	1.08		3.74	52	1.03		3.73	51	.96			3.39
Developing a record-keeping device to use	57	.94		3.72	57	1.00		3.67	50	.99		3.62	52	1.07			3.44
Measuring the current activity level of these indicators	55	.89	3.91		57	.95	3.95		51	.94		3.75	52	.98		3.54	
Deciding how the results, outcomes, or findings from the project could be shared with one another	56	.87	3.96		56	1.03	3.86		51	1.03		3.77	52	.99		3.67	

Note: Range of replies from very helpful (5.0) to hindered (1.0).

Thus, the participatory evaluation process was rated at the level "somewhat to usually helpful" for all project participants on these critical measurement issues. From the literature search, Drucker would argue that the evaluation measurement techniques need to be most helpful to the persons taking, recording and using the measures in the project operations (e.g., the community members involved in the project or the project committee, etc.). In that case, the mean-value scores confirm the helpfulness of the participatory evaluation process and techniques for community people to measure their own project results. However, in the case where equal participation is desired for all project participants, then the mean-value scores indicate that the process helps the partner agency less than other project participants on measurement issues.

The F-test analysis, however, shows that the participatory evaluation process was rated as more helpful to the critical issues of measurement by the Asia respondents than the Latin American respondents who have used the process longer. The large number of Asia respondents are influencing strongly the overall mean-value scores. The low ratings by Latin American respondents on initial measurements in designing the project could signal future difficulties in subsequent measurements.

It is very important, therefore, to recognize that selecting indicators to measure program activities, deciding how to record them, and developing recording keeping devices to use in monitoring these indicators is the point of origin for further success or problems with reporting project results. When good records are maintained, the direct project participants—the community, the project committee, and project staff—will be continuously aware of project results as they keep their record books, public charts, progress graphs, or whatever means they decide to use. However, if the participants have trouble designing a record-keeping device, poor or no records may be maintained, thus making performance assessment and reporting impossible. These suppositions will be explored later by the findings on reporting.

The response item "measuring current activity levels of indicators" was rated high for the WHA employee and for the community. The next question explores further their experiences with baseline measurement.

Baseline Measurements: Performance reports are most useful when they can be compared to some prior measure so changes can be noted. Thus, beginning information is essential to assessment. Moreover, when

WHA decides to fund a development project, the community may decide to pursue a number of activities at the same time. Thus, information may need to be gathered on several conditions at once: the community members' health, their food consumption, their housing, even the community's work and leisure activities. Thus sufficient information must be gathered at the beginning of a project from which to assess various changes.

To ascertain how helpful the participatory evaluation process was for measuring current activity levels on indicators selected to monitor project activities, question 9 asked respondents about their experiences with taking baseline measures. Response items are presented on a scale from strongly agree (5.0) to strongly disagree (2.0). Using the confidence interval size of .30, two categories emerged for the range of mean value scores; they are displayed in Table 24.

TABLE 24

AGREEMENT WITH BASELINE MEASUREMENT TECHNIQUES FOR
PARTICIPATORY EVALUATION PROCESS

*Based on your experience with using the participatory evaluation skills and techniques
to obtain baseline measures, do you agree/disagree with the following:*

Response Items	N	SD	$\bar{X}$ 4.08- 3.78	$\bar{X}$ 3.76- 3.46
More socio-economic, political, religious information was needed than was obtained in the baseline surveys	67	.59	4.08	
The communities baseline surveys were adequate for our needs	67	.86	3.93	
I know how to use the techniques well enough to collect meaningful data	68	.66	3.84	
The use of special evaluators would be wise for baseline assessments rather than the local community	63	.93		3.67

Note: Range of replies from strongly agree (5.0) to strongly disagree (2.0).

The four response items examined regarding baseline measurements all originated in the internal documents of WHA. However, they are also reflective of issues raised in the literature. The range of mean-value scores was 4.08 to 3.67. Examining these responses disclosed some interesting relationships between the ratings. WHA has designed baseline measurement techniques which they feel are the least obtrusive way to gather such information by having the community people measure their own activity levels. Even when adequate information is gathered and the respondents feel comfortable using the baseline techniques, they felt more information was needed, and the low standard deviation shows strong agreement among the respondents that more information was needed.

By contrast, however, the response item "the use of special evaluators would be wise for baseline assessments rather than the local community" was rated the lowest. The higher standard deviation for this item indicates that the respondents are not in as strong agreement concerning the use or exclusion of special evaluators to help with baseline measures. No significant differences in opinion were found by the F-test analysis among respondents from the different workshops. Their ratings on the project design issues and the baseline measurement techniques indicate that a participatory evaluation process is less helpful to measurement issues than program composition issues.

Organizing the Project Administration: Evaluation research is concerned with all phases of designing a program or project. Evaluators do, or review the organization's own, needs assessments to determine which problems were identified for an intervention and which resources were available to address them. They note which programs and activities were selected to be carried out in the project, what goals and objectives were set, and what baseline measurement were taken. In addition to programming considerations, evaluators also note the administration and funding budgets set for a program to test for efficiency. Thus, one facet of usefulness for an evaluation process is its ability to incorporate efficiency measures as well as effectiveness measures. At issue here is whether the type of project chosen and the strategies for the delivery system were the best for the context and problem.

To learn how helpful the participatory evaluation process was to project participants for organizing their project, question 4 asked respondents to rate how helpful they perceived the techniques to be for

TABLE 25

HELPFULNESS OF THE PARTICIPATORY EVALUATION PROCESS TO VARIOUS PROJECT PARTICIPANTS FOR ORGANIZING THE PROJECT ADMINISTRATIVELY

In organizing the project, how helpful were the skills you learned from the participatory evaluation workshop to each of these individuals or groups when:

Response Items	WHA STAFF N	SD	$\bar{X}$ 4.06-3.76	$\bar{X}$ 3.75-3.45	PROJECT COMMITTEE N	SD	$\bar{X}$ 4.06-3.76	$\bar{X}$ 3.75-3.45	PARTNER AGENCY N	SD	$\bar{X}$ 4.06-3.76	$\bar{X}$ 3.75-3.45	COMMUNITY N	SD	$\bar{X}$ 4.06-3.76	$\bar{X}$ 3.75-3.45	$\bar{X}$ 3.44-3.14
Deciding on what kind of MHS project would be best for this community	62	1.05	3.92		55	.90	3.89		54	.96		3.65	61	1.03	3.82		
Deciding what kind of project organizational structure to use	59	.88	3.98		53	.86	3.85		54	.95	3.76		57	.96		3.72	
Deciding what kind of project administration to use	62	.89	4.03		52	.94		3.79	54	1.08		3.67	60	1.01	3.80		
Deciding what kind of evangelism strategy was appropriate to use	58	.93	3.90		50	1.00	3.84		53	1.06	3.91		55	1.08			3.40
Considering alternative spending levels for these activities	55	.87	4.06		51	.90	3.86		53	1.01	3.83		55	.87	3.80		
Determining a funding amount that seemed most appropriate to achieve the project's goals	62	.98	4.00		53	.89	3.98		55	1.07	3.78		62	1.01	3.84		

Note: Range of replies from very helpful (5.0) to hindered (1.0).

various individuals and groups when organizing the project administratively. Response items were rated from helpful (5.0) to hindered (1.0).

The six response items examined for organizing the project represent management issues which evaluators use in assessing efficiency. The response items themselves emanated from the procedure manuals and other internal documents of WHA, but they portray the managerial decisions which need to be made in organizing any program. Their range of mean-value scores were 4.06 to 3.40; these were generally lower than the mean-values for needs assessment and project design. Table 25 displays the three categories of helpfulness which resulted for their mean-value scores; the response items are listed in their technical sequence.

Compounding these lower mean values, the standard deviations on response items for all six of these evaluation components are generally higher, indicating less agreement among the respondents on the helpfulness of the participatory evaluation process in accomplishing these functions when organizing a project administratively. The WHA staff reported the participatory evaluation process was helpful to them in fulfilling all the tasks examined. Furthermore, for the first time, the process was rated more helpful to the partner agency than to the community; in fact, it was least helpful to the community.

These findings are very reassuring to a management or accounting researcher because all functions in the management process should align people properly with their requisite role in accomplishing the task. Since WHA, the partner agency, and the project committee are instigating a development project to aid the community, these four project participants should each find the participatory evaluation process most helpful to them in fulfilling their respective proper role in the project. In this case, for example, the process was rated most helpful to the partner agency in deciding on an evangelism strategy. WHA's overriding corporate goal is to have the partner agency reach out to the community and share their religious views. Correspondingly, participatory evaluation was least helpful to the community when deciding on an evangelism strategy, as they are the ones to receive the evangelism. This is an encouraging pattern for both managers and evaluators.

To confirm the helpfulness of the participatory evaluation process to augment managerial objectives, in question 5 respondents were asked if participatory evaluation increased their awareness of other organizational concerns. Response items are presented on a scale from always (5.0) to never (2.0). The classifications for these confirming variables are presented in Table 26.

TABLE 26

CONFIRMING ITEMS ON THE HELPFULNESS OF THE
PARTICIPATORY EVALUATION PROCESS IN
ORGANIZING THE PROJECT ADMINISTRATIVELY

When preparing a new project proposal, the participatory evaluation process helps me consider how this new project will fit into:

Response Items	N	SD	$\overline{X}$ 4.48-4.18	$\overline{X}$ 4.17-3.87
WHA's organizational strategy	61	.67	4.48	
Our National Office strategy	54	.69	4.46	
Our National Office budget	56	.82	4.38	
WHA's organizational mission	59	.85	4.37	
Our National Office five year plan	58	.84	4.29	
WHA's budget	54	.86	4.28	
Our National Office quota for new children in programs	53	.95		4.15

Note: Range of replies from always (5.0) to never (2.0).

The range of mean-value scores for these response items is higher than the mean-value scores for the initial items on organizing the project's administration. The respondents reported usually to always being aware of the corporate WHA concerns.

Generally, the activities pursued in each program are the building blocks to achieve corporate plans. Therefore, programs must be designed and organized to contribute to the organizations' objectives while, at the same time, being compatible with the local context and culture. Likewise, preparing budgets generally help employees identify the appropriate resources to achieve their plans. Converting plans into budgets requires program administrators to consider alternative combinations of resources and spending levels needed to most efficiently accomplish their goals.

The respondents reported that the participatory evaluation process helps them consider the corporate goals of both the national and international offices. They also indicated that the process helped them consider how the request to fund this project fits into the national office budget and WHA's general budget, as they used the process in budgeting with the community. The participatory evaluation process was reported as helpful in augmenting the managerial task of properly aligning both the project participants with their requisite role in the project and the organizational and budgetary characteristics of a project with the cultural context and the problem being addressed. These are both very important to the acceptance and success of a program or project in any organization.

Analyzing the data by workshops using an F-test where $F_{(2,72)}=3.15$, $P<.05$, showed that the Latin American respondents reported the process to be more helpful to certain project participants in organizing the project than the Asian respondents. These differences are displayed in Table 27.

TABLE 27

VALUE OF THE PARTICIPATORY EVALUATION PROCESS TO DIFFERENT PROJECT PARTICIPANTS FOR ORGANIZING THE PROJECT IN VARIOUS REGIONS

Response Items	F	Latin America $\overline{X}$	Asia $\overline{X}$
Deciding what kind of WHA project would be best for this community by the project committee	3.96	4.4	3.8
Deciding what kind of project administration to use by the community	4.30	4.5	3.7
Determining a funding amount that seemed most appropriate to achieve the project's goals by the:			
community	6.56	4.8	3.7
project committee	4.50	4.8	3.9
partner agency	4.66	4.8	3.6
Consider WHA's budget	5.37	2.5	3.6

Note: Range of replies from very helpful (5.0) to hindered (1.0).
$^aF_{(2,72)}=3.15$, $P<.05$.

The reasons for these differences are not readily apparent, and several factors could be causing this finding. Perhaps group decisions on organization and funding are culturally more acceptable in Latin America than in Asia. Or perhaps, because they had used the process longer, Latin Americans have had more opportunities to recognize the benefits of participatory evaluation for organizing administratively and budgeting for the project. As would be expected, however, the helpfulness of the participatory evaluation process diminishes abruptly when considering budgets beyond their immediate national concern. The carry-over effect on budgeting (considering the international operations budget while preparing the project's budget) reported by the Asia respondents seems high.

This finding supports the literature on management by objectives, which contends that people will be aware of their immediate resource needs and that efficient resource allocation will occur only as each iteration of the budgeting process occurs throughout the organization. The increased awareness reported for all project participants is equally important as concurrently considering operating objectives and properly aligning participant roles. The results shown in Table 25 indicate that the process was more helpful for considering alternative spending levels than for deciding on the most appropriate spending levels. Since the partner agency technically requests the funds from WHA through the WHA staff member, a healthy tension may be created between these two as they fulfill cooperatively, adversarial roles—one requesting funds and desiring all their requests be met, the other taking the request and protecting the interest of their organization. The proper role for people who have authority and responsibility for budgeting is important, but increased awareness by all participants of how and why the money is being spent is an interesting finding on the usefulness of a participatory evaluation process.

The process seems to create an open system between the WHA project specialist and the other project participants; it appears to facilitate the tasks of different participants, accommodating their particular role in the project and their culture.

Monitoring the Project Outcomes: Evaluators often monitor programs using the sponsoring organization's, or the project's own, management reporting system. This is more efficient than maintaining two reporting systems. Outside measures, or evaluation specific measures, can be used to validate or confirm these reports. WHA's

TABLE 28

HELPFULNESS OF THE PARTICIPATORY
EVALUATION PROCESS FOR PROJECT MONITORING

How helpful were the participatory evaluation techniques
and skills in accomplishing these tasks?

Response Items	N	SD	$\bar{X}$ 4.30-4.00	$\bar{X}$ 3.99-3.69	$\bar{X}$ 3.68-3.38	$\bar{X}$ 3.37-3.07
DIALOGUE AND DISCUSSION						
Clarify issues	67	.78	4.30			
Discuss concerns expressed	67	.80	4.30			
Dialogue with the Partner Agency, Project Committee, Director, Staff, and Community	67	.83	4.30			
Find new issues concerning community development	67	.81	4.22			
REVIEW PROJECT PERFORMANCE						
Assess what the project has been doing	66	.84	4.14			
Note the community's progress toward achieving project's goals	62	.91	4.13			
Note the activity level of specific tasks	55	.98	4.04			
Note the results of particular activities	57	.94		3.97		
Observe the project's operations	66	.93		3.94		
VALIDATING PROJECT REPORTS						
Compare evaluation records to the original plan	57	.88		3.84		
Compare evangelism report to the visit dialogue	50	.94		3.76		
Compare monthly project reports to the milestone plan of action reports	62	.90			3.66	

TABLE 28 (Continued)

HELPFULNESS OF THE PARTICIPATORY
EVALUATION PROCESS FOR PROJECT MONITORING

*How helpful were the participatory evaluation techniques
and skills in accomplishing these tasks?*

Response Items	N	SD	$\bar{X}$ 4.30- 4.00	$\bar{X}$ 3.99- 3.69	$\bar{X}$ 3.68- 3.38	$\bar{X}$ 3.37- 3.07
Compare monthly project reports to accounting records	59	.94			3.64	
Compare monthly project reports to the project's budget	61	1.01			3.57	
Compare milestone reports to major expenditures	57	1.00			3.51	
Review sponsor relations department (SRD) correspondences for unresolved issues	48	1.05				3.27
Satisfy SRD discrepancies	47	1.15				3.19
MAKING EVALUATIVE DECISIONS						
Evaluate the operations, logistics, and coordination of this project	56	.89		3.96		
Identify project discrepancies for their correction	57	.98		3.84		
PREPARING FOR FUTURE ACTION						
Give the people advice	65	.89	4.20			
Involve the community members in these review and validation procedures	60	.89		3.98		
Give them training	67	.87		3.97		
Reach a consensus	64	.89		3.97		
Agree to the next monthly plan	56	1.00		3.80		
Discuss unresolved issues or discrepancies in the project	58	1.00		3.74		

Note: Range of replies from very helpful (5.0) to hindered (1.0).

project monitoring system requires monthly project visits by the WHA project specialist and the filing of various management reports. The information for these reports is compiled and validated by the staff member during the visit.

Evaluative decisions about a project are the judgments which evaluators and project administrators must make when they assess project outcomes and service accomplishments. Is the project proceeding in the direction and at the pace anticipated? Are the activities achieving the objectives and alleviating the problems? These decisions are based on various forms of information.

To discover how helpful the participatory evaluation process was in monitoring and reporting the project's progress and results, two sets of questions were asked. First, question 6 asked respondents how helpful (very, 5.0, to hindered, 1.0) the participatory evaluation techniques and skills were in accomplishing the monitoring tasks. The tasks are grouped by activities performed on the monthly project visit and Table 28 presents the responses on them in four categories of helpfulness for the range of mean-value scores.

The twenty-five response items examined for monitoring the project all originated in the procedure manuals and other internal WHA documents. However, they are representative of the monitoring and assessment procedures discussed in the literature and performed in most organizations. Their range of mean-value scores was 4.30 to 3.19. Overall, for the tasks of gathering needed information and having community members evaluate their project, the respondents rated the participatory evaluation techniques more helpful for dialogue, discussion, and review than for validation, making evaluative decisions, and preparing for future action.

The findings show the techniques to be least helpful in the documenting procedures, like noting the results of activities and comparing expected or observed results to actual or reported outcomes. Comparison of the evaluation plan has the highest mean value; but the low number of responses, the high standard deviations, and the difficulties reported earlier with developing record keeping devices, raise some doubt about the agreement on and validity of this finding.

The usefulness of participatory evaluation in providing substantive measures and facts on project results is essential if project participants are to make good evaluative decisions. The respondents reported that the participatory evaluation techniques and skills were less helpful to them when making evaluative decisions and preparing for future action, than when they conducted dialogue and discussion with the project participants. However, that finding does not speak to how helpful the techniques were to other project participants. Unfortunately the response items "reach a consensus," "involve the community members in these review and validation procedures," and "discuss unresolved issues or discrepancies in the project" indicate that the techniques and skills may not work as well for the evaluative aspects of the process (e.g., making a decision), as it does for the behavioral aspects (e.g.: dialogue, discussion, participation).

Later in the questionnaire, other response items were used in several questions to confirm the findings of question 6. Two categories of helpfulness were derived for their mean-value scores and they are presented in Table 29. Response items are presented on a scale from strongly agree (5.0) to strongly disagree (2.0). The response items are grouped by the major evaluation functions of interest in this study.

The confirming variables present an interesting paradox in this analysis of the utility of the participatory evaluation process in monitoring project performance. In the first analysis of question 6 on project site visits, dialogue and discussion were rated high while involving the project participants in the review procedures and reaching a consensus were rated lower. For the confirming variables, involving the project participants and in review assessment performance is rated higher, while the standard deviations on these variables are much lower, indicating greater general agreement. Perhaps the respondents did not understand question 6; or perhaps, asked in the context of questions on project site visits, the respondents answered in respect to their perceptions when they visit. But when asked later about the same issues, they responded as to how they feel about the process in more general terms. Others might explain this paradox as respondents "saying what they think researchers or management want to hear."

The F-test analysis further raises suspicions on these findings. For the 41 variables used to assess monitoring, 20 had statistically significant difference between workshop groups in their mean-value scores. For 18 of these, Latin American respondents were higher than the Asia respondents. Only for the validation procedure "compare milestone reports to major expenditures" were Latin American respondents' mean scores lower than the Asia respondents.

TABLE 29

CONFIRMING ITEMS ON HELPFULNESS OF THE PARTICIPATORY
EVALUATION PROCESS FOR PROJECT MONITORING

*Based on your experience using participatory evaluation skills and
techniques in a project, do you agree/disagree with the following:*

Response Items	N	SD	$\bar{X}$ 4.25- 3.95	$\bar{X}$ 3.94- 3.64
MONITORING PROJECT PERFORMANCE Activity outcomes measure programs	65	.53	4.19	
The techniques were helpful to continuously monitor project activities	62	.85	4.15	
The techniques are helpful to measure improvements	65	.94	4.11	
The techniques are helpful to review changes in the original plans	60	1.02		3.80
DETERMINING IMPACTS Project results are more relevant to the community	65	.56	4.25	
Involved community have more realistic expectations	65	.52	4.22	
Involved community more readily recognized changes resulting from the project	64	.54	4.16	
The techniques were helpful to identify key success areas	58	.81	4.10	
Partner agency more readily recognized changes resulting from the project	61	.44	4.07	
Partner agencies have more realistic expectations	59	.47	3.98	
The techniques are helpful to realize when training is needed	62	.90		3.94
Recognize when technical assistance was needed	60	.82		3.93
DISTRIBUTING EVALUATION FINDINGS Involved community better understand why the project is being done	65	.56	4.25	
Involved community used their evaluation information in carrying out the project	64	.52	4.13	
The involved community take corrective action sooner	64	.63	4.08	
Involved community routinely consider project results	64	.55	3.95	

Note: Range of replies from strongly agree (5.0) to strongly disagree (2.0).

No definite explanation is possible for these differences between the responses on the monitoring function variables and the confirming variables—or theseinconsistent results. The validating procedure of using confirming variables can only identify the paradox, but not explain it. A paradox such as this is one of the limitations of empirical survey research, however, it does focus administrator and staff attendention on regional differences.

Reporting the Project Evaluation Findings: When the monthly project visit is completed, the information gathered during the visit is reported to WHA in routine management reports. Reporting the evaluation findings is the final evaluation component analyzed in this research.

To determine how effective the participatory evaluation process was in reporting project evaluation findings to the WHA organization, question 10 in the expectations questionnaire asked all the employees about their experiences using the evaluation reports. Of the 320 respondents to that questionnaire, 116 (36%) reported receiving and reading the reports. The breakdown by job positions is shown below, in Table 30.

TABLE 30

EXPECTATIONS QUESTIONNAIRE RESPONDENTS
CLASSIFIED BY JOB POSITION

	Number of Respondents	% of Total Respondents
Management	25	22
Administration and Finance	6	5
Direct Operations	69	60
Support Staff	9	7
Evaluation and Training	7	6
	116	100

The reasons for asking the entire staff about their experiences are twofold: (1) reporting is of critical importance in large organizations; and (2) employees from throughout the organization will have to use the reports and the findings. Management reports are the vehicles organizations use to convey information routinely. Qualitative and quantitative information is collected throughout the organizational structure and transmitted to people who need to know how various parts of the organization are functioning.

Financial information is most often gathered because it is important, it is quantitative, and it is well suited to comparisons—budgeted to actual spending or costs incurred in one department versus another. In recent years, evaluators have realized the importance of comparing spending in programs or projects with outcomes or results for cost effectiveness. Operating performance has also been converted to quantitative measures which can be summed and compared like financial information. Unfortunately, incorporating qualitative information into the routine reporting mechanism of large, functionally diverse, and geographically dispersed non-profit organizations has not been as easily achieved.

The evaluation reports required for WHA's participatory evaluation process are expository, case-study reports created by each project specialist to share the results in their projects. No reporting form or format is required of national office staff members. Rather, they are given the freedom to incorporate project performance and result measures they feel appropriate and compatible with the project's evaluation plan and monitoring records. The experiences of WHA management-decision making employees in using these reports are presented in Table 31. The experiences of WHA project workers in preparing the reports are presented in Table 32. Replies are presented on a scale from strongly agree (5.0) to strongly disagree (2.0); they are categorized by the major evaluation function of interest in this study.

The experiences reported by WHA employees are consistent with the strengths and weaknesses of qualitative reporting often discussed in the literature. The worth of the reports to respondents is clear; both the project worker and the line managers report using them and confirm their value. However, the reports are cumbersome to prepare, to read, and to use. Therefore, their full potential utility to both the project specialists and the line managers is underdeveloped and not being achieved.

With respect to receiving and reading these reports, the ratings are high, indicating the respondents usually (4.0) to always (5.0) take the time to read them. The ratings are lower, however, for frequency of reading evaluation reports. The respondents report sometimes (3.0) to never (2.0), reading these reports more often than other reports. Thus they are not re-reading or regularly referencing the reports.

TABLE 31

USES OF EVALUATION REPORTS

Based on your experience with using the participatory evaluation reports, do you agree/disagree with the following:

Response Items	N	SD	$\bar{X}$ 4.21-3.91	$\bar{X}$ 3.90-3.60	$\bar{X}$ 3.59-3.29
DISTRIBUTION TO ORGANIZATION They are worth the effort to read	112	.89	4.21		
I read them	116	.93	4.09		
I read these more carefully than other evaluation reports	103	.93		3.60	
They require too much time to read	109	.90			3.45
I read these more often than other reports	100	.88			3.25
PROVIDING ROUTINE MANAGEMENT INFORMATION ON PROJECT EVALUATION They are good for the necessary required line management report	99	.94		3.88	
They help provide the necessary information for my management task	108	.94		3.83	
USEFUL FOR ASSESSING PROJECT EFFECTIVENESS I see the project impact on the community	114	.79	4.12		
I know more about the project from reading them	110	.92	4.06		
I can judge the project's operating performance	111	.91	3.94		
I take these more seriously than previous or other findings	110	.97		3.89	
I trust these reports	109	.82		3.84	
I can judge WHA management performance	105	.85		3.67	
USEFUL FOR MAKING DECISIONS They help me make decisions	110	1.05		3.86	
I now request evaluation reports (if available) on project results before making decisions about a project	90	1.08		3.74	
I refer to them when making routine decisions	107	1.03			3.49

Note: Range of replies from always (5.0) to never (2.0).

TABLE 32

VALUE OF THE PARTICIPATORY EVALUATION PROCESS IN PROVIDING EVALUATION REPORTS

Based on your experience with preparing the evaluation reports, do you agree/disagree with the following:

Response Items	N	SD	$\bar{X}$ 4.25- 3.95	$\bar{X}$ 3.94- 3.64	$\bar{X}$ 3.63- 3.33	$\bar{X}$ 3.32- 3.02
PROVIDE ROUTINE MANAGEMENT REPORTS ON PROJECT EVALUATIONS						
Techniques helped incorporate results' measures in my routine reporting	60	.97		3.68		
USEFUL FOR ARTICULATING WITH OTHER PARTS OF THE MANAGEMENT CONTROL PROCESS						
Techniques were helpful to prepare other project documents	55	1.04		3.67		
USEFUL FOR ASSESSING PROJECT EFFECTIVENESS						
Helped to make headway in solving the problem addressed by this project	61	.60	4.25			
GENERAL ASSESSMENT OF THE REPORTING PROCEDURES						
Worth the time	63	.68	4.22			
Laborious	61	.71		3.79		
Allowed for indepth information	61	.75		3.74		
Time consuming	62	.74		3.69		
Required no extra time	63	.85			3.40	
Too tedious	62	.62				3.18
Unrealistic	61	.70				3.06

Note: Range of replies from strongly agree (5.0) to strongly disagree (2.0).

The F-test analysis by job position ($F_{(4,115)}$=2.45, $P<.05$) supports this contention; it revealed only one significant difference, and that response item asks about using the reports. The variable "I read these more carefully than other evaluation reports" was rated higher by Evaluation and Training staff and the support staff ($\overline{X}$=3.4) than by management and operating staff ($\overline{X}$=2.6) or by Administration and Finance ($\overline{X}$=1.8). The farther removed a position is from the evaluation and support functions in a project, the less willing they are to read an expository report carefully.

The F-test analysis by geographic location where $F_{(3,115)}$=2.60, $P<.05$, revealed eleven significant differences. These F-test analysis are presented by the major categories of interest to this study. First, Table 33 shows the differences in the value of the participatory evaluation process for providing routine management information.

TABLE 33

VALUE OF THE PARTICIPATORY EVALUATION PROCESS FOR
PROVIDING ROUTINE MANAGEMENT INFORMATION ON
PROJECT EVALUATIONS IN VARIOUS REGIONS

Response Items	F	Latin America $\overline{X}$	Asia $\overline{X}$	Africa $\overline{X}$	International Head-quarters $\overline{X}$
They help provide the necessary information for my management task	2.66	4.0	3.9	3.9	3.0
I see the project impact on the community	3.04	4.4	4.0	4.5	3.7
I know more about the project from reading them	5.04	4.5	3.8	3.3	4.1
I can judge the project's operating performance	5.42	4.2	3.9	4.6	3.1
I take these reports more seriously than previous or other findings	4.36	4.5	3.8	4.2	3.3

Note: Range of replies from always (5.0) to never (2.0).
$^a F_{(3,115)}$=2.60, $P<.05$.

With respect to the amount of information contained in the reports and how helpful these were to assessing the project's performance, the ratings are high again, especially in the regions of the world where the project operations occur. However, the respondents from international headquarters gave generally lower ratings to their acceptance of the reports for providing routine information from which to judge the project's performance. Further, they report only sometimes taking these reports more seriously than other findings on a project, while the respondents from Africa gave lower ratings to knowing more about the project from reading the report. These findings are both of interest and concern to a researcher, because providing useful information which people trust for assessing project effectiveness is essential to decision making and to determining relevance. Table 34 shows the differences in reply scores by region on the value of the participatory evaluation process for providing reports which are useful for making decisions.

TABLE 34

VALUE OF THE PARTICIPATORY EVALUATION PROCESS
FOR PROVIDING USEFUL REPORTS
FOR MAKING DECISIONS IN VARIOUS REGIONS

Response Items	F	Latin America $\bar{X}$	Asia $\bar{X}$	Africa $\bar{X}$	International Head-quarters $\bar{X}$
They help me make decisions	4.36	4.2	3.9	4.0	2.8
I refer to them when making routine operating decisions	6.01	3.8	3.7	3.1	2.3
I now request evaluation reports on project results before making further decisions about a project	9.38	4.2	3.9	3.5	2.2

Note: Range of replies from always (5.0) to never (2.0).
* $F_{(3,119)}=2.60$, $P<.05$.

With respect to using the evaluation reports in their decision processes about projects, the respondents reported that they usually (4.0) use them; but the respondents from the international headquarters report that they almost never (2.0) use them routinely.

One field director wrote on his questionnaire that no reports had been produced by his office when, in fact, four reports were confirmed as having been produced by his office and his subordinates had rated using reports in their questionnaires. Allowing the reporting procedures to be determined in each national office could explain why such an important user was omitted from the report routing channels. Allowing each project specialist to prepare and write their own expository report on the projects could explain why they are not referred to as frequently, nor used by higher echelons of the organization for decision making. While respondents see the value of these reports for indepth insights into a project's operations, that is not a sufficient reason to use the reports.

The difficulty of designing individual, flexible, yet routine, reports for qualitative information is well recognized in the evaluation literature. Management researchers are also searching for efficient ways to convey qualitative performance reports to augment financial reports. WHA's experiences support the difficulty of incorporating indigenously designed result measures into a formal reporting system. Respondents reported that the helpfulness of participatory evaluation reports on assessing project performance accrues to themselves and the other immediate project participants. Correspondingly, respondents also reported the diminished managerial utility of participatory evaluation to administrators and operating personnel for making decisions about the project.

Summary of the Evaluation Component Analysis: The WHA staff found the participatory evaluation process, and its techniques and skills, generally helpful for all the evaluation components. The range of mean value scores for the various evaluation components is displayed as a bar graph in Figure 17. For needs assessment and program design, the process was rated most helpful to the community members and the WHA staff members. For organizing the project, the respondents reported it helped them, the project committee and the partner agency most. This finding is consistent with the nature of the tasks done and the decisions made to organize a project administratively (e.g., deciding on delivery system strategy and budgeting). For monitoring the project,

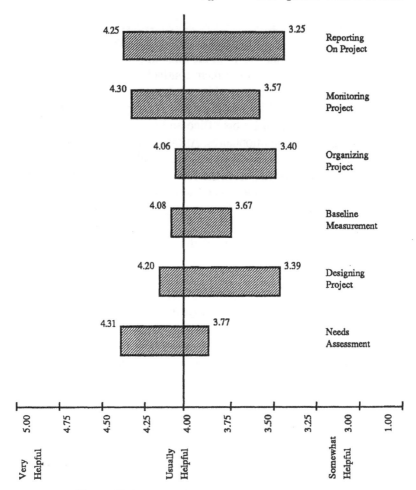

Figure 17: Range of Mean-Value Scores—Evaluation
Components of Participatory Evaluation

the process was rated more helpful for dialogue and discussion, reaching a consensus, and making evaluative decisions about the project outcome, than for measuring and validating outcomes from project activities.

One noteworthy exception to these reports of helpfulness is the difficulty of designing a record keeping device for community members to use when maintaining information on various project activities. The low scores for project design pertain to measuring and recording the project activities. This difficulty may contribute to the subsequent difficulty of validating and reporting evaluation findings—both to the community during project visits and to the organization. If the changes occurring in indicators selected to measure project activities are not regularly and routinely recorded, then assessing and reporting outcomes may be impossible even though the participatory evaluation process produces many of the other benefits attributed to it in this study.

Further, the reporting component may be shown as less helpful because of the information reporting system design. Expository reports drafted by individual project specialists and circulated by each national office may explain why respondents state that they do not use the reports. To confirm when the participatory evaluation process, techniques, and skills were used with the community, question 14 asked respondents if they had used them for various functions. Replies are presented on the scale from always (5.0) to never (2.0). Table 35 presents the three classifications for usefulness which emerged.

The mean values for these functions are consistent with the mean-values reported for the various evaluation components. The

TABLE 35

CONFIRMING ITEMS ON THE USEFULNESS
OF THE PARTICIPATORY EVALUATION PROCESS
FOR PROJECT MANAGEMENT

I used the participatory evaluation techniques and skills with the community for:

Response Items	N	SD	$\bar{X}$ 4.32-4.02	$\bar{X}$ 4.01-3.71	$\bar{X}$ 3.70-3.40
Preparing the project plan of action	73	.78	4.32		
Project improvement	60	.84	4.27		
Assessing project outcomes/results	60	.92	4.22		
Project planning	64	.90	4.22		
Project revisions	60	.90	4.12		
Project budgeting/resource allocation	59	.97	4.02		
Project administration	61	.94		3.98	
Project funding	55	1.13			3.62

Note: Range of replies from always (5.0) to never (2.0).

variables in the first confidence interval show that the process is used more for project programming than for project administration.
Perhaps the respondents had not used the process long enough to have realized the benefits of an evaluation process to the administrative tasks.

The F-test analysis by workshop did not reveal any significant differences between the respondents, however. Thus in eighteen months, the cross-over benefits of evaluation to project structure, strategy, budgeting, and reporting were not perceived by these respondents.

Behavioral Aspects of the Participatory Evaluation Process

When an evaluation process allows all the stakeholders involved in the project or program to collectively design and use the evaluation research function, the behavioral aspects of the participation can be equally as important to management as the evaluative aspects. How well the people work together, communicate with one another, share responsibilities, make decisions, and together take control of their experience all affect the management process. Management tools and procedures must allow people to behave in an acceptable manner for their context and culture and in a way which is conducive to accomplishing the task at hand. This is especially true for a value-rational, non-profit organization engaged in human resource development.

The utility of participatory evaluation for several behavioral characteristics was assessed in order to discover where the process was more helpful and where it was less helpful. These replies were not asked in response to one particular question, but they were interspersed throughout the last half of the questionnaire (See Appendix A, Experience Questionnaire, questions 7 to 15).

Group Dynamics: A participatory process must be conducive to dynamic interaction among all effected parties. To determine how helpful the participatory evaluation process was to project participants working together as a group, respondents were asked to rate several response items based on their own experiences, perceptions, and opinions compared to other projects in which they worked. Replies are presented on a scale from strongly agree (5.0) to strongly disagree (2.0) Three classifications of usefulness from group interactions emerged; they are displayed in Table 36.

TABLE 36

USEFULNESS OF THE PARTICIPATORY EVALUATION
PROCESS FOR GROUP DYNAMICS

*Based on your experience using the participatory evaluation
skills and techniques, do you agree with the following?*

Response Items	N	SD	$\bar{X}$ 4.50- 4.20	$\bar{X}$ 4.19- 3.89	$\bar{X}$ 3.88- 3.58
Mutual trust increased	30	.51	4.50		
Create an environment in which people can express themselves and grow	69	.76	4.45		
Team building is increased within the project	66	.59	4.32		
Communities are more incorporated into the project rather than just receiving the project	65	.61	4.31		
The community shows enthusiasm for the process	64	.56		4.06	
The partner agency shows enthusiasm for the process	58	.52		3.90	
Conflicts of interest (do not) increase between WHA's standards and the community's desires	67	.70			3.82
The community (does not) show indifference to the process	62	.71			3.77
The community (does not) show resistance to the process	59	.66			3.75
The partner agency (does not) show indifference to the process	56	.59			3.73
The partner agency (does not) show resistance to the process	57	.62			3.72

Note: Range of replies from strongly agree (5.0) to strongly disagree (2.0).

The respondents rated the response items representing group interaction higher than the response items on the project participants' response to the process. They report the process most helpful for creating an environment which incorporates the community people into the project, where these people can express themselves, and where mutual trust and team building are increased.

The low response rate to the variable "mutual trust increased" is especially interesting to note. Perhaps only 30 people had experienced an "increase" in trust; if so, then the other 43 respondents could have replied that they disagreed. Instead they chose to reply "have not experienced." These results would therefore indicate that, rather than increasing mutual trust ($\bar{X}$=4.5, N=30), in actuality, no experience with trust is occurring (N=43).

The community's and partner agency's response and reaction to the process was rated lowest. The mean-value scores in the lower two categories, while far enough apart to statistically indicate a difference in opinion, are similar enough to warrant consideration and discussion together. Respondents agreed (4.0) that the participants showed enthusiasm for the process, but they did not completely disagree (3.0) that the participants show resistance or indifference to the process. Not as many employees responded to these questions, but the standard deviations are low enough to show strong agreement among those who did respond.

The F-test analysis by workshop ($F_{(2,72)}$=3.15, P<.05) indicates that Asian respondents assigned lower mean value scores to the variables "create an environment in which people can express themselves and grow" (F=5.02) and "team building is increased within the project" (F=4.96). The Latin American respondents assigned a lower mean value to the variable "conflicts of interest (do not) increase between WHA's standards and the community's desires" (F=3.22, $\bar{X}$=3.2).

These behavioral reactions to the process could be a result of the cultural difference in these countries. Awareness of this closeness in responses between enthusiasm and indifference allows management and project workers to be sensitive to the cultural context of their work and to implement the process in accordance with the participants' responses to it—more quickly where enthusiasm is the response and more slowly where indifference is the response. Communications is an important element of people working together.

Communication: To function and be useful, a participatory evaluation process must allow communication to occur between the project participants. To ascertain how helpful the participatory evaluation process was to project participants communicating with one another, respondents were asked to rate various items. Replies are presented on a scale from strongly agree (5.0) to strongly disagree (2.0). Table 37 presents the one category of helpfulness for communicating which emerged.

The respondents rated these variables consistently high. They reported that the process allows people to speak out about the project,

TABLE 37

VALUE OF THE PARTICIPATORY EVALUATION PROCESS
TO COMMUNICATION

Based on your experience using the participatory evaluation process, do you agree/disagree with the following:

Response Items	N	SD	$\bar{X}$ 4.39-4.09
This process allows anyone from the community who wishes to be involved to speak out about the project	70	.60	4.39
Understanding is increased among and with all the participants	65	.56	4.31
The community appears to be more informed	66	.57	4.27
The information flow is improved between the community and the Project Specialist	65	.55	4.22
The information flow is improved within the community	66	.50	4.20
The partner agency appears to be more informed	63	.52	4.16
The information flow is improved within WHA	62	.59	4.13
The information flow is improved with the partner agency	61	.53	4.09

Note: Range of replies from strongly agree (5.0) to strongly disagree (2.0).

that understanding is increased, and that the information flow is improved for the community. No statistically significant differences were found between respondent groups by the F-test analysis.

The literature review emphasized the importance of communications and the flow of information to people who had to make decisions. Since the project participants are making the evaluative decisions on the impacts of a project on their community, these findings are significant. They indicate a critical element to participative decision making is present. The low standard deviations further indicate strong agreement among the respondents on these replies.

Participants Relationships: To learn how helpful the participatory evaluation process was in developing the project participants' relationship towards the project and their relationships among themselves, the respondents were asked to rate several response items assessing how the process affects the way project participants feel about the project, each other, and themselves. Replies are presented on a scale from strongly agree (5.0) to strongly disagree (2.0). Using the confidence interval size of .30, two categories of helpfulness for developing relationships were derived for both the relationship towards the project and with other individuals. These findings are presented in Table 38.

The respondents rated both the relationship towards the project and interpersonal relationships generally the same. With respect to the project, they reported the community members' relationship to be higher in all specific cases than the partner agency's, but they do not feel the partner agency is ignored in the process. The communication variables were rated the same way.

Initial examination of the mean scores would indicate that the interpersonal relationships between the WHA project specialist and the community members are also enhanced. The low standard deviations would indicate strong agreement among the respondents on these replies. The F-test analysis by workshop groups ($F_{(2,72)}$=3.15, $P<.05$) revealed, however, that the respondents from Asia rated three of the interpersonal relationship variables lower than the respondents from the other workshops: "I feel closer to the people in this project" (F=10.61), "the process enhanced my relationship with the people involved" (F=7.95), and "the process helped me be sensitive to my own behaviors during participation" (F=7.93).

TABLE 38

HELPFULNESS OF THE PARTICIPATORY
EVALUATION PROCESS FOR DEVELOPING
PARTICIPANT RELATIONSHIPS

Based on your experience using the participatory evaluation process, do you agree/disagree with the following:

Response Items	N	SD	$\bar{X}$ 4.38-4.08	$\bar{X}$ 4.07-3.77
RELATIONSHIP TOWARDS THE PROJECT				
The community appears to be more involved	66	.53	4.30	
The community appears to be more interested	66	.51	4.27	
The partner agency appears to be more involved	61	.48	4.20	
The community people involved feel respected	63	.50	4.19	
The partner agency appears to be more interested	61	.49	4.16	
I am more committed to this project	65	.59		3.97
The community people involved feel independent	65	.75		3.88
The partner agency (does not) appear to feel ignored in the process	58	.70		3.79
INTERPERSONAL RELATIONSHIPS				
I feel closer to the people in this project	66	.55	4.38	
The community people involved feel closer to one another	65	.57	4.26	
The process enhances my relationship with the people involved	68	.86	4.22	
The process helps me be sensitive to my own behaviors during participation	70	.96	4.09	

Note: Range of replies from strongly agree (5.0) to strongly disagree (2.0).

These findings cast doubt on whether the project specialists' interpersonal relationship with the community members is enhanced, or whether the participatory evaluation process simply realigns the working relationship between WHA, the partner agency, and the community people. The process moves the WHA project worker directly closer to the community people than they were before. This does not mean that the partner agency is by-passed. It does indicate, however, that their role changes and that the community people are more proactive in their relationship towards the project when WHA's participatory evaluation process is used.

The remaining questions build on these initial findings. The next group of questions examine the decision process and behavior, (i.e., As people begin to work together, communicate, and build relationships, is the decision process enhanced as well?). Furthermore, the explicit incorporation of values into decision making is a unique characteristic of non-profit organizations.

Values: In the literature search, it was noted that Thompson introduced values into rationality theory and Maynard-Moody argued that non-profit organizations were value-rational rather than economically rational. Therefore, if the participatory evaluation process enhanced the participants' understanding of one another's values, its utility would be enlarged. To discover if values are transmitted between the project participants, the respondents were asked about their experiences with understanding the values of various project participants. Replies are presented on a scale from strongly agree (5.0) to strongly disagree (2.0). Two categories of helpfulness for understanding the values of other project participants were derived for the range of mean-value scores. They are presented in Table 39.

The respondents reported that the process was most helpful for them to understand the values of the community, secondly the values of the partner agency, and lastly, their own values. Here again, the community is rated higher than the partner agency, but this seems reasonable since WHA and the partner agency would share some common values before they began working together.

The standard deviations would indicate that the respondents did not strongly agree among themselves with these mean value scores. Further, the F-test analysis by workshop ($F_{(2,72)}=3.15$, $P<.05$) revealed that the respondents from Asia, again rated two of these variables lower than the other respondents: "understand the values of the community" (F=5.63) and "understand my own values" (F=5.07).

TABLE 39

HELPFULNESS OF THE PARTICIPATORY EVALUATION
PROCESS FOR UNDERSTANDING PROJECT
PARTICIPANTS' VALUES

			$\bar{X}$ 4.33-4.03	$\bar{X}$ 4.02-3.72
The participatory evaluation process helped me:				
Response Items	N	SD		
Understand the values of the community	69	.80	4.33	
Understand the values of the partner agency	62	.90	4.10	
Understand my own values	68	1.07		3.79

Note: Range of replies from strongly agree (5.0) to strongly disagree (2.0).

The respondents may have rated the variable, "understand my own values" lower because they feel that they already understand their own values adequately, rather than an alternative interpretation that the process does not help individuals understand their own values, but only the values of others. Conversely, since the respondents are primarily young nationals, working in their home country, the Asian respondents might feel they already understand the values in the communities well. Another possibility is that transmission and understanding of values takes longer than the 18 or 12 month time frame examined in this study.

However, understanding the values of the community is the first step to incorporating those values into the decision process and creating an open-system between the community and WHA. Discovering how responsibility is distributed among the project participants is another important element to understanding how participatory evaluation affects the decision making process in a project.

Responsibility: In the literature review on management by objectives and self-control, it was noted that Drucker argued that individuals must be responsible for their own work. Further he argued that an effective management process and information system would enhance the responsibility of the individual and the work group closest to the productive activity. To ascertain how responsibility is affected by the participatory evaluation process, respondents were asked to rate eight items about responsibility in three different questions. Their replies are presented on a scale from strongly agree (5.0) to strongly disagree (2.0). Again, only one category of conduciveness to enhance responsibility emerged; it is presented in Table 40.

TABLE 40

CONDUCIVENESS OF PARTICIPATORY EVALUATION
PROCESS TO ENHANCE RESPONSIBILITY

Based on your experiences using the participatory evaluation
process, do you agree/disagree with the following:

Response Items	N	SD	$\bar{X}$ 4.26-3.96
Responsibility is enhanced for the Project Specialist	62	.57	4.26
The participatory evaluation process helped maximize local responsibility for the project	62	.88	4.23
Responsibility is enhanced for the community	64	.57	4.20
Who is responsible for outcomes is clearer	63	.56	4.19
Responsibility is enhanced for the project committee	61	.51	4.15
Responsibility is enhanced for WHA	60	.57	4.10
Responsibility is enhanced for the partner agency	60	.57	4.05
Responsibility is enhanced for the National Office	59	.62	4.03

Note: Range of replies from strongly agree (5.0) to strongly disagree (2.0).

The respondents reported that responsibility is enhanced most for the WHA project specialist, then for the community, the project committee, the WHA organization, the partner agency, and lastly for the WHA National Office. Moreover, the respondents reported that the process helped maximize local responsibility and clarify who is responsible for project outcomes. These characteristics should further enhance evaluation and self-control in the projects.

The low standard deviations for most of the replies indicate that the respondents strongly agree with these mean-value scores. One exception is the response item, "the participatory evaluation process helped maximize local responsibility for the project;" it was also the only item to have significantly different mean values between the respondents from different workshops. The F-test ($F_{(2,72)}$=3.15, P<.05) revealed Asia respondents rated it lower (F=3.36) than the other respondents. Responsibility can only be fulfilled as people are allowed to make decisions concerning their work, and are thereby given authority to act responsibly. Thus, the logically succeeding issue is the effect of the participatory evaluation process on patterns of decision-making.

Decision-Making: Participation, self-control, and the development of open-systems can only occur in environments where decentralized decision-making is encouraged and facilitated by the management process. The procedures designed to carry out each function in the management process must allow participants to recognize gaps between desired and actual conditions (e.g., opportunities and present operations, targeted and actual output, budgeted and actual spending, etc.) and to decide to take some action. To determine how the participatory evaluation process affected decision-making in WHA projects, the respondents were asked to rate four response items about the decision process in two different questions. The two categories which emerged for these items are present in Table 41. Their relatively close mean values and their low standard deviations indicate strong agreement among the respondents on the effects of the participatory evaluation process on the decision-making in WHA projects.

The respondents reported that foremost the participatory evaluation process is a tool to help communities make decisions for the future. Secondly, they report that the local people begin to realize and experience the outcomes of their decisions. These findings support the claim that the goal of promoting the andragogical (adult learning) process of human development, identified in the description of the WHA Organization in Chapter III, is being met.

Further, the finding that willingness to make decisions shifts to the community supports the contentions in the management literature that participation, self-control, and open-systems can only occur in

TABLE 41

EFFECTS OF THE PARTICIPATORY EVALUATION
PROCESS ON DECISION MAKING

*Based on your experiences with the participatory evaluation
process, do you agree/disagree with the following:*

Response Items	N	SD	$\bar{X}$ 4.49-4.19	$\bar{X}$ 4.18-3.88
This process is a tool to help communities make decisions for the future	70	.56	4.49	
The local people begin to realize and experience the outcomes of their decisions	65	.59	4.32	
Willingness to make decisions shifts to the community	65	.56	4.25	
The decision process changes within the community	65	.55		4.17

Note: Range of replies from strongly agree (5.0) to strongly disagree (2.0).

environments where decentralized decision making is encouraged and facilitated by the management process. The fact that changing the decision process within the community is rated lower is interesting, but not surprising. The reason for using an indigenous evaluation process is to make it contextually compatible. Therefore, the culturally acceptable way to make decisions would be expected to continue; however, the willingness of the participants to make decisions themselves rather than have someone else (e.g.: WHA, the partner agency, the project committee, or the project staff) make decisions for them is important. Ideally, the decision process within the community should change slowly, in congruence with the community members' own development.

Power: Open-system theory and Maciariello's cybernetic management control model contended that the decision process drives the management process. When people make decisions and take actions based on those decisions, they have both power and control in that situation. To partially discover how the participatory evaluation process effected power within the project, the respondents were asked to rate their perceptions on power changes in the project. Only two response items were asked in one question, and their mean values were classified in one category. These results are presented in Table 42.

TABLE 42

EFFECTS OF THE PARTICIPATORY EVALUATION
PROCESS ON POWER WITHIN A PROJECT

Based on your experiences with the participatory evaluation process, do you agree/disagree with the following:

Response Items	N	SD	$\overline{X}$ 4.15- 3.85
The project's power structure shifts to the community	65	.54	4.15
The project's power relationships are altered within the community	65	.61	4.06

Note: Range of replies from strongly agree (5.0) to strongly disagree (2.0).

The mean value scores indicate that the respondents agreed (4.0) with the statements. The relatively close mean values and low standard deviations indicate that the respondents generally agree with each other. No statistically significant differences in the mean-value scores of respondents from the various workshops was discovered by the F-test analysis.

Note that the shift in power to the community is not perceived to be as high by the respondents ($\overline{X}$=4.15) as the shift in decision making ($\overline{X}$=4.49, from Table 41) indicating that the change in power had not yet been recognized by the WHA employees. Also, a shift in power towards one group may take power away from another group, but total control may be increased.

Control: In the literature search, it was noted that Tannenbaum argued that total control is not fixed but rather it is dynamic. Therefore, increases in control for one group may actually increase total control for the organization. Thus, low perceived shifts in power may alienate the fewest number of people, thereby making the process more acceptable to the project participants. At the same time, accepting Tannenbaum's contention that control is dynamic and more people can be accountable for the same activities, then total control will be increased for the organization. To learn how participatory evaluation effects accountability and control, the respondents were asked to rate three response items in two different questions. The results are presented in Table 43.

TABLE 43

EFFECTS OF THE PARTICIPATORY EVALUATION
PROCESS ON CONTROL IN A PROJECT

Based on your experiences with the participatory evaluation process, do you agree/disagree with the following:

Response Items	N	SD	$\bar{\mathrm{X}}$ 4.12- 3.82
The partner agency appears to be more accountable	60	.52	4.12
The community appears to be more accountable	64	.54	4.08
The community people involved feel in control	63	.70	3.84

Note: Range of replies from strongly agree (5.0) to strongly disagree (2.0).

Only one category of effects on control was derived for the range of mean-value scores on these response items, so they are all inferred as increasing similarly. Thus, while there is no statistically significant difference between these response items, the relative positions of the variables is most interesting. The respondents rate the partner agency first as appearing to be more accountable when using the participatory evaluation process and the community second. Since the partner agency is the organization which operates the project, increasing their accountability would improve effectiveness in the project and improve WHA's effectiveness as a funding agency. The respondents reported that accountability is increased for both the partner agency and the community. This finding seems to support Tannenbaum's control model that total control is dynamic.

During the field study interviews and in written documents, concern had been expressed by staff and administrators in both the national offices and at international headquarters, that the participatory evaluation process may be "by-passing" the partner agency and putting WHA in too direct a contact with the community. These findings would not support that concern. In fact, while the findings indicate that total control is increased, they also indicate that the community people do not appear to the respondents to feel in control. Even though the other findings in this study indicate that the conditions necessary for participation and self-control are present, the community people involved do not yet feel in control. The realization of control seems to take longer than the longest time frame (18 months) of this study.

Summary of the Behavioral Aspects of the Participatory Evaluation Process: The participatory evaluation process was usually helpful for each behavioral aspect investigated. Figure 18 presents the range of mean-value scores in a bar graph. The noteworthy exceptions may be in the response items at the low end of the intervals.

First, the negative aspects of participation are not felt strongly by these respondents. In the case of group dynamics, the project participants do not show resistance or indifference to the process, rather they allow a cohesive group to form. Conflicts of interest do not increase as project participants actively represent their interest in the project. With regard to relationships towards the project, the partner agency is not perceived as feeling ignored.

Second, the WHA employees do not report the benefits of participation accruing to themselves but to the community people involved in the project and the partner agency. In the area of relationships, the process was less helpful for them to be sensitive to their own behaviors during participation and for their commitment to this project. With respect to values, the process was less helpful for them to understand their own values than the values of others.

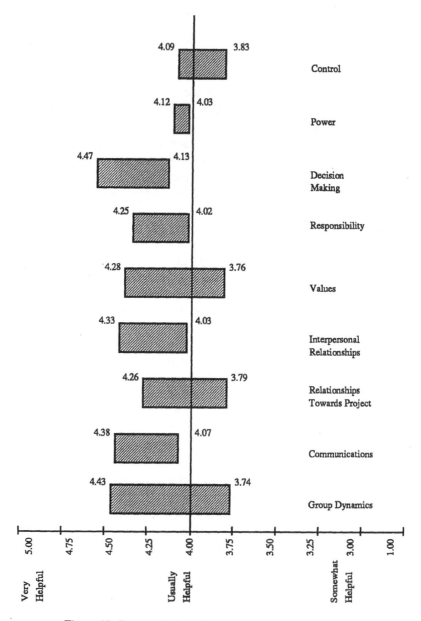

Figure 18: Range of Mean-Value Scores Behavioral
Aspects of Participatory Evaluation

Finally, the community people are not experiencing all of the positive aspects of participation. In the case of group dynamics, the community and partner agency are not showing high enthusiasm for the process. In their relationship towards the project, the community people involved are reported as not feeling very independent. With respect to control, the community people involved are also not feeling in control.

The participatory evaluation process designed by WHA was helpful for: group interactions, communications, interpersonal relationship, establishing responsibility, and decision making. The power and control inherent in decision making was not recognized by the respondents. Understanding where the benefits often attributed to participation were not being fulfilled for the WHA staff and the community suggests some areas of discord between these findings and the literature review. Here further thought, investigation, design, and even research may be warranted. The respondents' conclusions summarize their feelings on the participatory evaluation process.

Respondent Conclusions on the Participatory Evaluation Process

How the respondents felt about the process in general will suggest a great deal about its success or failure. If workers like a particular management technique, find it to be worthwhile, find it to be transferable or adaptable to other management functions, or find that it facilitates and complements other tasks which they must do, then they will modify and refine the technique until it works well. If, on the other hand, they do not like the technique and it does not fulfill their needs, then they will neglect and not use the process until it become irrelevant.

To ascertain how the WHA employees felt in general about the evaluation process four concluding issues were examined: (1) What is your general assessment of the process? (2) When have you used the participatory evaluation skills and techniques in your work? (3) How helpful have you found them to be when incorporating them as part of your other tasks? (4) What are your general conclusions about the process? The findings on each of these questions is presented and discussed.

TABLE 44

GENERAL ASSESSMENT OF THE
PARTICIPATORY EVALUATION PROCESS

*Based on your experiences with the participatory evaluation
process, do you agree/disagree with the following:*

Response Items	N	SD	$\bar{X}$ 4.38- 4.08	$\bar{X}$ 4.07- 3.77	$\bar{X}$ 3.76- 3.46	$\bar{X}$ 3.45- 3.15
Process takes patience	68	.57	4.38			
The whole process has been worth the:						
Efforts required	63	.57	4.29			
Time for visits	63	.58	4.29			
Preparation of materials	63	.58	4.29			
Committee meetings	62	.55	4.27			
The workshop has helped me establish an understanding of evaluation	71	.55	4.24			
The workshop is not enough training; I need more	70	.58	4.20			
The whole process has been worth the journal keeping	59	.53	4.17			
Process takes too much time	68	.74	4.12			
I have flexibility to adapt and develop methods suitable to my project and area	66	.50	4.08			
I (am) comfortable with the techniques and process	67	.83			3.63	
I have (no) difficulty with the techniques and process	69	.78			3.58	
I have adequate skills to use the participatory evaluation techniques with the community	68	.58				3.42

Note: Range of replies from strongly agree (5.0) to strongly disagree (2.0).

General Assessment of the Process: In two different questions the respondents were asked to rate response items on their general assessment of the process; their replies are presented on a scale from strongly agree (5.0) to strongly disagree (2.0). Table 44 presents the four categories of assessment which emerged from the range of mean-value scores.

The respondents reported that the process takes time and patience, but it is worthwhile. The lower rated response items identify trouble spots for the process's survival. The WHA staff rated very low their flexibility to adapt and develop methods suitable to their project and area. They do not feel that they have adequate skills to use the techniques with the community.

Finally, they are not comfortable using the techniques, and they are experiencing some difficulty with the techniques and process. Therefore, in general, the respondents agree that they like the process; but the workshops only introduced them to the concepts, and they need more training and support to overcome their discomforts and to ensure the survival of the process.

Use of the Process: In question 8 the respondents were asked when they had used the participatory evaluation skills and techniques in their project work. Response items were rated from very helpful (5.0) to hindered (1.0). Table 45 presents the two categories of uses for the participatory evaluation process in WHA projects.

The respondents reported generally lower mean scores on these uses of the skills and techniques in their work. The higher standard deviations suggest they do not agree strongly among themselves on these uses. The F-test analysis by workshop ($F_{(2,72)}$=3.15, P<.05) confirms these differences of opinion between the respondent groups. The respondents from Asia reported a lower mean value on the first four variables: "recognize when the community has accepted the project as their own" (F=6.84), "focus my efforts on critical issues" (F=10.07), "integrate my ministry work with co-workers, community members, and others who share responsibility for this project" (F=5.86), and "assess my task in the project" (F=6.56). These differences may be due to the short length of experience for the Asia respondents, to the way the process is being implemented, or to the fact that these respondents see fewer uses for the process.

Further, all the respondents rate the process as least helpful for facilitating or complementing their other tasks in the project. If they do not find the techniques and skills transferable to their management tasks, this is unfortunate, as the techniques and skills seem to have a potential synergy with other management tasks.

TABLE 45

USES OF PARTICIPATORY EVALUATION SKILLS
AND TECHNIQUES IN PROJECT WORK

The participatory evaluation techniques and skills were helpful to:

Response Items	N	SD	$\bar{X}$ 4.17-3.87	$\bar{X}$ 3.86-3.56
Recognize when the community has accepted the project as their own enterprise	59	.85	4.17	
Focus my efforts on critical issues	63	.87	4.08	
Integrate my ministry work with co-workers, community members, and others who share responsibility for this project	64	.98	4.05	
Assess my tasks in the project	60	.88	4.03	
Supervise the project	60	.92	3.93	
Integrate my management tasks	63	.94		3.71

Note: Range of replies from very helpful (5.0) to hindered (1.0).

Transferability of the Skills and Techniques to Other Management Functions: In question 7 the respondents were asked to rate how helpful they found the participatory evaluation techniques and skills to be when working with all people and incorporating the methods into various management functions. Response were rated from very helpful (5.0) to hindered (1.0). Table 46 presents the one classification of helpfulness which was derived for their transferability of the participatory evaluation skills and techniques to other management functions.

All the response items being classified in one category of helpfulness infers that the respondents found the skills and techniques equally helpful to all the management functions examined in this question. The respondents reported generally lower mean-value scores, however, on the transferability of these skills and techniques to other management functions. While there is no statistically significant difference between these items, their relative positions and statistical characteristics are enlightening.

TABLE 46

TRANSFERABILITY OF THE PARTICIPATORY
EVALUATION SKILLS AND TECHNIQUES
TO OTHER MANAGEMENT FUNCTIONS

*How helpful have you found the participatory evaluation techniques and skills to be
when working with all people and incorporating the techniques as part of your:*

Response Items	N	SD	$\overline{X}$ 4.25- 3.95
Regular project practices	65	.77	4.25
Personal ministry	67	1.01	4.06
Routine project reporting	63	.93	3.97
Management responsibilities	67	.95	3.97
Professional conduct	69	.96	3.96

Note: Range of replies from very helpful (5.0) to hindered (1.0).

The respondents gave regular project practices the highest mean-value score ($\overline{X}$=4.25). They did not rate as highly the transferability of the participatory evaluation skills to other management functions. Further, the higher standard deviations on the last four items indicates less agreement among the respondents on these functions. These findings suggest: (1) that the skills and techniques are most helpful to the routine project practices for which they were designed, and (2) that they are usually helpful to carry out other tasks for which the respondents are responsible and for their other professional interactions.

Transferability of the skills is important to management because development and training for any participatory process is labor and time intensive, and therefore, expensive. Ideally the process for each management function would augment, facilitate, and articulate with the other functions. The respondents are reporting that this evaluation process is complementing the other management functions, at least in its early stages of development.

Identifying whether employees are incorporating the skill into their other tasks is an important indicator of their acceptance or rejection of the process itself. The higher standard deviations for these variables indicates there is a diversity of opinions among the respondents. The F-test analysis by workshop ($F_{(2,72)}=3.15$, $P<.05$) confirms these findings. The Asia respondents again rated three mean-value scores lower than the respondents from Africa and Latin America: "regular project practices" (F=5.65), "personal ministry" (F=6.54), and "professional conduct" (F=6.61).

This suggests that: (1) the WHA staff may need more assistance in applying and adapting the concept, process, skills, and techniques to other management functions; (2) that the transferability will take longer to occur; or (3) that people do not readily recognize when transferability of skills and techniques are occurring, but they rate them as equally helpful to various management functions. In either of the last two cases, the development costs and efforts for a participatory evaluation process brings benefits to the entire management control process. The lower mean-value scores for these response items in the general conclusions section, the higher standard deviations, and the lower ratings from the Asian respondents indicate that the respondents rated transferability less favorably than their other concluding assessments of the participatory evaluation process.

General Conclusions: In two questions the respondents were asked to rate response items on their overall conclusions about the process. The mean values of their replies are presented on a scale from strongly agree (5.0) to strongly disagree (2.0). The two categories of agreement which emerged are displayed in Table 47.

The respondents concluded that the participatory evaluation process has really helped the community members participate in their own development and that it is a window to help WHA see the realities of the world it wants to help. These are very positive findings and indicate the participatory evaluation process is worthy of further development, refinement, and support. The respondents further indicate that they plan to use the techniques in other projects, and that it increases the possibility of eventually turning the project over to the local people. But as the earlier findings suggest, several refinements are needed in the techniques, and the WHA staff implementing the process need continued training and support in using the skills.

TABLE 47

GENERAL CONCLUSIONS ON
PARTICIPATORY EVALUATIONS

Based on your experiences with the participatory evaluation process, do you agree/disagree with the following:

Response Items	N	SD	$\bar{X}$ 4.53-4.23	$\bar{X}$ 4.22-3.92
The participatory evaluation process has really helped community members to participate in their own development	66	.56	4.53	
These techniques will be a window to help WHA better see the realities of the world it wants to help	64	.62	4.45	
This process helps me be more effective in doing the work God has called me to do	69	.67	4.30	
I plan to use these techniques in other projects	70	.58		4.20
The possibility of eventual turn over of the project to local people is increased	65	.61		4.14

Note: Range of replies from strongly agree (5.0) to strongly disagree (2.0).

SUMMARY OF THE PARTICIPATORY EVALUATION PROCESS

Participatory evaluation research is a pluralistic evaluation model. All stakeholders are invited to work together to design and implement the project's evaluation plan. The groups' evaluation activities are facilitated by the sponsoring organization's own project worker, without the aid or supervision of an evaluation specialist.

The evaluation plan is designed at the project's inception, and used throughout the project's life-cycle. Monitoring the project activities occurs through the record keeping efforts of the project participants. Record keeping devices are designed and maintained by the host community members. The project specialist reviews and collects the evaluation data on monthly project visits. All of the project participants assess the project's outcomes, and together they decide on the next month's plans and activities. The evaluation findings are reported to the sponsoring organization through the national office, in case studies describing the project's progress.

The process was generally helpful for all the evaluation components. The process was more conducive to dialogue, discussion and design than to review, evaluation, and creation of a consensus for decisions. It aided more the planning and programming aspects of the project evaluation than the administration and budgeting aspects. However, in each aspect, the process aids most the persons or groups responsible for that requisite function. This matching, of helpfulness to the persons or groups responsible for a task with the proper task to be accomplished, increases the general applicability of the participatory evaluation process to various situations, contexts, and tasks.

In addition, the process was usually helpful for each of the behavioral aspects of participation investigated. It improved group dynamics, communications, interpersonal relationships, responsibility, and decision-making. Control and accountability are expanded in the project setting. However, many of these correlative benefits to participation, such as control and power, were not recognized as strongly by the respondents.

In general, the respondents liked using the process and felt it assisted in involving the project participants and incorporating their context into the development process. However, they reported feelings of inadequacy in adapting, adopting, and fulfilling all the evaluation tasks required of them.

The immediate value of the participatory evaluation process lies in how well it fulfills the sponsoring organization's strategic goals and objectives for development work. If the process functions well as an andragogical learning experience for participants by allowing them to assess their project's performance, and at the same time to learn decision-making in their own host community, then it contributes to the human development process which is the main business of WHA. Therefore, any difficulties in compiling and reporting the evaluation findings are worth overcoming. The findings from the evaluation process must feed into the organization's custodial accounting and reporting system. Only then can the potential benefits of the evaluation process be manifested in the entire management control process of the organization. When this is accomplished, then the ultimate value of the process could be as a standard of service effort and accomplishment in external accounting information as well.

SUMMARY OF THE FINDINGS

The last two chapters have presented the findings of this field study research on participatory evaluation. The findings were arranged according to the research strategy outlined in Chapter III. The research methodology included a description of the WHA organization and a description of the participatory evaluation process designed and developed by WHA to assess the outcomes of their development projects.

WHA is a funding institution which supports human development projects world-wide. Its goal is to develop self-reliance and create a community life where mutual long-term survival and growth can occur. Its approach to development requires a decentralized management style in each national office which is sensitive to both the cultural context within which it operates and to the constituencies with whom it works. Its evaluation mandate required it to develop a capacity for participatory evaluation which would influence staff selection and training, program design, innovation, planning, and educational materials for project participants.

The results of the expectations questionnaire were displayed and discussed in Chapter IV. Table 15 summarized the expectations of WHA employees from participatory evaluation. The strategic policy characteristics of what evaluation should be in WHA appear to be better formulated in the minds of WHA employees than the operational characteristics.

The findings of the experience questionnaire were displayed and discussed in this chapter. The evaluation process has been designed to allow any persons in a community where a development project is sponsored by WHA to participate in developing the evaluation research plan for that project. The WHA employees reported finding participatory evaluation techniques and skills generally helpful for all functional components of the evaluation and equally helpful for all the behavioral aspects of participation.

Participatory evaluation may indeed be an outstanding evaluation process for indigenous programs, if some way can be found for recording project activities in the community and then incorporating evaluation findings into the project reporting system. Presently, however, the usefulness of participatory evaluation is found in the components which can be achieved through dialogue, discussion, and community interaction.

A word of caution is necessary with consistently high findings from self-administered questionnaires. WHA may hire only optimistic employees who have a "missionary zeal" for new ideas presented to them. Further, since WHA is a funding institution for development projects, employees may have a "social welfare" attitude of confirming new approaches by saying what is expected of them, or what they think management or the researcher wants to hear, in order to sustain the funding. Consistently high findings need to be viewed in light of these "halo" effect biases.

Small deviations in patterns or values have been noted in order to identify important, if not statistically significant, differences. Conversely, however, the large number of F-test analysis done by job position, geographic location, and workshop groups will produce some spurious statistical significance; thus, these inferences should also be viewed with caution. Patterns of findings are the most indicative results from which to assess how participatory evaluation affects the management control process.

CHAPTER VI

Results of the Research

The participatory evaluation method described in Chapter III was designed and developed by World Humanitarian Aid to assess the outcomes of their development projects. In Concepts Statement No. 4 the Financial Accounting Standards Board concluded that information about service efforts and accomplishments was an indicator of performance for non-business entities.

> Information about service accomplishments in terms of goods or services produced (outputs) and of program results may enhance significantly the value of information provided about service efforts. However, the ability to measure service accomplishments, particularly program results, is generally underdeveloped. . . . Research should be conducted to determine if measures of service accomplishment with the requisite characteristics of relevance, reliability, comparability, verifiability, and neutrality can be developed.

One purpose of this research was to prepare initial assessments on the characteristics attributed to self-control in the management literature which should be present in a participatory evaluation process and which would indicate if relevance and reliability are present in the evaluation findings. These characteristics could help develop an interdisciplinary theory of service accomplishment in non-profit organizations involving accounting and evaluation research. This chapter will discuss the results of the field study conducted at WHA to examine how participatory evaluation affects the management control process of a multinational non-profit organization.

The findings will be organized around the research questions raised in Chapter II. These questions were:

I.   Can members of a host community design and use their own project evaluation plan?

II.   Can evaluation findings be incorporated into the formal management control system of a multinational non-profit organization?

III. Does the participatory evaluation process provide the benefits attributed to management by objectives and self-control in decentralized operations?

Each of these questions will be analyzed in the following sections by comparing the expectations from participatory evaluations expressed by WHA employees with the experiences of their colleagues who are using the process. The implications of these results will be discussed in the concluding chapter.

HOST COMMUNITY MEMBERS DESIGN AND USE OF THEIR OWN EVALUATION PLAN

Can members of a host community design and use their own project evaluation plan? The intent of this research question was to determine if the participatory evaluation process was functioning, and if so, whether it was producing an open-system environment as well as requisite operating information for assessment. An open-system environment would be created by the participatory evaluation process if the organization was interacting with its external environment for planning and resource allocation. Requisite operating information would be provided by the process if the various stakeholders could evaluate and control the project through a mutual decision process. The participatory evaluation process by which WHA evaluates their development projects was studied to ascertain if adequate information could be included in and provided by the participatively designed and used evaluation plan. Parameters of both design and implementation of the evaluation plan were analyzed.

Environmental Information for Planning and Resource Allocation

After the literature review, this research questioned whether environmental information for planning and resource allocation could be provided by a participatory evaluation process, thereby creating an open system between the organization and its total environment. Four characteristics of contextual information exchange were studied: (1) environmental scanning; (2) involving all audiences affected by the operations; (3) incorporating these audiences' context, culture, and values into the evaluation process; (4) incorporating the organization's purpose, goals, and strategies into the process.

Environmental Scanning: In order for the various parts of a multinational organization to respond to their individual contexts and for their evaluation findings to be relevant in their individual cultures, the participatory evaluation process must solicit information from the project's total environment. It must systematically require host community members to gather and use information from the portion of their own environment that is external to the WHA project. To appraise the utility of the participatory evaluation process for environmental scanning, an informative comparison can be made between some findings from the WHA employees' expectations questionnaire with findings from the experiences questionnaire.

In Chapter IV, one of the policy characteristics examined to help define the ideal participatory process expected by WHA employees was critical issues important for evaluators to understand. From the list of possible critical issues displayed in Table 9, respondents rated the response item, an understanding of the individual community where the project was being conducted, as very important.

The useful comparative findings from the experiences questionnaire are those about the needs assessment component of participatory evaluation. This component was described in Chapter V as involving the community members, the project committee, the partner agency, and the WHA project specialist in recognizing, identifying, and deciding which problems to address, which resources to utilize, and which talents to employ. Respondents reported that all project participant groups were involved in the evaluation process and that this process caused more potentials and possibilities for the project to be considered. The process was reported as being usually helpful for the 41 variables analyzed in needs assessment. However, the mean-value scores of these experience response items were generally lower than the mean-value score reported for the expectation response item, importance of an evaluator understanding the community. Thus, the participatory evaluation process was helpful for environmental scanning but not to the extent expected by this organization.

Involving all audiences affected by the operations: In order for effective participation to be occurring in a multinational non-profit organization, all people effected by the project must be encouraged to help design and implement their project evaluation plan. The participatory evaluation process should structurally involve all interested host community members and facilitate the interaction of all these stakeholders as a cohesive work group.

In Chapter IV, Table 16 summarizes the persons respondents rated on the expectations questionnaire as important to particular tasks in the participatory evaluation process. In all four tasks, the persons classified in the category of most importance were the local people who are directly involved in the project. To assess the utility of the participatory evaluation process for involving all audiences affected by the operations, these expectations were compared to responses on the experiences questionnaire regarding the behavioral characteristics of group dynamics and relationships developed among project participants. These responses recorded the WHA staff's experiences and perceptions of how involved the various audiences were and how they worked together.

For group dynamics, the respondents reported that mutual trust increased, that an environment was created in which people could express themselves, that team building was increased, and that communities were more incorporated into the project rather than just receiving the project. For the project participants' relationship towards the project, both the community and the partner agency were reported to be more involved, interested, and respected in projects where the participatory evaluation process was being used than in projects where it was not. For the project participants' relationship toward each other, the respondents reported that they felt closer to the people, the community people involved felt closer to one another, and that the process enhanced their relationship with the people involved.

The expectations of the WHA employees were that the participatory evaluation process would involve all the project participants in assessing their project's outcomes and results. The experiences reported by WHA staff members using the process were that it facilitated the project participants' interaction and enhanced their working relationship. The community members became proactive in their projects. Thus the participatory evaluation process was useful for involving all audiences affected by the project operations. As people begin to work together and build mutual trust, then they can begin to share their ideas and incorporate their values into their collective efforts.

Incorporating these audiences' context, culture, and values into the process: In order for an open-system environment to be created, where a multinational non-profit organization responds, adapts, and grows in its varied operating locations, the stakeholders in a program or project must be sharing their ideas, norms, and values. The procedures for participatory evaluation should require community members to consider their own context when designing and implementing their evaluation plan for assessing the project's performance. This will allow stakeholders to cybernetically control their project through the decisions they make.

The expectations questionnaire results defined one major purpose of participatory evaluation as community examination of performance. The literature review on rationality theory contended that decisions are made: (1) within the social norms of the decision context and the decision maker; (2) based on the information available and in the circumstance present at the time; and (3) after a discrepancy is identified, as a result of which an analysis takes place, and some acceptable, alternative choice is found. When communities examine the project's performance using their indigenous evaluation plan, they would be incorporating their own context, culture, and values into the evaluation process through their decisions. To assess the utility of the participatory evaluation process for incorporating all audiences' context, culture, and values into the evaluation process, this expectation of community examination of its own project was compared with the experiences of project participants using the process to design their evaluation plan.

WHA employees evaluated their experiences in designing the project evaluation plan as helpful in allowing the project participants to consider alternative evaluation techniques in order to make an informed decision. Only for deciding how to record indicators of project activities and developing a record keeping device were the techniques less helpful. The confirming items on designing the project evaluation plan suggest that the project plans are better because the activities are more related to the goals and they are more compatible with the communities' talents and resources. The respondents also reported that the participatory evaluation was helpful to the community members for recognizing measurable operating plans which were related to the project goals. Their responses to the behavioral characteristics questions on values indicate that the participants' values are better understood with this process. These findings suggest that (1) the participatory evaluation process was useful in fulfilling WHA's expectations for community examination of projects, and (2) all audiences' context, culture, and values are being incorporated into the evaluation process and would therefore be reflected in the environmental information used for planning and resource allocation. Incorporating the community's environment needs to be reciprocated by incorporating the supporting organization's interests as well.

Incorporating the organization's purpose, goals, and strategies into the process: While incorporating the host communities' context, culture, and values is a necessary condition for creating an open-system environment, it is not a sufficient condition. The sponsoring organization's purpose, goals, and strategies must also be incorporated into the evaluation process. The participatory evaluation process should procedurally lead the project participants to consider the sponsoring organization's corporate interests and administrative requirements.

In Chapter IV, two of the critical issues respondents expected evaluators to understand were WHA's mission in doing its development work and WHA's management requirements. Understanding WHA's mission was classified in the most important category of issues, while understanding the management requirements was classified as less important. To assess the utility of the participatory evaluation process for incorporating the sponsoring organization's corporate interests into the evaluation process, these expectations were compared to the experiences of respondents using the process when organizing the project.

The project organizing component of the questionnaire on experiences asked how WHA's strategy and operating elements were considered when developing the evaluation plan. The respondents reported that the process was helpful to the project participants in deciding what kind of project would be best, what organizational structure and administration to use, what evangelism strategy would be appropriate, and what funding amount would be most appropriate to achieve the project's goals. Respondents reported that the evaluation process was even more helpful to themselves for considering how this project fit into the National and International office's strategies, budgets, missions, and five-year plans. These findings indicate that the participatory evaluation process is useful for incorporating the sponsoring organization's purpose, goals, and strategies into program evaluations. Therefore these corporate interests would be reflected in the environmental information used for planning and resources allocation by the host community members in designing their evaluation plan but not to the extent expected by this organization or achieved for the community. Incorporating the organization's interest into the evaluation plan is more difficult than incorporating the community's interest.

Summary: The mean-value scores of the expectations questionnaire response items are generally higher than the scores on the experience questionnaire response items. Thus, while the findings reported helpful experiences with using the participatory evaluation process to gather information, the process appears not to be meeting the organization's expectations for providing environmental information for planning and resource allocation. The open-system characteristics of involving all audiences effected by the operations and incorporating these audience's context, culture, and values into the process come very close to meeting expectations for opening the organization to its external environment and to specific contextual settings where operations occur.

While expectations for environmental scanning and for incorporating the organization's concerns into the process appear to be met less satisfactorily, a reason for this needs to be considered. The expectations expressed through the mean values for these characteristics may be so unrealistically high as to cause this conclusion to be misleading. A problem often cited with management by objectives programs is that organizations have excessively high initial expectations from the programs. Because the programs take so long to develop fully, they are often discontinued based on an initial gap between expectations and experiences, without an adequate testing period during which expectations could be realistically modified and the process made fully functional. This situation appears to be present in these results. These initial findings indicate that the participatory evaluation process is helpful for providing environmental information for planning and resource allocation.

Operating Information for Assessment and Control

This dissertation further questioned whether operating information for assessment and control could be provided by a participatory evaluation process, thereby allowing self-control in the project and management control in the organization. Four characteristics of operational information were studied: (1) providing beginning baseline measures, (2) monitoring operating performance, (3) determining impacts caused by the project, and (4) distribution of evaluation findings.

Providing beginning baseline measures: In order for host community members to evaluate the outcomes of the development project conducted in their location, they must have beginning or current measures from which to judge the changes that are occurring. The participatory evaluation process should systemically solicit, gather, and report beginning baseline measures on environmental factors and indicators selected to monitor project activities.

As noted in the literature review, several models of evaluation research exist. Even though they represent different processes and technical requirements, they all include some form of baseline measures. Two of the critical issues respondents expected evaluators at WHA to understand were the evaluation process and the technical requirements of evaluation. Both of these expectations would provide meaningful measures from which changes could be determined. To examine the utility of the participatory evaluation process for providing baseline measures, these expectations were compared to the experiences reported for using the baseline measurement procedures developed at WHA.

The baseline measurement component of the questionnaire on the participatory evaluation process described the WHA staff's experiences when designing the evaluation plans with communities. The respondents reported that more socio-economic-religious data were usually needed, but they should be gathered by the community people themselves. They reported that they usually knew how to use the techniques well enough to collect meaningful data and that the data collected were adequate for their needs. However, they felt more information would be beneficial. These findings indicate that the participatory evaluation process systemically provided beginning operating measures from which to assess changes due to the project and that the information gathered through techniques used was meaningful for evaluation purposes.

Monitoring Operating Performance: During a project's implementation and operation, host community members must routinely and systematically keep track of and check the quality and quantity of outputs from all project activities. The structure of the participatory evaluation process should insure that record keeping devices are designed and used to keep track of outputs on all indicators selected to measure project activities.

Periodic measuring of impacts or changes caused by projects was the highest-rated expected purpose of the participatory evaluation process, while continuous assessment of project performance was one of the most desirable goals and a major reason why evaluation was needed in development projects. To assess the utility of the participatory evaluation process for monitoring operating performance of projects, these two expectations were compared to the respondents' experiences with monitoring projects.

Monitoring of development projects by the WHA staff is done through monthly project visits to observe the operation and gather information about the project. The monitoring component of the participatory evaluation process involved three steps: (1) dialogue and discussion, (2) review of project performance, and (3) validation of project reports. These steps are used to measure operating performance and assign a value to the project's output. The participatory evaluation process (its skills and techniques) were most helpful for dialogue and discussion and for reviewing the project's performance. The process was reported to be less helpful for noting the results of particular activities, for observing the project's operations, and for validating the project's reports by comparing the project's records to the original plans.

These findings indicate that (1) the participatory evaluation process fulfills partically the respondents' expectations, and (2) the structure of the participatory evaluation process should be refined to insure that record keeping devices are designed and used by the host community members to keep track of outputs on all project activities. No techniques are inherently present in the process to monitor project activities in order to determine project impacts, therefore community monitoring is imperative for the process to measure and report service accomplishments.

Determining Impacts Caused By The Project: Ultimately, an evaluation research process must allow people to use the information, measurements, and incremental changes which have been identified to assess the results of a project or program.

In Chapter IV, respondents identified continuous awareness of project results as one of the most important purposes of evaluation, and determining impacts resulting from projects as an important goal. To assess the utility of the participatory evaluation process for determining impacts caused by the project, these two expectations were compared with the experiences of making evaluative decisions.

Making evaluative decisions which determine impacts from the project is another function of project monitoring completed during monthly project visits. The respondents agreed that as a result of participatory evaluation, project results were more relevant to the community and the partner agency, both of these groups had more realistic expectations, and they more readily recognized changes resulting from the project. These findings indicate that the community's awareness of results is increased when the participatory evaluation process is used. Unfortunately, the respondents classified the process as less helpful for evaluating the operations, logistics, and coordination of the project, as well as for identifying and discussing project discrepancies for their correction. These findings indicate that evaluative decisions are difficult for the project participants to make.

Distribution of Evaluation Findings: Evaluation findings must be distributed both among community members and to the organization. The participatory evaluation process should produce evaluation reports which present the findings of the constituents from the host community on the project's performance. The mechanisms used to present these findings should be compatible with the context, the problem, the capabilities of the constituents, and the reporting requirements of the sponsoring organization.

In Chapter IV, the most important reason respondents gave for why WHA should conduct project evaluation was to share lessons learned. To assess the utility of the participatory evaluation process for distributing evaluation findings within the host community, this expectation of sharing lessons learned was compared with the experiences of the community members preparing for future action during the project monitoring visit.

The respondents classified the process as less helpful for involving community members in the review and validation procedures in general, but comparing the evaluation records to the original plan had the highest mean-value score for these procedures. The process was also less helpful for discussing unresolved issues or discrepancies, for reaching a consensus, and for agreeing to the next monthly plan. The confirming response items show that the host community members understand why the project is being done, they use their evaluation information in carrying out the project, they routinely consider project results, and they take corrective action sooner when using the participatory evaluation process. Thus, they use the evaluation information given them, but reaching a consensus on the next month's plans is still difficult. These findings indicate that the participatory evaluation process produces and distributes evaluation findings within the host community for assessment of project outcomes and self-control.

In addition, findings must be distributed to the organization if the results are to be incorporated in the formal management reporting system. The highest expectations on how lessons learned should be shared with the entire international organization was by annual evaluation reports for each project. To examine the utility of the participatory evaluation process for distributing evaluation findings to the organization, this expectation was compared to the experiences of WHA employees with distributing evaluation findings.

At the time of this study, evaluation findings were prepared by each WHA project specialist in case study reports. Selecting persons to receive these reports was left to the discretion of each individual national office for their distribution. The reporting component of the participatory evaluation process described how the organization received and used these written case study reports.

About one-third of the expectation questionnaire respondents reported receiving and reading the reports. These respondents included all managerial decision makers in the organization, and they indicated that the reports were usually worth the effort to read, but that they did not read them more carefully than other evaluation reports nor more often than other reports in general. Thus the participatory evaluation process produces and distributes worthwhile evaluation findings to the organizations. However, these reports are not the annual evaluation reports expected by the organization and they are not referenced frequently by these users.

Summary: In analyzing these results on operating information for assessment and control, similar patterns to the environmental information results are present. The participatory evaluation process was helpful for the project participants to gather their own beginning baseline measures, but more information is needed than is gathered presently. The process was helpful for dialogue and discussion during the WHA staff members' monthly visit to the project site, but the project participants had difficulty developing record keeping devices for monitoring the outcomes of project activities. The process was also less helpful than expected for the participants to make evaluative decisions on these outcomes and reach a consensus on the next month's plans. Nevertheless, community members were reported as being more aware of project results by using the participatory evaluation process. Furthermore, case study evaluation reports were prepared on projects and distributed to the organization. Respondents reported referring to these reports less frequently than other reports, but this may be due to their form rather than their substance.

Based on an analysis of the mean-value scores, the participatory evaluation process does not appear to be fulfilling the organization's expectation for providing operating information on project performance. However, the mean values for expectations from this process may indicate unrealistically high expectations rather than inadequate performance. The results provide evidence that the participatory evaluation process was functioning, that it was creating an open-system environment in the project, and that it was providing operating information for program assessment and self-control to various audiences in both project operations and organizational administration.

Conclusions On The Host Community Members Designing and Using Their Own Evaluation Plan

The participatory evaluation process works well in the project site for developing a cohesive work group among project participants who consider environmental concerns which are both internal and external to the project. The logistical difficulties of measuring, summarizing and reporting project outcomes begin when the project evaluation plan is designed and the record keeping devices are developed. Once the process has been verified as functioning in the projects, then further analysis is needed, to more fully describe how evaluation research affects the management control process of a multinational non-profit organization.

INCORPORATING EVALUATION FINDINGS INTO THE MANAGEMENT CONTROL SYSTEM

The second research question posed in Chapter II was: Can evaluation findings be incorporated into the formal management control system of a multinational, non-profit organization? This question was asked to determine if the formal management control system of a multinational non-profit organization is capable of incorporating indigenous evaluation reports. The process by which WHA distributes and uses their evaluation findings was studied to ascertain if adequate information was provided to assess project effectiveness and to make the decisions necessary for managerial control.

Four characteristics of information in a management control system were studied: (1) providing routine evaluation reports on operating performance, (2) articulating with other parts of the management control system, (3) allowing for assessment of effectiveness in achieving stated goals, (4) supplying information necessary for making managerial decisions.

Providing Routine Evaluation Reports on Operating Performance

The custodial accounting and management reporting system of a multinational non-profit organization must incorporate evaluation findings into its routine information gathering, summarizing, and distributing process for them to be effectively used by all members of the sponsoring organization. The length of the routine evaluation reporting cycle may be different than other operating reporting cycles due to the nature of evaluation research, but it should at least coincide with the annual budgeting, funding approval, and program operating cycle. The reporting aspect of the participatory evaluation process should provide routine assessment reports on the operating performance of development projects at time intervals suitable to show service accomplishments in the project and to augment the annual reporting cycle of the sponsoring organization.

In the previous analysis, annual evaluation reports were identified by respondents as the most desirable method to distribute evaluation reports. From the expectations reported in Chapter IV, it appears that the WHA employees did not expect the participatory evaluation process to provide routine evaluation reports. They rated routine assessment of project results as an unimportant purpose for doing evaluations and routine management reports as a less desirable way to distribute evaluation findings and to share lessons learned. To assess the capability of the sponsoring organization's management control system to provide routine evaluation reports on operating performance, these expectations were compared with experiences in providing routine management information on project evaluations.

The WHA staff rated the case-study evaluation reports as usually less helpful for providing routine management information both for their own tasks and for the necessary line management reporting; further, they rated the reports as usually helpful for incorporating result measures in the routine reports. These findings on the reporting component of participatory evaluation indicate that routine evaluation reports are not expected and that the case reports now prepared are helpful in providing management information. However, this finding does not support the original contention of this question that maximum utility of the participatory evaluation process would require that data and findings be reported to, maintained by, and distributed through the custodial accounting and management information system.

Articulating With Other Parts of the Management Control System

For the management control system to be efficient and effective, information and reports on each management function in the system should complement and augment the other functions. Planning should lead into programming, and the reporting done on programming should help determine if plans have been achieved. The evaluation models reviewed from the literature showed that evaluation research parallels the management control process. Therefore, the participatory evaluation process should complement other management functions, and evaluation reports should augment the financial reporting with service accomplishment measures which are meaningful to both the community and the organization.

The respondents did not expect the participatory evaluation process to articulate with other parts of the management control process. With respect to the community, the findings displayed in Table 6 show that the goal of helping integrate the management activities in projects was rated low, as was the critical issue for evaluators to understand WHA's management requirements from Table 9. To assess how complementary the participatory evaluation process was to other management control functions performed in the community, these expectations were compared to the summary variables relating when respondents had used the evaluation process with community people. Respondents reported having used the participatory evaluation skills and techniques with the community for preparing plan-of-action reports, project improvement, assessing outcomes/results, planning, and program revisions. These findings are displayed in Table 35.

With respect to the organization's expected uses of evaluation reports, the findings in Table 8 showed that the respondents desired to use the evaluation reports in conjunction with other management reports. They expected to use participatory evaluation reports most when assessing project performance, reviewing monthly plan-of-action reports, reviewing annual goals, reviewing five-year plans, and before deciding on continued funding. These uses represent the organization's expectations for how evaluation reports should articulate with other parts of the management control system. These expected uses were compared to the actual uses to determine how well the participatory evaluation process reports articulated with reports from other management functions. The experiences of using evaluation reports, showed (1) that WHA staff members who are using the process in projects have used the skills and techniques to help prepare other project documents, but (2) that WHA staff members who use the reports in their management tasks refer to them only sometimes when making routine decisions.

These findings indicate that the organization did not expect the process to be complementary with and help integrate the other management's functions. However, it was helpful and frequently used to complete these tasks and fulfill reporting requirements from the community. Conversely, the respondents desired to use the evaluation reports when reviewing other management documents, and they reported only sometimes using them to augment these other reports. The case-study report design does not articulate with the other parts of the management reporting system. The overall process, however, exceeds the respondent's expectations for articulating with other parts of the management control process.

Allowing for Assessment of Effectiveness in Achieving Stated Goals

Profit represents management's ability to use its resources efficiently to effectively provide the best product for their customers. A service accomplishment measure for non-profit organizations must represent management's stewardship in employing its resources effectively and efficiently. Findings from the participatory evaluation process should allow managers to assess the effectiveness of individual projects in achieving their stated goals and in contributing to the general well being of the sponsoring organization.

When analyzing the expectations of participatory evaluation for assessing project effectiveness, a contradiction occurs between the respondent's ratings on goals and uses. Focusing management's attention on outcomes and results was rated very low as a less important goal for the participatory evaluation process, while assessing project performance was rated the most desirable, highest expected use for evaluation reports. Thus, at WHA management assessment of projects is a secondary goal to indigenous assessment for participatory evaluation. Nevertheless, the reports which are finally produced by the process should allow management to assess the project's performance in effectively achieving its stated goals and efficiently using its resources. To examine the capability of the sponsoring organization's management control system to provide routine evaluation reports which allow management to assess the effectiveness of projects, these two expectations were compared to the experiences reported by managerial users of evaluation reports.

For assessing project effectiveness, the managerial users of evaluation reports said that they usually could see the project's impact on the community, that they knew more about the project, and that they could judge the project's operating performance from reading these reports. However, they rated the reports less favorably for trusting them, for taking them more seriously than other or previous findings, and for judging WHA's managerial performance in the project.

The respondents working directly with the project rated the process more favorably for helping them to make headway in solving the problems addressed by this project. Thus, preparing the reports helped focus the first-line employees' attention on project effectiveness. The subsequent managerial users reported improved knowledge about the project and ability to judge or assess project performance. This was the most desirable expected use for evaluation reports. These results indicate that the management control system of a sponsoring organization is capable of providing routine evaluation reports to assess the effectiveness of projects. The form and content of that report is critical to aggregating, compiling, and distributing the evaluation findings to decision-makers throughout an organization.

Supplying Information Necessary for Making Managerial Decisions

Ultimately, every management tool must help employees make decisions about their organization. This is especially true about an evaluation tool; it must supply the necessary information for people to reach a conclusion and take an action. Open-systems theory, rationality theory, and cybernetics all contend that an organization can only survive, prosper, and grow as people's decisions drive the management process. Participatory evaluation is a specialized mechanism for multinational non-profit organizations to support their unique business and to provide equal potentials in all their diverse locations. A participatory evaluation process should supply information necessary for making managerial decisions within the sponsoring organization.

Making decisions about the project outcomes was among the most important goals specified for the participatory evaluation process. To assess the utility of the participatory evaluation process to supply information necessary for making managerial decisions, this expectation was compared to the experiences reported by managerial users of this information.

The managerial users of evaluation reports agreed that the reports were helpful for making managerial decisions, and that they now request the reports when they are available before making decisions about a project. Unfortunately, these users report that they do not refer to evaluation reports when making routine decisions. Comparing the expectation for making decisions about the project's outcomes with the experiences of these same respondents when using the reports for decision making indicates that the information generated by the participatory evaluation process and supplied to the sponsoring organization has a low utility or limited usefulness in its present form. The managerial information system is not systemically capable of distributing these reports and no synopsis is currently supplied for routine reference by these managerial users.

Respondents reported seeing the impacts of projects on communities but they did not agree that they trust these reports and find them helpful for making decisions. This indicates that the reports do not contain the operative criteria needed by these decision makers and that the data are not considered reliable. On the other hand, the behavioral aspects of participatory evaluation examined in Table 41 indicate that the information generated by the process is relevant to the project participants in the community and is very helpful to them for operating their project.

Conclusions On Incorporating Evaluation Findings Into The Management Control System

The management control system of a multinational, non-profit organization is capable of incorporating evaluation findings into its regular reporting. The utility of evaluation reports, however, does not seem to be manifested in routine management reports but rather in periodic reports disbursed in regular time segments, such as annual reports. Such longer time frames would allow for a larger increment of change to be reported. Furthermore, the content of these reports should be tailored to the unique characteristics of evaluation information and the specific reporting procedures of the sponsoring organization.

For the first characteristic analyzed on the capability of the management reporting to incorporate the participatory evaluation process into its formal reporting system, the process appears to be exceeding the organization's expectations for providing routine evaluation reports on operating performance. Part of this may be due to the fact that the organization reported low expectations for the process providing routine evaluation reports. With respect to the other three characteristics studied, the respondents had high expectations. In the cases of articulating with other parts of the management control process for the community and allowing for assessment of effectiveness in achieving stated goals, these high expectations are nearly being met and will possibly be achieved more fully as the process matures and is refined.

These findings support one of the original issues raised in this research. The literature review established that the evaluation components and the management process functions parallel one another. Evaluation research reports can augment financial reports to aid managerial decision makers in assessing program performance and effectiveness in achieving stated goals. However, the characteristics of articulating with other parts of the management control process for the organization and supplying information necessary for making managerial decisions are not being met.

The substantive content of reports is critical to the acceptance, utilization, and success of participatory evaluation as a management tool. The evaluation reports subsections should cross reference to the annual plans, program activities, and budgets approved for each project. They should include beginning baseline measures, and anticipated or expected outcomes for that year. The record keeping devices should be designed to monitor the activities approved for the year, and then the case-study report should provide disclosures which explain and expand the quantitative data.

The comparative advantage of evaluation research over the other functions in the management control process is that it reexamines each of the other functions and brings them together in a juxtaposition for presentation to management. A participatory evaluation process is relevant to the indigenous population, so its product, a report for the sponsoring organization, should be designed to maximize this advantage. It should articulate with all parts of the management control process, and contain quantitative measures and qualitative explanations on the program content management approved for the current year and on any unanticipated outcomes the project participants identified during their evaluation activities. Then managers in the National and International Offices will be able to see the rate and direction of changes occurring when making decisions which will propel the organization during coming years.

The advantages of managers in decentralized locations being able to see the magnitude and direction of changes occurring in the community as a result of WHA's development projects is important for efficient allocation of resources and the commonweal of the total organization. The philosophy of management by objectives contends that self-control will enhance both the process and the content of decentralized operations.

PARTICIPATORY EVALUATIONS AND THE BENEFITS OF SELF-CONTROL

The third research question posed in Chapter II was: Does the participatory evaluation process provide the benefits attributed to management by objectives and self-control in decentralized operations? The participatory evaluation process was studied to ascertain if it displayed the three characteristics suggested by the literature for self-control: (1) alignment of functional tasks nearest to the point of performance; (2) enhancement of staff performance and project effectiveness; (3) efficient resource allocation decisions in both the long-run and the short-run.

Alignment of Functional Tasks Nearest to the Point of Performance

The literature on self-control contended that functional tasks should be planned, completed, and assessed by the persons closest to the point of performance. Table 16 in Chapter IV summarizes the expected location of persons associated with various evaluation characteristics; the alignment begins at the project and progresses away from the project site through the organizational hierarchy. The expected alignments of who should manage the evaluation process, do the technical evaluation tasks, provide support or assistance when needed, and who should benefit from the findings all begin with the people directly involved in the project and end with the International Office staff. Thus people and positions in the participatory evaluation process are properly aligned for self-control to occur.

The helpfulness of the participatory evaluation process to the project participants was reported for needs assessment, designing the project and evaluation plans, and organizing the project. Reviewing these findings shows that the process was almost equally helpful to the involved community, project committee, and to WHA project specialists. The process was slightly less helpful to the partner agency, but the process did assist project participants with their respective roles and tasks in the project. For example, for organizing the project administratively, the process was least helpful to the community and most helpful to the other participants.

Thus, the participatory evaluation process appears to be meeting the organization's expectations for aligning the functional tasks of evaluation nearest to the point of performance and benefitting helpfully each project participant group with their respective tasks. However, properly aligning project participants and helping fulfill their tasks in a project is only the first step to determining if self-control is occurring in the project. The process must also assist participants in doing their jobs well and with the fewest resources.

Enhance staff performance and project effectiveness

This research further questioned if project effectiveness and participant performance would be enhanced by using the participatory evaluation process for self-control in the project. Four characteristics of self-control were examined: (1) concentrating flow of information at the point of performance, (2) concentrating responsibility at the point of performance, (3) shifting operating decision power to the point of performance, and (4) shifting operating control to the point of performance.

Concentrating flow of information at the point of performance: For self-control to occur, the people closest to the project operations must have the highest concentration of information readily available to them. The literature review contended that the flow of information should be to the people who had set their own goals and recorded the outcomes of their activities through monitoring. For optimal effectiveness, these people could take corrective action sooner and share their experiences and lessons learned with their immediate work group and their supervisor. The participatory evaluation process should procedurally require that project participants have full access to the information about their project and use it to assess their own performance.

The highest rated goal for participatory evaluation at WHA was to share lessons learned. To examine the utility of the participatory evaluation process for concentrating the flow of information at the point of performance, this expectation was compared to the communication patterns reported for the process.

The variables reported in Table 37 on the behavioral characteristics of communication report the respondents' experiences with the flow of information at the point of performance. The respondents reported that the process was especially helpful for communication in the project. They said that the process allows anyone from the community who wishes to be involved to speak out about the project, that the information flow is improved for all project participants, that understanding is increased, and that the community and the partner agency both appear to be more informed. Comparing the high expectation to share lessons learned with the high rating on helpfulness for communication among the project participants indicates that the process is useful for concentrating the flow of information at the point of performance for self-control.

Concentrating responsibility at the point of performance: For self-control to occur, the people closest to the project operations must have the greatest responsibility for project outcomes. The literature review of management by objectives and self-control asserted that true accountability occurred when each individual was responsible to themselves for their own actions and decisions. For optimal effectiveness in the project, each individual would also be responsible to their immediate work group, and together they would control the operations. The participatory evaluation process should assign responsibility to individuals through the procedures designed for people to account to themselves and to their work group. One of the primary purposes given for participatory evaluation was to provide self-examination by the people involved in the project. To assess the utility of the participatory evaluation process for concentrating responsibility at the point of performance, this expectation was compared to experiences reported on responsibility.

The variables reported in Table 40 on the behavioral characteristics of responsibility report the respondents' experiences with responsibility at the point of performance. The participatory evaluation process helped maximize local responsibility for the project, it enhanced responsibility for all project participants as well as for the respective national offices, and it made clearer who is responsible for outcomes. The comparison of the high expectation for this process to provide self-examination by the people involved with these experiences of maximizing local responsibility for the project indicates that the participatory evaluation process is useful for concentrating responsibility at the point of performance for self-control.

Operating decision power shifts to the point of performance: Another characteristic which needs to be present for self-control to occur is that the people closest to the project must be making the operating decisions about the project. Learning to make decisions and to live with the ramifications of those decisions is one of the most important outcomes of an andragogical learning process. The literature on decentralization argued that young managers become more self-reliant as they learn to think through their situation or conditions and decide how to change their circumstances in order to control their operations. In development work, the local community members have the requisite knowledge to make project operations contextually appropriate. Therefore, the participatory evaluation process should empower the project participants systemically to make decisions concerning their project's operations.

Developing self-reliance skills in the community was rated as a secondary goal for participatory evaluation by the WHA employees, even though WHA identifies developing self-reliance in project participants as one of their organizational goals. To assess the utility of the participatory evaluation process for developing self-reliance through shifting the operating decision power to the point of performance, this variable was compared to the behavioral characteristics of decisions making and power.

The respondents' experiences with decision making are displayed in Table 41. The process is reported to be a tool to help communities make decisions for their future and for the local people to begin to realize and experience the outcomes of their decisions; further, willingness to make decisions shifts to the community when the participatory evaluation process is used. Making decisions empowers people to act on their assessments. The respondents reported that the project's power structure shifts to the community members when this evaluation process is being used and that the power relationships within the community are altered. With respect to decision power, the participatory evaluation process provides an unanticipated benefit. The experiences with the shifting of operating decision power to the point of performance for self-control exceed the expectations for developing self-reliance in the participants.

Operating control shifts to the point of performance: The final characteristic required for self-control to be occurring was that operating control shifts to the persons closest to the project.

Being held accountable to one's self and to one's co-workers is a reason often cited for self-control. In the literature search, Tannenbaum argued that total control could be increased as it was more widely distributed throughout an organization. References to Drucker argued that control would be enhanced as people were accountable to themselves and to their immediate work group. However, accountability was another reason rated as a secondary goal of participatory evaluation at WHA. To assess the utility of the participatory evaluation process for shifting operating control to the point of performance, this expectation was compared to the experiences reported for control.

The variables reported for control as a behavioral characteristic of participatory evaluation were displayed in Table 43. The respondents reported that both the partner agency and the community appear to be more accountable for this project where the participatory evaluation process is being used. Further, the community people involved feel in control of their project. Comparing the expectations and experiences on the shifting of operating control to the point of performance indicates that the participatory evaluation process is useful for enhancing accountability in the project. This is another unanticipated benefit of the process.

Summary: The participatory evaluation process appears to be enhancing project effectiveness and participant performance to a greater extent than was anticipated by WHA employees. These results address another of the central issues raised by this dissertation. The process did increase the knowledge of project participants by improving the flow of information among themselves as well as between them and the organization. This improved flow of information was not to the full extent expected by the organization, but the organization's high expectation for sharing lessons learned may be unrealistically high for this early stage of development in the participatory evaluation process. Moreover, the increased knowledge about the project was also reported as then being used to make decisions about the project and to take actions to control the projects' outcomes. This result showed that increased responsibility, decision power, and self-control were all unanticipated benefits of using the participatory evaluation process.

Efficient resource allocation decisions in both the long-run and the short-run

The final issue of concern in this dissertation was whether participatory evaluation facilitated efficient resource allocation. Hopwood's model on budgeting in the management control process contended that allocation of resources is more efficient when the operations specialist and the budgeting officer jointly develop budgets. This research inquired into the helpfulness of the participatory evaluation process in facilitating joint examination by project participants and management of resource allocations for both the long run and the short run.

Since capital formation can only occur in the long run, an efficient resource allocation process must require decision makers to anticipate capital needs for infrastructure such as plant, property, equipment, roads, wells, etc. The participatory evaluation process should require participants to examine and assess resource allocation for capital investment expenditures. Further, the evaluation reports should allow management to monitor the effectiveness of long-term capital formation in projects. Reviewing the participatory evaluation reports before deciding on capital expenditures and continued capital funding was a secondary use of evaluation reports. This expectation for the evaluation process was compared to the reported experiences with monitoring capital formation in the project to assess whether efficient long-run resource allocation was occurring. Respondents reported the evaluation process to be less helpful when considering and requesting capital expenditures for their project than for considering other aspects of the project.

For the short run, a primary expected use of evaluation reports was for decisions on continued funding; usage as information inputs before decisions to offer new funding or to stop funding were secondary. These expected uses were compared to the experiences reported by respondents for resource allocations. The process was reported as helpful for considering alternative spending levels for activities, determining a funding amount that seemed most appropriate for the goals, comparing the project reports to the accounting records, comparing spending in the project to the budget, and considering their own office's annual budget.

The participatory evaluation process appears not to be meeting WHA's expectations for resource allocation in the long run, but to be slightly exceeding their expectations in the short run. The experiences reported support the contention in the literature that budgeting can be a joint process between people performing the operations and the people from whom resources are requested, in this case the WHA project specialist.

Conclusions On Participatory Evaluation and the Benefits of Self-Control

The participatory evaluation process appears to be providing the benefits attributed to management by objectives and self-control in decentralized operations. The process aligns the effected audiences assigned to do evaluation tasks beginning at the point of performance closest to the project and ends in the organizational hierarchy. The process enhances project effectiveness and staff performance by increasing responsibility for the project and its outcomes to the people involved in the project, thereby allowing decision making and operating control to occur at the point of performance. The process facilitates efficient resource allocation in the short run as alternative spending levels are considered to achieve program activity goals.

SUMMARY OF THE RESULTS

The participatory evaluation process described in Chapter IV was designed and developed by WHA to assess the outcomes of their development projects. This chapter has discussed the results of a field study conducted to examine how participatory evaluation affects the management control process of a multinational non-profit organization.

Non-profit organizations were described as value-rational enterprises operating within a human welfare ethic in which all their outcomes are achieved by a mutual causation process. Human beings are the source of acts; they innovate new techniques, they identify more efficient methods, they recognize resources available, they decide how activities will be performed, and they adjust the process to achieve their desired results. The purpose of management in an andragogical model of human resource development is two-fold: (1) to create environments in which continuous development of individuals towards their full and unique potential can occur, along with (2) the continuous renewal of the larger economic and social systems through constructive interaction between people and their environment.

Necessarily following from this two-fold purpose, four key characteristic are identified from this research for the management process of a non-profit organization engaged in human resource development: (1) a flexible control system geared to competency development, (2) emphasis on the significance of the intervening process over the immediate products, (3) appreciation of qualitative change over quantitative change, and (4) stressing the role of experience in facilitating the course of development rather than the role of the intervention as the source of development.

The process of human resource development requires that managers facilitate selection by employees and program recipients of program components which are best suited to their circumstances and adaption of these components to their particular situation. Here an organic open-system organization is created between the human-services enterprise and the recipient local community. Value-rational decisions are made, albeit at a sub-optimum level. Alternative management and operating processes are selectively adapted to the cultural context in which they are imbedded.

The results indicate that a host community can design and use its own evaluation plan. The community's plan can involve all audiences effected by the operation. Incorporating the community's context, values, and culture will be easier than incorporating the organization's purpose, goals, and strategies.

Implementing the evaluation plan, however, did not provide all the operating information needed for assessment and control. For example, the participatory evaluation process was helpful for dialogue and discussion on project monitoring, but measuring and recording project outcomes for assessment was difficult for the project participants. Distributing the findings from this evaluation process is easier in the community than in the formal reporting system of the organization.

The results for incorporating evaluation findings into the management control system of a multinational, non-profit organization also show this pattern of helping the community more than the formal organization reporting system. The process provided routine evaluation reports and articulated with other parts of the management control system for the community, but not for the organization.

These results represent issues relevant to evaluation and control in multinational non-profit organizations where functions in the management process must be selectively adapted to dispersed and varied operating contexts. They indicate that managers must be willing to accept the ambiguity and loose coupling inherent in human resource development processes that have a dual role of performing a management task and teaching participants self-reliance skills. This is how human services organizations invest in human capital. The findings show the greatest benefits of the participatory evaluation process occur by instilling attributes of the management by objectives and self-control philosophy in the community and in the project. Local responsibility, decision power, and control all met or exceeded the organization's expectation.

The participatory evaluation process developed by WHA fulfills the management needs of a non-profit multinational organization because it: (1) is flexible enough to accept qualitative and quantitative information, (2) encourages individual and group exploration of alternative approaches to solving problems and needs, (3) accepts multiple or compound goals which mutually cause change to occur in the community and the people, (4) appreciates and captures the patterns and processes of change occurring in communities, and (5) holds the community people accountable for results in the long run.

Chapter VI summarized the findings and results of this study. It assessed the research questions posed in Chapter II and found positive answers to each of these prerequisite questions on the effectiveness of the participatory evaluation process in providing control in a multinational non-profit organization. Empirical propositions on the operating relationships inherent to this process will be presented in the concluding chapter. The possibility of participatory evaluation research findings being further developed and ultimately incorporated into the accounting information published by non-profit organizations will also be discussed. Finally, possibilities for further study on evaluation research as a service accomplishment measure in the non-profit environment will be explored.

CHAPTER VII

Summary and Conclusion

Participatory evaluation research has been studied in this dissertation to determine how it affects the management control process of a multinational non-profit organization. Surveys were prepared to explore three conditions of internal accounting and management reporting. This dissertation asserts that only when all three of the conditions are present can participatory evaluation effectively augment other forms of assessment in internal reporting and be considered as a potential service effort and accomplishment measure in accounting information.

This chapter summarizes the results and conclusions of the study with some suggestions for future research. The first section restates the purposes and objectives of this research. The next section of the chapter reviews the methodology employed with the constraints and boundaries imposed. The third section summarizes the findings and states implications. The fourth section states the operational definitions of participatory evaluation as empirical propositions inferred from these findings. The fifth section pertains to possibilities for future research. Finally, the last section contains some concluding remarks.

STATEMENT OF PURPOSES

A major theme stressed in this study was that different conditions, assumptions, and normative possibilities are present in multinational non-profit organizations than in for-profit organizations. Their non-market environment for the goods and services which they provide makes assessing management's stewardship of resources difficult since no standard indicator of performance has been developed for reporting accounting information on these entities.

Evaluation research is one form of performance assessment commonly used by non-profit organizations to measure and value both their effectiveness and their efficiency in providing goods and services. Therefore, the questions posed were, can evaluation research function as a surrogate market measure for non-profit organizations and can findings from evaluation research be incorporated as a service effort and accomplishment measure in accounting information? One pluralistic form of evaluation research was studied to explore these questions.

Participatory evaluation allows all stakeholders affected by a program to collectively design, implement, and use the evaluation research plan for their project or program. The fundamental values associated with participatory evaluation are closely associated with modern management thinking. Much of the current business literature has been devoted to the benefits derived from incorporating all people involved with an organization into its management process, thereby creating an open-system effect between the organization's internal and external environments.

Another fundamental value associated with modern management thinking is self-control. The philosophy of management by objectives advocates making individuals responsible for themselves and accountable to their immediate work group. The decisions these individuals and work groups make will drive the management control process, while reflecting the values and conditions simultaneously present in various geographic locations and program settings. How participatory evaluations affect the management control process of a multinational non-profit organization will also influence how the overall management process provides structure and impetus for other management tasks.

Thus, for internal users of management information, evaluation research findings would not only be used to assess performance; but they would also be used to evaluate decisions, thereby, allowing managers to improve goals, perceptions, and performance in the organization's responsiveness to various environments. External users of accounting information also need a service effort and accomplishment measure from which to compare their predictions on management's stewardship and with which to evaluate their decision to contribute resources to an eleemosynary organization. Therefore, understanding how a participatory evaluation process affects the management control process is a necessary prerequisite to further understanding of the internal and external benefits from incorporating evaluation research findings into management and accounting information.

From this rationale, three major research questions were addressed by this dissertation. Each of these questions must be affirmatively answered before any further analysis on the potentials of evaluation research can be reasonably discussed. The first question asked if host community members could design and use their own evaluation plan. The second question asked if participatory research findings could be incorporated into the formal reporting system of a multinational non-profit organization for distribution and utilization. The third question asked if the attributes and benefits of self-control were present in both the indigenous location and the organizational hierarchy when a participatory evaluation process was used. The first two questions focus on how the participatory evaluation process functions in the community and the organization. The last question relates the process to the behavioral and organizational consequences of self-control to determine if the information characteristics of relevance and reliability are present in participatory evaluation findings.

Effective control, first within the project and then in the immediate contact with the organization, is an essential prerequisite for participatory evaluation research to have further potential as a service effort and accomplishment measure in internal and external reporting. These themes have been stressed throughout this dissertation. Acquisition of knowledge about the process and elementary measurements on various aspects of the process were the first steps to developing a theory concerning participatory evaluation management control in non-profit organizations and to developing an interdisciplinary theory on evaluation research and accounting information.

RESEARCH METHODOLOGY

A field study was conducted in one multinational non-profit organization and involved employees from five separate groups:

(1) management, (2) administration and finance, (3) direct operations staff, (4) support staff, and (5) evaluation and training; the employees were located in thirty-two regional or national offices and the international headquarters. These groups were utilized to make comparisons between what they expected from a participatory evaluation research process for their organization and the experiences of their own field staff who are using the process in development projects.

Descriptions of the organizational setting for this research and of the participatory evaluation process studies were presented based on numerous observations over a five year period. Two self-administered questionnaires were constructed and utilized for empirical analysis. The open-ended questions could not be analyzed due to the difficulty of translating the many languages represented. The directed questions and demographic questions were analyzed to provide elementary measurements of the variables representing different aspects of the process. These variables were sorted and classified into descriptive statements on the parameters of participatory evaluation, its characteristics, conditions, and components. These parameters were then compared to their effects on the management control process according to the three research questions asked in this study.

The conclusions of this dissertation are intended to be informative, initial explorations on participatory evaluations which are generalizable to other similar institutions. Despite some inherent limitations of scope and results from an inductive field-study of one multinational non-profit organization, the study was designed to contribute to the overall knowledge of evaluation research, the management control process, and accounting information. The operational definitions proposed from the empirical findings and results of this research attempt to integrate and "knit-together" these disciplines. Uniting these specializations also increases general understanding of self-control in non-profit organizations.

SUMMARY OF THE RESULTS AND IMPLICATIONS

The results of the field-study may be summarized as follows: First, members of the host community were able to design and use their own evaluation plan; however, they were not able to fully create the open-system environment anticipated from a participatory evaluation process. The process did allow all project participants to be included in designing and using the evaluation plan. The process was not reported to be as helpful as the organizational respondents had expected it to be for environmental scanning of the entire local context. The values and culture of the local community were incorporated into the evaluation plan and project content. Unfortunately, the process did not incorporate the organization's goals, objectives, and values into the evaluation plans and project operations to the extent expected by the respondents.

The process was able to provide operating information on the project for assessment and control. The respondents reported that beginning baseline measurement techniques needed to include more data and different types of information, which, however, could be collected by the project participants. Monitoring the project's operating performance through dialogue and discussion were helpful for the behavioral aspects of the evaluation process; but it was not as helpful for monitoring activities, determining the impacts of the project outcomes, and deciding on the next month's plans and program activities. Finally, the process was also helpful for distributing results among the community members but not to the organization.

Second, the information which was provided fulfilled the respondents' expectations for routine evaluation reports. It articulated with other information required from the project participants by the management reporting system. However, the process did not articulate well with information required in the organization for the management reporting system. The process was helpful for assessing project performance in achieving stated goals and making managerial decisions concerning the project.

Third, the attributes and benefits of self-control confirm the previous findings. The behavioral aspects of management by objectives and self-control in decentralized operations were present in the process. The alignment of project participants and functional tasks begins nearest to the point of performance and progresses upward through the organizational hierarchy. Responsibility, decision power, and control were all present, and reported as enhance, in the project. The flow of information among the project participants and to the organization is improved by using the process. It was also helpful for efficient resource allocations in the short-run.

OPERATIONAL RELATIONSHIPS OF THE PARTICIPATORY EVALUATION PROCESS

Evaluators present their findings, supported by facts, figures, and illustrations which they have gathered. Ordinarily, only program administrators or managers can actually assess and evaluate, make decisions, and take future actions. However, proponents of pluralistic evaluation processes argue that routinely involving stakeholders in the project evaluation process improves the contextual relevance of evaluation findings. They contend that regularly reporting evaluation findings to managers improves the decisions made by all affected parties and allows evaluation findings to affect the form and content of programs. Participatory evaluation allows project participants to assess whether the project is meeting their expectations and achieving its goals without the involvement of a trained evaluation specialist. Several operating relationships are present in this evaluation model.

Role of the Organization's Project Staff: The project specialist from WHA functions as a facilitator when the project participants meet to design the evaluation plan, use it to assess project outcomes, and to decide on further actions. Therefore this person fulfills several important roles at one time: (1) they teach the evaluation process to the other project participants; (2) they represent the intervening organization's interest in the project; (3) they facilitate the entire process; and (4) they must carry out their other project tasks as well. In addition, they make critical decisions concerning the project, its funding and its form.

This multiplicity of roles could be a design weakness which does not allow the participatory evaluation process to function as effectively as it might with another person to facilitate the process or to represent the organization during the evaluation process. The process would still be participatory and unobtrusive if another WHA employee was assigned any responsibilities which are incongruent with the project specialists' overall role in the project, (e.g., representing WHA's interest in the evaluation process).

> *Empirical Proposition 1:* The project specialist role in the participatory evaluation process as a facilitator to the entire process has a consequence to his/her other roles in the project.

Monitoring Projects: In monitoring project activities, participatory evaluation techniques and skills helped the project participants more in their dialogue, discussion, and review procedures than to make evaluative decisions or to prepare for the next month's plans and activities. The techniques did help involve the community members in the review and validation procedures. However, the reliability of the participatory evaluation process to supply substantive measures is an important element in the utility of the process for making evaluative decisions and for reporting service effort and accomplishment.

The problem of stakeholder evaluation having low marginal impacts on the project decision process was substantiated in the literature review. WHA may be able to overcome this problem and improve the utility of participatory evaluation if meaningful, useful, and effective monitoring devices can be designed by the project participants in their communities, which are suitable to the participants' context and capabilities. Only then can project outcome results be routinely measured and reported to all the project participants. Then subsequently, they can be summarized for the project, reported to the intervening organization, and incorporated into the management information system and control process.

Designing participatory processes which facilitate dialogue, discussion, decision-making, *and* documentation is a recurring difficulty discussed in the literature review and corroborated in these findings. Participatory evaluation techniques were reported as least helpful for validation procedures which require comparison of expected to actual results. The techniques and skills were found to be "somewhat helpful" for comparison of the evaluation records. Such procedures as these are essential, however, for participatory evaluation findings to have the qualitative characteristic of reliability required for externally reported accounting information.

> *Empirical Proposition 2:* Reliable reporting of project evaluations is dependent upon project participants designing and using effective monitoring devices which are suitable to their capabilities, context, and the indicator of project outcomes being monitored.

Timing of Corrective Actions: Allowing the community to design the project evaluation plan prepares them to also be involved in changing or maintaining the project's activities. As the project is implemented and performance results become available, the community members decide if the project should be revised or how it could be improved. Since the evaluation functions parallel the management functions, participatory evaluation allows all the project participants to be concurrently involved in the project management as well as the project evaluation. The efficiency of accomplishing these two functions at the same time is valuable to the sponsoring organization.

Participating as a community and designing the evaluation plan was helpful in implementing decentralized management of project operations by increasing understanding and awareness of key project elements. Having designed the evaluation plan together, the project participants know the specific problems the project is addressing, the activities selected to alleviate or modify these problems, and the changes anticipated in key areas. This prior knowledge allows them to take corrective action sooner. Fewer resources are, therefore, used on unproductive activities.

> *Empirical Proposition 3:* Project participants being able to take corrective action sooner is a function of their involvement in planning and designing the project evaluation plan.

Egalitarian Nature of the Process: WHA chooses to have the community assess the project's performance for the self-reliance skills such assessment develops. Participatively designing the evaluation plan clearly helps the community assess the project's performance and become more involved in the development project. Moreover, designing the evaluation plan was equally helpful to everyone involved for their particular area of interest. Thus, participatory evaluation benefits all affected populations—the community, the project committee, the partner agency, and the WHA project specialist—as they assessed the activities and evaluated if they were achieving the desired results.

Usually program administrators make decisions to change or maintain program activities. In WHA, the project director, under the guidance of the project committee and in concurrence with the partner agency, would ordinarily have responsibility for this management function. However, the chain of command and lines of authority are not absolutely specified, and participatory evaluation allows the community members to be actively involved as equals in formatively changing the project.

> *Empirical Proposition 4:* Active involvement of all project participants to plan, design, and use the project evaluation plan has a consequence of creating an egalitarian environment for the evaluation process.

Participatory Evaluation Research Reports: Regular reporting of evaluation findings is dependent on adequate and systematic collection of project outcomes at their point of origin. Requiring each project participant group to design their own record keeping devices to accumulate data on indicators which measure program goals and objectives, debilitates the reporting process before it can begin.

Where evaluation reporting was functioning, the process was cumbersome and unstructured. Periodic case study reports provided insights into the respective projects, but the reports were neither widely distributed nor routinely used during decision making. Therefore, the behavioral aspects of participatory evaluation were present for self-control in the community, while the technical aspects of self-control were not present in the organization's management process.

Evaluation research is only one evaluative tool management has at its disposal. Therefore, it should be compatible with, complement, and augment other financial and managerial control tools. The process did articulate with other parts of the management control process in the community but not in the organization. Not correlating with other management control functions has a potential consequence of evaluation reports being under utilized in decision making. Record keeping devices which are compatible with the host community members' abilities must be designed and developed in each project. Correspondingly, standardized forms which are flexible and can be adapted for use with various indicators should be uniformly produced throughout the organization and incorporated in the routine project management reporting process at regular intervals.

> *Empirical Proposition 5:* Optimum utilization of participatory evaluation research reports is dependent on the findings of these reports being uniformly produced, systematically collected, and routinely distributed through the organization's management information system at regular time intervals.

Timing of Evaluation Research Assessments: An overriding issue which emerged from these research findings is that evaluation research information is formative only in the long-run (e.g., annual periods or longer). The types of changes which evaluation research measures, are incrementally small in the short-run (e.g., monthly or quarterly). Development project outcomes require the passage of time in order to accumulate noticeable changes resulting from the project.

Monthly, quarterly, or sporadically prepared evaluation reports do not contain enough information to influence the decision process. Comparative annual evaluation reports would focus the attention of both the preparer and the reader on key project activities at sufficiently long intervals to recognize changes. Drucker contends attention of the preparer is essential for self-control. This would occur as project participants maintain their record-keeping devices and report their progress to the community during the monthly visits of the project specialist. This way, both the community and the local WHA office would be aware of the progress in the project, but cumulative annual reports would convey an adequate increment of change to affect the management decision process in the organization, as well.

> *Empirical Proposition 6:* The participatory evaluation research reports conveying information on adequately large increments of change to affect the managerial decision process in the organization is dependent on the passage of an adequately long period of time to allow the changes to reflect magnitude, rate and direction of the program toward achieving its goals.

Inclusion of Participatory Research Into A Management Control Model: The American Accounting Association, in ASOBAT, their monograph on basic accounting theory, contended that management can be segregated into two processes: the planning process and the control process. Anthony proposed a management process model which began with an overall corporate strategic planning process, then formulated these strategic plans into operations through the management control process, and finally implemented them through the operations control process. Dermer, Maciariello, Hopwood, Tannenbaum, Herzlinger, and Ramanathan further developed these processes for both profit and non-profit organizations.

From these models, certain common functions have evolved to comprise the management control process. These functions include environment scanning, program planning, allocating resources, measuring, reporting, assessing, and deciding to take future actions. Some of these models represent merely how information flows through an organization to support these processes. Other models represent the decision making relationships which drive the management process.

Actual information reporting systems and decision support systems must be designed to coordinate the organization's work efforts and to solidify the organizational structure. A participatory evaluation process could be made compatible with various reporting relationships and decision schemes.

Every management tool must fit the task for which it is designed. Participatory evaluation research is no exception. It would fit best with modern organizational structures, reporting relationships, and decision schemes, (e.g.: matrix organizational structures and reporting systems, horizontally integrated work groups, federally decentralize operations, ad hoc or task force management styles).

It would also fit best in organizations which have externally oriented corporate strategies. Organizations where the nature of their business and the goods or services they provide, require innovative responsiveness to external conditions. Organizations where the experiences of external constituents in the transformation process, (e.g., human resource and infrastructure development through andragonous learning) is more valuable than specific procedures being used to implement a process or precise measures resulting from a process.

Many management control models and information systems are conducive to such a process. The effects of participatory evaluation on these models would primarily be in the area of adaptive reporting procedures. The effects of participatory evaluation on these models would be in the loose-coupling of their components, in the consideration of measurement, assessment, and evaluation of outcomes in each function of the process, and in the creations of the management process as a joint exercise between all project participants.

> *Empirical Proposition 7:* Participatively designing and using the project evaluation plan has three major consequences for the management control process: (1) of loosely-coupling the management control functions into a more fluid process; (2) of considering measurement, evaluation, and control assessment of project outcomes when performing each of the other management functions; and (3) of creating a joint

exercise between all project participants for each of the
management functions in the project.

Creating Negative Entropy for the Organization: Entropy is the
second law of thermodynamics and measures unavailable energy or
information in a closed system or message. The law infers that the
degradation of matter and energy in the universe is an ultimate state of
inert uniformity. The literature review on open-system theory for
organizations asserted that organizations must create negative entropy
in order to survive, prosper, and grow.

Nine conditions necessary for an open-system organization to exist
were presented. Katz and Kahn argued that the first three conditions
were present in all biological systems; but organizations had the
potential to create negative entropy and, thereby, both protect
themselves from the natural degradation process and produce for
themselves an environment in which are present the remaining five
conditions necessary for an open-system organization to survive, adapt,
and grow.

Therefore, arresting the entropic process is essential. Enterprises
must import more energy from their environment than they expend to
provide goods and services. Multinational non-profit organizations can
only acquire and store energy to improve their survival position when
they develop a comfortable margin of operation as well as a margin of
available financial resources.

The participatory evaluation process allowed WHA to acquire
energy from its external environments at the various project sites where
its operations occurred. This energy came in the forms of: (1) contextual
information about the operating locations, (2) increased human resource
utilization by involving all project participants in designing and using
the evaluation plan, (3) increased and more effective utilization of
talents, abilities, and natural resources available in the operating
location, (4) increased potential to respond to all opportunities equally,
and (5) more efficient allocation of financial resources in the short-run.
Importation, utilization, and retention of these new sources of energy for
the organization help arrest the entropic process and assure a growth
process in the long-run.

Empirical Proposition 8: Participatory evaluation creates
the condition of negative entropy and therefore has a
consequence of producing an open-system environment

between multinational non-profit organizations and their geographically dispersed operating locations.

Long-term Commitment: A word of caution is required when research on participative, stakeholder involvement is conducted. Mazmanian and Nienaber, in studying a community involvement program conduct by the Army Corp of Engineers, found that even when the community participated in the project's development and implementation, they did not "take ownership" in the project's content or its outcomes.[106] Therefore, while this initial research shows increased involvement and interest in the project, long-term commitment to and ownership in the project, and in the development efforts in total, can not be inferred from these findings and results. They can only be determined by continuing to studying them in longitudinal research.

Empirical Proposition 9: Positive responses to the participatory evaluation process do not necessarily correlate with long-term commitment by the project participants to either the project itself nor to the development efforts in total.

These empirical propositions identify the operational definitions for the parameters of participatory evaluation research. The process is strongest in its behavioral aspects. It is weakest in measuring, collecting, and compiling project outcome data at the point of origin. The attributes and benefits of self-control are present in the process at the indigenous location but not in the organization.

The process affects the management control process by facilitating the interactions of project participants to plan, design, organize, and implement the development project as well as the evaluation plan for the project. The process creates a joint exercise between respective project participant groups for these management functions. The process provides enough benefits to be worthy of further development, continued refinement, and future research.

FUTURE RESEARCH

The general methodology (Chapter III) of this dissertation was subject to limitations. Scope limitations included restriction of this study to one organization, albeit large, and the inherent limitations of field-based research.

The first suggestion, for future research, which will improve similar studies, is that replication of this study with other non-profit organizations be made. These replications can improve this study by constructing the questionnaires with more association between variables, especially those identified in this research. In addition, the study could be improved by conducting the surveys in phases to narrow the focus of particular questions and identify specific circumstances where the process is most effective or efficient. This could be done by repeated data collection on a longitudinal basis, (i.e., giving the questionnaires to particular subjects at given intervals of time). Another possibility is conducting surveys in phases, (i.e., giving portions of the questionnaire at various times and then building the next portion of the questionnaire based upon the results). For example, in a delphi technique manner, open-ended questions used in the first phase, would then be analyzed to improve the directed questions in the second phase. These improvements could also be applied to continued longitudinal research with this organization as it continues to develop and refine its participatory evaluation process.

Another improvement might be to utilize different research strategies, such as experimental methods to test the validity of these elementary measures and operational relationships. For example, if it is true that participatory evaluation is helpful for particular project participant groups to fulfill their specific tasks in the project, then this suggests that standardized policies, procedures, and segregation of duties is possible with the process because people may recognize the benefits accruing to them and other participants. Further research with more controlled design methodology is warranted to test this proposition that the process benefits all participants equally by testing for between group differences.

The case study descriptions, elementary measurements, operational relationships, and empirical propositions developed in this initial research provide a reference and element of objectivity to any subsequent research efforts.

CONCLUDING REMARKS

Human services organizations are value-rational enterprises which use human resource development processes to interact with their environment. They financially support and engage in development work in the third world to aid in the transition of those societies from primitive or under-developed agrarian societies into the industrial and information societies of the twenty-first century. Their purpose is to minimize the inherent inequities of economic and social development, while maximizing the incentives for innovation, efficiency, learning, and personal development. Their objectives are to create justice and equal opportunity for every human which is effected and/or affected by their development process.

These values and their resulting operating processes are manifestations of the philosophy of management by objectives and self-control. Participatory evaluation was designed to open WHA's complex and geographically dispersed operations to its total environment; thereby, serving the needs of internal users for operating information. This dissertation introduced the additional possibility of this information serving the needs of external users for service effort and accomplishment information as well.

Information about service accomplishments for non-profit organizations in providing goods and services or in achieving desired program results would enhance the usefulness of both internal and external reports. External users of accounting information need to assess how well managers have discharged their stewardship responsibilities. Ultimately, stewardship is intergenerational equity; one generation of managers leaving an organization as well off as they received it plus real economic and operational growth. A service accomplishment element could be useful for external users to determine if management has improved the wealth and stability of a non-profit organization.

The findings and results of this research infer that participatory evaluation can open a highly developed, complex, geographically dispersed organization to it constituents, their values, and their cultural context; but reciprocally sharing the organization's values, philosophy, purpose, and goals with the community was not as easily achieved. The primary weaknesses identified in the process were measuring project outcomes and distributing evaluation information. These difficulties could be overcome with further development and refinement of the evaluation process.

The attributes and benefits of management by objectives and self-control are partially present. However, they are not adequately present to consider the process an internal control device in the management process of the total organization. The process has the potential to be a service effort and accomplishment element for internal accounting information when the process is refined. These refinements would allow the process to provide relevant data for intra-project performance assessment. However an intrinsic tension is present in the inherent nature of participatory evaluation between individually derived reports on evaluation findings and inter-project comparisons of performance necessary for managerial stewardship as well as with the need to compile and aggregate findings for organization-wide reporting. A compilation and comparison mechanism is needed to summarize these individual findings into some comparable and aggregate indicators of performance, like profit, for participatory evaluation results to be considered a surrogate market measure in non-profit organizations. Therefore, in its early state of development at WHA, the findings would indicate that participatory evaluation is not presently a potential service accomplishment measure for external accounting information. The requisite conditions of relevance, reliability, comparability, verifiability, and neutrality are only partially present. Future research could examine further if these characteristics emerge as the process advances through maturation.

NOTES

106. Mazmanian, Daniel A. and Jeanne Nienaber, *Can Organizations Change?*, (Washington, D.C.: The Brookings Institution) 1979.

APPENDIX A

Questionnaires

EXPECTATIONS QUESTIONNAIRE

Please give us your personal responses and ideas about evaluation. We are most interested in your assessments, opinions, and judgments based on your experiences. In the following pages you are asked to read each of the following questions and using a scale of lowest to highest rate each item by circling the response which best represents your opinion and views. We are grateful for the time and effort you will spend helping us in the next few minutes.

I. Evaluation Issues

Several issues have been raised by people throughout the WHA Partnership about evaluation and the participatory evaluation skills and techniques being developed, taught in the workshops, and adapted in the projects. To keep you informed of one another's thoughts and help us assess these concerns and issues, please share your responses to *each* item by circling the response which best represents your opinion.

1. Listed below are several definitions people in WHA have given to evaluation; to what extent do you agree or disagree with each one? To me evaluation means:

	Strongly disagree	Disagree	Agree	Strongly agree
Continuous awareness of project results and outcomes	1	2	3	4
Routine assessment of project performance	1	2	3	4
Periodic measuring of impacts or changes caused by project results	1	2	3	4
Regular checking up on project performance	1	2	3	4
Regular checking up on people's performance	1	2	3	4
Management examination of projects	1	2	3	4
Management examination of people	1	2	3	4
Self-examination by people involved in projects	1	2	3	4
Community examination of project performance	1	2	3	4
Other:_____	1	2	3	4

2. Listed below are several reasons people have given why WHA needs to conduct project evaluations. Rate each reason by how important you think it is for evaluating development projects.

	Not important	Somewhat important	Usually important	Very important	Does not apply / Do not know
Needed for accountability	1	2	3	4	0
Needed for credibility in the international development community	1	2	3	4	0
Needed for developing self-reliance skills in the community	1	2	3	4	0
Needed for continuous assessment of project performance	1	2	3	4	0
Needed for making decisions about project outcomes	1	2	3	4	0
Needed to learn lessons from project activities and results	1	2	3	4	0
Needed to determine the impacts resulting from project activities	1	2	3	4	0
Needed to identify exceptional projects	1	2	3	4	0
Needed to help integrate the management activities in projects (planning, setting goals, selecting activities, budgeting, etc.)	1	2	3	4	0
Needed to focus management's attention on the project's outcomes and results	1	2	3	4	0
Needed to identify successful projects	1	2	3	4	0
Needed to identify projects that are not meeting our expectations	1	2	3	4	0
Other:_____	1	2	3	4	0

3. Listed below are various people involved in WHA projects. For each of the people (groups) listed, how desirable do you think it would be for them to manage the evaluation of development projects?

	Not desirable	Somewhat desirable	Usually desirable	Very desirable	Does not apply / Do not know
Entire Community	1	2	3	4	0
Community members involved in the project	1	2	3	4	0
Project partner	1	2	3	4	0
Project committee	1	2	3	4	0
Project director/manager	1	2	3	4	0
Project staff	1	2	3	4	0
Project specialist	1	2	3	4	0
Sub-office/DAC center	1	2	3	4	0
Operations Coordinator	1	2	3	4	0
Administrative Coordinator	1	2	3	4	0
Evaluation Coordinator	1	2	3	4	0
Field Director	1	2	3	4	0
Regional Director/Field Development Director	1	2	3	4	0
International Field Development Office	1	2	3	4	0
International Evaluation Office	1	2	3	4	0
International Vice President for Field Ministries Office	1	2	3	4	0
International Systems Audit	1	2	3	4	0
Support Offices	1	2	3	4	0
Outside Evaluation Consultants	1	2	3	4	0
Other:_____	1	2	3	4	0

4. I think it is most desirable that requests from the community, project staff, or area supervisor (project coordinator) for help or assistance in meeting evaluation requirements should be directed to:

	Not desirable	Somewhat desirable	Usually desirable	Very desirable	Does not apply Do not know
Sub-office/DAC Center	1	2	3	4	0
Field Office	1	2	3	4	0
Regional Office/Desk	1	2	3	4	0
International Office	1	2	3	4	0
Other:_____	1	2	3	4	0

5. To what extent do you think it is important that the people doing the technical work of evaluation should understand the following:

	Not important	Somewhat important	Usually important	Very important	Does not apply Do not know
Understand WHA's mission	1	2	3	4	0
Understand the evaluation process	1	2	3	4	0
Understand development projects	1	2	3	4	0
Understand the community	1	2	3	4	0
Understand the technical requirements of evaluation	1	2	3	4	0
Understand WHA's management requirements	1	2	3	4	0
Other:_____	1	2	3	4	0

6. To what extent do you think it is desirable for each of these people (group) to provide support or assistance for meeting evaluation requirements?

	Not desirable	Somewhat desirable	Usually desirable	Very desirable	Does not apply Do not know
Entire Community	1	2	3	4	0
Community members involved in the project	1	2	3	4	0
Community leaders	1	2	3	4	0
Government agencies	1	2	3	4	0
Project partner	1	2	3	4	0
Project committee	1	2	3	4	0
Project director/manager	1	2	3	4	0
Project staff	1	2	3	4	0
Project specialist	1	2	3	4	0
Sub-office/DAC center	1	2	3	4	0
Operations Coordinator	1	2	3	4	0
Administrative Coordinator	1	2	3	4	0
Evaluation Coordinator	1	2	3	4	0
Field Director	1	2	3	4	0
Regional Director/Field Development Director	1	2	3	4	0
International Field Development Office	1	2	3	4	0
International Evaluation Office	1	2	3	4	0
International Vice President for Field Ministries Office	1	2	3	4	0
International Systems Audit	1	2	3	4	0
Support Offices	1	2	3	4	0
Outside evaluation consultants	1	2	3	4	0
Other:_____	1	2	3	4	0

7. To what extent do you think each of the following people are desirable to do the technical work of evaluation (such as gathering data about the community, keeping records on the project's activities. confirming the changes in the community because of the project)?

	Not desirable	Somewhat desirable	Usually desirable	Very desirable	Does not apply / Do not know
Entire Community	1	2	3	4	0
Community members involved in the project	1	2	3	4	0
Community leaders	1	2	3	4	0
Government agencies	1	2	3	4	0
Project partner	1	2	3	4	0
Project committee	1	2	3	4	0
Project director/manager	1	2	3	4	0
Project staff	1	2	3	4	0
Project specialist	1	2	3	4	0
Sub-office/DAC center	1	2	3	4	0
Operations Coordinator	1	2	3	4	0
Administrative Coordinator	1	2	3	4	0
Evaluation Coordinator	1	2	3	4	0
Field Director	1	2	3	4	0
Regional Director/Field Development Director	1	2	3	4	0
International Field Development Office	1	2	3	4	0
International Evaluation Office	1	2	3	4	0
International Vice President for Field Ministries Office	1	2	3	4	0
International Systems Audit	1	2	3	4	0
Outside evaluation consultants	1	2	3	4	0
Other:_____	1	2	3	4	0

8. Listed below are several ways people have suggested for sharing the lessons learned from project evaluations. Rate each item by how desirable you think it is for sharing lessons learned from individual development project evaluations with the entire WHA partnership.

	Not desirable	Somewhat desirable	Usually desirable	Very desirable	Does not apply / Do not know
Evaluation integration task forces	1	2	3	4	0
Annual evaluation reports for each project	1	2	3	4	0
Annual evaluation reports for each region	1	2	3	4	0
Regional Field Directors conference reports	1	2	3	4	0
International Partnership Planning Meeting reports	1	2	3	4	0
Routine management reports (like plan of action reports or milestone reports)	1	2	3	4	0
Informal discussion between staff	1	2	3	4	0
International Affairs Committee meeting reports	1	2	3	4	0
WHA Board meeting reports	1	2	3	4	0
WHA Partnership teams doing indept evaluation reports	1	2	3	4	0
Other:_____	1	2	3	4	0

9. To what extent do you think each of the following people (group) should benefit from development project evaluation's results, findings, conclusions, and reports?

	Least benefit	Somewhat benefit	Usually benefit	Most benefit	Does not apply Do not know
Entire Community	1	2	3	4	0
Community members involved in the project	1	2	3	4	0
Project partner	1	2	3	4	0
Project committee	1	2	3	4	0
Project director/manager	1	2	3	4	0
Project staff	1	2	3	4	0
Project specialist	1	2	3	4	0
Sub-office/DAC center	1	2	3	4	0
Operations Coordinator	1	2	3	4	0
Administrative Coordinator	1	2	3	4	0
Evaluation Coordinator	1	2	3	4	0
Field Director	1	2	3	4	0
Regional Director/Field Development Director	1	2	3	4	0
International Field Development Office	1	2	3	4	0
International Evaluation Office	1	2	3	4	9
International Vice President for Field Ministries Office	1	2	3	4	0
International Systems Audit	1	2	3	4	0
Support Offices	1	2	3	4	0
Individual WHA donors	1	2	3	4	0
Agency/Foundation/WHA donors	1	2	3	4	0
Other:_____	1	2	3	4	0

II. Developing Useful Evaluation Reports

During the past year, many area supervisors have been learning about and beginning to use participatory evaluation techniques in their development projects. These techniques affect both their direct work in projects and other peoples' tasks at WHA who work indirectly for the projects. The next series of questions concern the issues of participatory evaluation and ask your opinion how evaluation reports can be most useful to you.

Have you ever heard of the participatory evaluation?   YES____   NO____
(IF NO, PLEASE SKIP TO PAGE 11 PART 2)

How did you first hear of participatory evaluation?

	(Check/tick)
Field office communications	_____
Regional Field Directors conference	_____
IPPM meeting	_____
International Field Directors conference	_____
International Evaluation Office	_____
Informally from other staff	_____
Other:_____	_____

In one sentence define what you perceive participatory evaluation to be:

Have you attended a participatory evaluation workshop?   YES____   NO____

Have you ever visited a project where participatory evaluation techniques were being used?
YES____   NO____

Do you see the participatory evaluation reports that have been received by your office?
YES____ NO____

In the following pages, you are asked to read two questions, and using a scale of never to always, rate each item by circling the response which best represents your opinion and views. If YES, you see the participatory evaluation reports, answer both questions; if NO, please answer question 2 on the next page as you *think* you would use evaluation reports.

1. From my experiences with using participatory evaluation reports:

	Never	Sometimes	Usually	Always	Does not apply / Do not know
I read them	1	2	3	4	0
They require too much time to read	1	2	3	4	0
They are worth the effort to read	1	2	3	4	0
They are good for the necessary, required line management reports	1	2	3	4	0
I refer to them when making routine operating decisions	1	2	3	4	0
They help me make decisions	1	2	3	4	0
They help provide the necessary information for my management task	1	2	3	4	0
I see the project's impacts on the community	1	2	3	4	0
I can judge the project's operating performance	1	2	3	4	0
I can judge WHA's management performance	1	2	3	4	0
I read these more often than other reports	1	2	3	4	0
I read these more carefully than other evaluation reports	1	2	3	4	0
I know more about the project from reading them	1	2	3	4	0
I trust these reports	1	2	3	4	0
I now request evaluation reports (if available) on project results before making further decisions about the project	1	2	3	4	0
I take these more seriously than previous or other findings	1	2	3	4	0
Other:_____	1	2	3	4	0

2. I use them/or think I would use them when:

	Never	Sometimes	Usually	Always	Does not apply / Do not know
Reviewing budget reports	1	2	3	4	0
Reviewing milestone/plan of action reports	1	2	3	4	0
Assessing project performance	1	2	3	4	0
Reviewing project appropriateness/conformity to our annual goals and/or five year plan	1	2	3	4	0
Before returning for additional explanation a project report or a project request	1	2	3	4	0
Before preparing SRD correspondence and discrepancies	1	2	3	4	0
Before preparing an internal audit report	1	2	3	4	0
Deciding on continued funding	1	2	3	4	0
Deciding on new funding	1	2	3	4	0
Deciding to stop funding	1	2	3	4	0
Deciding on capital expenditures	1	2	3	4	0
Other:_____	1	2	3	4	0

III. Your Ideas and Suggestions

The ideal way to have you share your ideas, thoughts, and suggestions would be to have individual interviews or to meet in small groups. Then a lively discussion could follow until we could achieve a consensus. In the absence of that "ideal" setting, hearing from you in writing is the next best way. The next set of questions asks you to tell us what *you* think is "best" for evaluations at WHA. There are no right or wrong answers; there are no particular number of answers. If you have only one idea, that is fine; if you have several ideas, write down quickly, yet clearly, as many as you care to. You can take as long as you want to for this section, but we intend very quick thoughts of immediate reaction to the questions. Therefore, you might take just 10 minutes or less to answer the following:

What purpose do you think evaluation should have in WHA projects?

_____
_____

What do you expect evaluation reports to tell you about project performance?

_____
_____

What do you expect evaluation reports to tell you about project management?

_____
_____

For whom do you think evaluation information is critical?

_____
_____

How can evaluation results, findings, conclusions, information, and reports help you do your job?

_____
_____

What other issues, questions, insights, and concerns do you think evaluation should consider?

_____
_____

PLEASE BE SURE TO ANSWER THE QUESTIONS IN PART IV ON THE NEXT
PAGE SO WE CAN SHARE WITH YOU THE INFORMATION WE HAVE GATHERED.

IV. Information About You

All the information requested in this questionnaire will be held in confidence by the independent researcher. All of the results will be reported using aggregate or grouped responses. No information will be disclosed about individuals or their responses. The following information will be used to group the replies and to analyze the responses. Your name, title, and office will be used to mail you the results and ask your help again as together we monitor the evaluation activities.

Name (optional)_____ Office (optional)_____
Job Title_____
Name of project(s) where participatory evaluation is being used_____
How long have you been involved with this project(s)?_____
How long have you been in your current position?_____
How long have you been with WHA?_____
Sex: M_____ F_____ Age: Under 20_____ 21-35_____ 36-50_____ 51-65_____ Over 65_____

Educational attainment: Level (check/tick)   Location
    Primary   _____   _____
    Elementary   _____   _____
    Secondary   _____   _____
    University   _____   _____

Thank you for the time, thought, energy, ideas, and opinions you have shared with us. We appreciate your contribution to helping us get to know one another better and the ministry work we are doing. We will inform you of the results and ask for your help again, as together we analyze each other's responses and share each other's concerns.

EXPERIENCE QUESTIONNAIRE

EVALUATION WORKSHOP PARTICIPANTS' RESPONSES
TO PARTICIPATORY EVALUATION TECHNIQUES
USED IN DEVELOPMENT PROJECTS
(SHARING EVALUATION EXPERIENCES)

Many changes have been predicted for yourself and for the community because of using participatory evaluation techniques in development projects. People throughout the WHA Partnership have asked the questions or raised the issues you are about to consider. Answering these questions serves to keep you informed about other peoples' concerns, and it allows all of you to share your experiences as well as respond to each others' ideas.

1. Consider the activities you routinely perform in development projects. Please identify or list as many of these activities as you can now recall in which you have been able to use the participatory evaluation techniques and skills you learned in the evaluation workshop. There are no right or wrong answers; there are no particular number of answers. If you can think of only one activity, that is fine. If you think of several activities, write down as many as you care to. Take only a few minutes; write quickly, yet clearly; the categories are provided only to help you sort the activities into a particular group.

With regard to project planning, design and application for support:
_____
_____

With regard to getting approval for the project:
_____
_____

Which regard to project funding:
_____
_____

With regard to project implementation:
_____
_____

With regard to project monitoring and control:
_____
_____

With regard to annual planning and budgeting tasks for the project:

_____

_____

We are interested in your opinion after having used the participatory evaluation techniques. You may still be in the process of introducing many of the skills and techniques and not yet experienced all of the events listed. Please base your answers on your experiences thus far. There are no right or wrong answers; we want to learn about your experiences and perceptions. In the following pages, you are asked to read each of the following questions and using a scale of lowest to highest, rate each item by circling the response which best represents your opinions and views. Comparing projects where you are using participatory evaluation techniques with other projects where you are not, rate the following items based on your experiences.

2. In assessing the community's needs, how helpful were the participatory evaluation techniques for each of the following individuals or groups when:

	Hindered	Not very helpful	Somewhat helpful	Usually helpful	Very helpful	Have not experienced
Recognizing problems or needs of the community						
Yourself	1	2	3	4	5	0
Community	1	2	3	4	5	0
Committee	1	2	3	4	5	0
Partner Agency	1	2	3	4	5	0
Identifying possible ways the problem or needs could be corrected						
Yourself	1	2	3	4	5	0
Community	1	2	3	4	5	0
Committee	1	2	3	4	5	0
Partner Agency	1	2	3	4	5	0
Deciding on certain project activities to resolve the problem or need						
Yourself	1	2	3	4	5	0
Community	1	2	3	4	5	0
Committee	1	2	3	4	5	0
Partner Agency	1	2	3	4	5	0
Recognizing talents and abilities present in the community						
Yourself	1	2	3	4	5	0
Community	1	2	3	4	5	0
Committee	1	2	3	4	5	0
Partner Agency	1	2	3	4	5	0
Identifying possible ways to use these talents and abilities in the project						
Yourself	1	2	3	4	5	0
Community	1	2	3	4	5	0
Committee	1	2	3	4	5	0
Partner Agency	1	2	3	4	5	0
Deciding on project activities to develop these talents and abilities						
Yourself	1	2	3	4	5	0
Community	1	2	3	4	5	0
Committee	1	2	3	4	5	0
Partner Agency	1	2	3	4	5	0
Recognizing resources present in the community						
Yourself	1	2	3	4	5	0
Community	1	2	3	4	5	0
Committee	1	2	3	4	5	0
Partner Agency	1	2	3	4	5	0

2. (Continued) In assessing the community's needs, how helpful were the participatory evaluation techniques for each of the following individuals or groups when:

	Hindered	Not very helpful	Somewhat helpful	Usually helpful	Very helpful	Have not experienced
Identifying possible ways to use these resources in the project						
Yourself	1	2	3	4	5	0
Community	1	2	3	4	5	0
Committee	1	2	3	4	5	0
Partner Agency	1	2	3	4	5	0
Deciding on project activities which include these resources						
Yourself	1	2	3	4	5	0
Community	1	2	3	4	5	0
Committee	1	2	3	4	5	0
Partner Agency	1	2	3	4	5	0

3. In designing the project, how helpful were the participatory evaluation techniques to each of the following individuals or groups when:

	Hindered	Not very helpful	Somewhat helpful	Usually helpful	Very helpful	Have not experienced
Considering the different activity levels that were possible for the tasks						
Yourself	1	2	3	4	5	0
Community	1	2	3	4	5	0
Committee	1	2	3	4	5	0
Partner Agency	1	2	3	4	5	0
Selecting a reasonable objective for these activity levels						
Yourself	1	2	3	4	5	0
Community	1	2	3	4	5	0
Committee	1	2	3	4	5	0
Partner Agency	1	2	3	4	5	0
Setting measurable goals for the project's activities						
Yourself	1	2	3	4	5	0
Community	1	2	3	4	5	0
Committee	1	2	3	4	5	0
Partner Agency	1	2	3	4	5	0
Agreeing upon task quotas (or work levels) for people involved in the project						
Yourself	1	2	3	4	5	0
Community	1	2	3	4	5	0
Committee	1	2	3	4	5	0
Partner Agency	1	2	3	4	5	0
Selecting indicators which we thought would best monitor these activities						
Yourself	1	2	3	4	5	0
Community	1	2	3	4	5	0
Committee	1	2	3	4	5	0
Partner Agency	1	2	3	4	5	0
Deciding how to record these indicators						
Yourself	1	2	3	4	5	0
Community	1	2	3	4	5	0
Committee	1	2	3	4	5	0
Partner Agency	1	2	3	4	5	0

3. (Continued) In designing the project, how helpful were the participatory evaluation techniques to each of the following individuals or groups when:

	Hindered	Not very helpful	Somewhat helpful	Usually helpful	Very helpful	Have not experienced
Developing a record keeping devise to use						
Yourself	1	2	3	4	5	0
Community	1	2	3	4	5	0
Committee	1	2	3	4	5	0
Partner Agency	1	2	3	4	5	0
Measuring the current activity level of these indicators						
Yourself	1	2	3	4	5	0
Community	1	2	3	4	5	0
Committee	1	2	3	4	5	0
Partner Agency	1	2	3	4	5	0
Deciding how the results, outcomes, or findings from the project could be shared with one another						
Yourself	1	2	3	4	5	0
Community	1	2	3	4	5	0
Committee	1	2	3	4	5	0
Partner Agency	1	2	3	4	5	0

4. In organizing the project, how helpful were the skills that you learned from the participatory evaluation workshop to each of the follow individuals or groups when:

	Hindered	Not very helpful	Somewhat helpful	Usually helpful	Very helpful	Have not experienced
Deciding on what kind of WHA project would be best for the community						
Yourself	1	2	3	4	5	0
Community	1	2	3	4	5	0
Committee	1	2	3	4	5	0
Partner Agency	1	2	3	4	5	0
Deciding what kind of project organizational structure to use						
Yourself	1	2	3	4	5	0
Community	1	2	3	4	5	0
Committee	1	2	3	4	5	0
Partner Agency	1	2	3	4	5	0
Deciding what kind of project administration to use						
Yourself	1	2	3	4	5	0
Community	1	2	3	4	5	0
Committee	1	2	3	4	5	0
Partner Agency	1	2	3	4	5	0
Deciding what kind of evangelism strategy was appropriate to use						
Yourself	1	2	3	4	5	0
Community	1	2	3	4	5	0
Committee	1	2	3	4	5	0
Partner Agency	1	2	3	4	5	0
Considering alternative spending levels for these activities						
Yourself	1	2	3	4	5	0
Community	1	2	3	4	5	0
Committee	1	2	3	4	5	0
Partner Agency	1	2	3	4	5	0
Determining a funding amount that seemed most appropriate to achieve the project's goals						
Yourself	1	2	3	4	5	0
Community	1	2	3	4	5	0
Committee	1	2	3	4	5	0
Partner Agency	1	2	3	4	5	0

5. When preparing a new project proposal, the participatory evaluation process helps me consider how this new project will fit into:

	Never	Sometimes	Usually	Always	Does not apply Do not know
Our field office strategy	1	2	3	4	0
Our field office quota for new children in programs (CIP)	1	2	3	4	0
Our field office five-year plan	1	2	3	4	0
Our field office budget	1	2	3	4	0
WHA's strategy	1	2	3	4	0
WHA's budget	1	2	3	4	0
WHA's mission	1	2	3	4	0
Other:_____	1	2	3	4	0

6. Listed below are several activities you perform during a project visit, how helpful were the participatory evaluation techniques and skills in accomplishing these tasks?

	Hindered	Not very helpful	Somewhat helpful	Usually helpful	Very helpful	Have not experienced
Dialogue with the partner agency, project committee, director, staff, and community	1	2	3	4	5	0
Discuss concerns expressed	1	2	3	4	5	0
Clarify issues	1	2	3	4	5	0
Find new issues concerning community development	1	2	3	4	5	0
Observe project operations	1	2	3	4	5	0
Compare monthly project reports to milestone/plan of action reports	1	2	3	4	5	0
Compare months project reports to accounting records	1	2	3	4	5	0
Compare monthly project reports to the project's budget	1	2	3	4	5	0
Compare milestone reports to major expenditures	1	2	3	4	5	0
Compare evaluation records to the original evaluation plan	1	2	3	4	5	0
Note the community's progress towards achieving the project's goals	1	2	3	4	5	0
Note the activity level of specific tasks	1	2	3	4	5	0
Note the results of particular activities	1	2	3	4	5	0
Compare evangelism report to visit dialogue	1	2	3	4	5	0
Evaluate the operations, logistics, and coordination of this project	1	2	3	4	5	0
Assess what the project has been doing	1	2	3	4	5	0
Note the direction of the project	1	2	3	4	5	0
Give the people advice	1	2	3	4	5	0
Give them training	1	2	3	4	5	0
Review Sponsor Relations Department (SRD) correspondence for unresolved issues	1	2	3	4	5	0
Satisfy SRD discrepancies	1	2	3	4	5	0
Identify project discrepancies for their corrections	1	2	3	4	5	0
Discuss unresolved issues or discrepancies in the project	1	2	3	4	5	0
Involve the community members in these review and validation procedures	1	2	3	4	5	0
Reach a consensus	1	2	3	4	5	0
Agree to the next monthly plan	1	2	3	4	5	0
Other:_____	1	2	3	4	5	0

7. How helpful have you found the participatory evaluation techniques and skills to be when working with all people and incorporating the techniques as part of your:

	Hindered	Not very helpful	Somewhat helpful	Usually helpful	Very helpful	Have not experienced
Management responsibilities	1	2	3	4	5	0
Professional conduct	1	2	3	4	5	0
Personal ministry	1	2	3	4	5	0
Regular project practices	1	2	3	4	5	0
Routine project reporting	1	2	3	4	5	0
Other:_____	1	2	3	4	5	0

8. Listed below are some of the ways people who attended the workshops have used the participatory evaluation techniques in their work. Based on your experience, how would you rate the helpfulness of these techniques for each of the following items:

	Hindered	Not very helpful	Somewhat helpful	Usually helpful	Very helpful	Have not experienced
Integrate my ministry work with co-workers, community members, and others who share responsibility for this project	1	2	3	4	5	0
Integrate my management tasks	1	2	3	4	5	0
Recognize measurable, operating plans related to project goals	1	2	3	4	5	0
Measure improvements	1	2	3	4	5	0
Continuously monitor project activities	1	2	3	4	5	0
Assess my task in the project	1	2	3	4	5	0
Supervise the project	1	2	3	4	5	0
Make assessments for the Project Planning Workbook checklist	1	2	3	4	5	0
Make judgments for the checklist	1	2	3	4	5	0
Document the checklist	1	2	3	4	5	0
Review changes in the original plan	1	2	3	4	5	0
Prepare other project documents	1	2	3	4	5	0
Identify key success areas	1	2	3	4	5	0
Focus my efforts on critical issues	1	2	3	4	5	0
Recognize when the community has accepted the project as their own enterprise	1	2	3	4	5	0
Incorporate result measures in my routine reporting	1	2	3	4	5	0
Recognize when technical assistance was needed	1	2	3	4	5	0
Realize when training was needed	1	2	3	4	5	0
Maximize local responsibility for the project	1	2	3	4	5	0
Understand the values of the community	1	2	3	4	5	0
Understand values of the partner agency	1	2	3	4	5	0
Understand my own values	1	2	3	4	5	0
Enhance my relationship with the people involved	1	2	3	4	5	0
Be sensitive to my own behaviors during participation	1	2	3	4	5	0
Create an environment in which people can express themselves and grow	1	2	3	4	5	0
Other:_____	1	2	3	4	5	0

9. Based on your experience with the baseline survey techniques, to what extent do you agree or disagree with the following statements?

	Strongly disagree	Disagree	Agree	Strongly agree
The community's baseline surveys were adequate for our needs	1	2	3	4
More socio-economic-religious information was needed than was obtained by the community in the baseline surveys	1	2	3	4
I know how to use the techniques well enough to collect meaningful data	1	2	3	4
The use of special evaluators would be wise for baseline assessments rather than the local community	1	2	3	4
Other:_____	1	2	3	4

10. You were asked to make evaluation reports to the Field Director and Evaluation Departments. Some people have used the following words or phrases to describe the reporting requirements for the participatory evaluation process. Please indicate what your experience has been:

	Strongly disagree	Disagree	Agree	Strongly agree
Allowed for in-depth information	1	2	3	4
Helped me to make headway in solving the problems addressed in this project	1	2	3	4
Laborious	1	2	3	4
Required no extra time	1	2	3	4
Time consuming	1	2	3	4
Too tedious	1	2	3	4
Unrealistic	1	2	3	4
Worth the time	1	2	3	4
Other:_____	1	2	3	4

11. For each of the following statements, indicate the level to which you agree or disagree with it based on your experience using the participatory evaluation techniques in projects.

	Strongly disagree	Disagree	Agree	Strongly agree
I have flexibility to adapt and develop methods suitable to my project and area	1	2	3	4
I have adequate skills to use the participatory evaluation techniques with the community	1	2	3	4
Process takes too much time	1	2	3	4
Process takes patience	1	2	3	4
The workshop is not enough training; I need more	1	2	3	4
I am not comfortable with the techniques and process	1	2	3	4
I have difficulty with the techniques and process	1	2	3	4
The workshop helped me establish an understanding of evaluation	1	2	3	4
I plan to use these techniques in other projects	1	2	3	4
I am more committed to this project	1	2	3	4
This process helps me be more effective in doing the work God has called me to do	1	2	3	4

12. From your experiences after using the participatory evaluation techniques in this project and compared to other projects in which you are involved, do you agree or disagree with the following statements?

	Strongly disagree	Disagree	Agree	Strongly agree
a. The community shows:				
resistance to the process	1	2	3	4
indifference to the process	1	2	3	4
enthusiasm for the process	1	2	3	4
b. The partner agency shows:				
resistance to the process	1	2	3	4
indifference to the process	1	2	3	4
enthusiasm for the process	1	2	3	4
c. Responsibility is enhanced for:				
myself	1	2	3	4
community	1	2	3	4
committee	1	2	3	4
partner agency	1	2	3	4
field office	1	2	3	4
WHA	1	2	3	4
d. The community people involved feel:				
independent	1	2	3	4
respected	1	2	3	4
in control	1	2	3	4
closer to one another	1	2	3	4
e. The information flow is improved:				
between the community and me	1	2	3	4
within the community	1	2	3	4
with the partner agency	1	2	3	4
within WHA	1	2	3	4
f. The community appears to:				
be more informed	1	2	3	4
be more involved	1	2	3	4
be more accountable	1	2	3	4
be more interested	1	2	3	4
have more realistic expectations	1	2	3	4
better understand why the project is being done	1	2	3	4
use their evaluation information in				
carrying out the project	1	2	3	4
routinely consider project results	1	2	3	4
take corrective action sooner	1	2	3	4
more readily recognize changes resulting				
from the project	1	2	3	4
g. The partner agency appears to:				
be more informed	1	2	3	4
be more involved	1	2	3	4
be more accountable	1	2	3	4
be more interested	1	2	3	4
have more realistic expectations	1	2	3	4
more readily recognize changes resulting				
from the project	1	2	3	4
feel ignored in the process	1	2	3	4

13. Based on your experience after using the participatory
    evaluation techniques in this project and compared to other
    projects in which you are involved, when the community
    designs their own evaluation plan together using the
    participatory evaluation techniques, do you agree or disagree
    with the following statements?

	Strongly disagree	Disagree	Agree	Strongly agree
They identify more potentials and possibilities for the project	1	2	3	4
Project plans are clearer	1	2	3	4
Project activities are more related to the goals	1	2	3	4
Project activities are more compatible with the community's talents and resources	1	2	3	4
Activity outcomes measure progress	1	2	3	4
Project results are more relevant to the community	1	2	3	4
Who is responsible for outcomes is clearer	1	2	3	4
Communities are more incorporated into the project rather than just receiving the project	1	2	3	4
Willingness to make decisions shifts to the community	1	2	3	4
Decision process changes within the community	1	2	3	4
The project's power structure shifts to the community	1	2	3	4
The project's power relationships are altered within the community	1	2	3	4
Understanding is increased among and with all the participants	1	2	3	4
Team building is increased within the project	1	2	3	4
Mutual trust increased	1	2	3	4
The local people begin to realize and experience the outcomes of their decisions	1	2	3	4
The possibility of eventual turnover of the project to the local people is increased	1	2	3	4

14. I have used the participatory evaluation techniques and
    skills with the community for:

	Never	Sometimes	Usually	Always	Does not apply Do not know
Project planning	1	2	3	4	0
Project plan of action	1	2	3	4	0
Project funding	1	2	3	4	0
Project budgeting/resource allocation	1	2	3	4	0
Project administration	1	2	3	4	0
Project assessing outcomes/results	1	2	3	4	0
Project revisions	1	2	3	4	0
Project improvements	1	2	3	4	0
Other: _____	1	2	3	4	0

15. Now that you have used the participatory evaluation techniques and experienced the process with the community, do you agree or disagree with the following conclusions?

	Strongly disagree	Disagree	Agree	Strongly agree
This process is a tool to help communities make decisions for the future	1	2	3	4
This process allows anyone from the community who wishes to be involved to speak out about the project	1	2	3	4
The process allows the community participants to consider the needs of *all* the community members in general who may be affected by the project	1	2	3	4
Conflicts of interest *increase* between WHA standards and the community's desires	1	2	3	4
I feel closer to the people in this project	1	2	3	4
The techniques will be a window to help WHA better see the realities of the world it wants to help	1	2	3	4
The whole process has been worth:				
the efforts required	1	2	3	4
the time for visits	1	2	3	4
the preparation of materials	1	2	3	4
the committee meetings	1	2	3	4
the journal-keeping	1	2	3	4
The participatory evaluation process has really helped community members to participate in their own development	1	2	3	4

PLEASE BE SURE TO ANSWER THE QUESTIONS IN PART 16 ON THE NEXT PAGE
SO WE CAN SHARE WITH YOU THE INFORMATION WE HAVE GATHERED

16. Information About You

All the information requested in this questionnaire will be held in confidence by the independent researcher. All of the results will be reported using aggregate or grouped responses. No information will be disclosed about individuals or their responses. The following information will be used to group the replies and to analyze the responses. Your name, title, and office will be used to mail you the results and ask your help again as together we monitor the evaluation activities.

Name (optional)_____ Office (optional)_____
Job Title_____._____
Name of project(s) where participatory evaluation is being used_____
How long have you been involved with this project(s)?_____
How long have you been in your current position?_____
How long have you been with WHA?_____
Sex: M_____ F_____ Age: Under 20_____ 21-35_____ 36-50_____ 51-65_____ Over 65_____
Educational attainment: Level (check/tick)   Location

Primary   _____   _____
Elementary   _____   _____
Secondary   _____   _____
University   _____   _____

Thank you for the time, thought, energy, ideas, and opinions you have shared with us. We appreciate your contribution to helping us get to know one another better and the ministry work we are doing. We will inform you of the results and ask for your help again, as together we analyze each other's responses and share each other's concerns.

APPENDIX B

Confidence Interval Derivations

The purpose of this appendix is to describe the confidence intervals presented in the text. To discover which characteristics and parameters are of most importance to the participatory evaluation process and to the management control process, confidence intervals were constructed for each questionnaire and its respective sample size. The purpose of these intervals was to determine if the spread between mean-value scores of response items representing similar evaluation characteristics was statistically significant.

In Chapters IV and V of the text, the confidence intervals presented compare different response items within one questionnaire in order to sort and classify items representing various evaluation components, functions, and characteristics. In Chapter IV, expectations questionnaire response items are compared and classified; and in Chapter V the experience questionnaire response items are compared and classified.

The purpose of these intervals was to determine if the spread between mean-value scores of response items representing similar evaluation characteristics and components was statistically significant. To be statistically significant at the .05 probability level, t must be greater than or equal to ($\geq$) 1.96 where t is:

$$(B.1) \qquad t = \frac{\overline{X_1} - \overline{X_2}}{\sqrt{\dfrac{S_1^2}{N_1} + \dfrac{S_2^2}{N_2} - \dfrac{2rS_1S_2}{N}}} \geq 1.96$$

and where,

$\bar{X}$ = the mean-value scores of a response item
S = the standard error of response items
N = the number of respondents
r = the intercorrelation between response items

An adjustment in the t value is required according to the correlation between the response items at issue. The response items in these samples are intercorrelated positively, which means that the t value denominator in equation (B.1) decreases. Therefore, smaller differences between mean-value scores will be statistically significant, as opposed to the case of uncorrelated response items.

In this research, the standard deviations were generally less than or equal to ($\leq$) 1.0. Where the standard deviation (SD) is equal to 1.0, and variance is $SD^2=(1)^2=1$, the numerical working formula for these response items was as follows:

$$(B.2) \qquad t = \frac{\bar{X}_1 - \bar{X}_2}{\sqrt{\dfrac{1}{N} + \dfrac{1}{N} - \dfrac{2r}{N}}}$$

$$= \frac{\bar{X}_1 - \bar{X}_2}{\sqrt{\dfrac{2 - 2r}{N}}}$$

$$= \frac{\bar{X}_1 - \bar{X}_2}{\sqrt{\dfrac{2(1 - r)}{N}}}$$

Under these conditions, for t to be statistically significant at $P \leq .05$, the derived value of t must be greater than 1.96 and $\bar{X}_1 - \bar{X}_2$ must be greater than

(B.3)
$$1.96\sqrt{\frac{2(1-r)}{N}}$$

For the expectations questionnaire with a sample size of N=320,

(B.4)
$$t = 1.96\sqrt{\frac{2(1-r)}{320}}$$

$$t = .155\sqrt{1-r}$$

Where r can be calculated (or estimated) for each group of response items being compared using the equation:

(B.5)
$$r = \frac{\sum (X_1 - \overline{X_1})(X_2 - \overline{X_2})}{\sqrt{\sum (X_1 - \overline{X_1})^2 \sum (X_2 - \overline{X_2})^2}}$$

With a large positive r, the differences between mean-value scores required for statistical significance would be very small. For example, in this sample population on organizational expectations, where r was estimated to be .15, then substituting that value into equation (B.4) yields:

(B.6)
$$t = .155\sqrt{1 - .15}$$

$$t = .143$$

Therefore, modest differences in mean-value scores from variable to variable (i.e. > .14) are statistically significant, even though the patterns underlying the response items could be very similar.

For the experience questionnaire with the sample size of N=73 using equation (B.3) yields:

$$\textbf{(B.7)} \qquad t = 1.96\sqrt{\frac{2(1 - r)}{73}}$$

$$t = .324\sqrt{1 - r}$$

With a positive r, the difference between mean-value scores required for statistical significance would again be small, but larger than the difference required for significance in the expectations questionnaire. For this sample population on organizational experiences, where r was also estimated to be .15, then substituting that value into equation (B.7) yields:

$$\textbf{(B.8)} \qquad t = .324\sqrt{1 - .15}$$

$$t = .299$$

Here again, modest differences in mean-value scores from response item to response item are statistically significant. As a practical matter, larger differences between response item mean-value scores are also statistically significant at the $P \le .05$. Therefore, the larger difference between mean-value scores, .30, was used to classify response items into confidence intervals for both the expectations and experience questionnaires where $N_1=320$ and where $N_2=73$.

Here the larger effect size difference in mean-value scores for the expectations questionnaire (i.e., .30 rather than .14) is a more stringent level of significance based on the larger sample size in this questionnaire. This allows the number of confidence intervals used to classify response items in the expectations questionnaire to be smaller, and it corresponds to the confidence interval size derived for the experience questionnaire which facilitates between questionnaire analysis of expectations and experiences.

BIBLIOGRAPHY

A. BOOKS

Adelman, Irma and C.T. Morris *Society, Politics and Economic Development*. Baltimore, Maryland: The Johns Hopkins Press, 1967.

Allen, Louis A. *Making Managerial Planning More Effective*. New York, New York, New York: McGraw-Hill Book Co., 1982.

American Accounting Association. *A Statement of Basic Accounting Theory*. Sarasota, Florida: American Accounting Association, 1966.

American Council of Voluntary Agencies for Foreign Service. *Evaluation Sourcebook*. New York, New York: American Council of Voluntary Agencies for Foreign Service, Inc., 1983.

Anthony, Robert N. *Planning and Control Systems—A Framework For Analysis*. Boston, Massachusetts: Division of Research, Harvard University, 1965.

_____. *Financial Accounting in Nonbusiness Organizations*. Stamford, Connecticut: Financial Accounting Standards Board, 1978.

Anthony, Robert N. and John Dearden *Management Control Systems—Text and Cases*. Homewood, Illinois: Richard D. Irwin, Inc., 1976.

Anthony, Robert N. and Regina E. Herzlinger *Management Control in Nonprofit Organizations*. Homewood, Illinois: Richard D. Irwin, Inc., 1980.

Argyris, Chris. *Integrating the Individual and the Organization*. New York, New York: John Wiley & Sons, Inc., 1964.

Belkaoui, Ahmed. *Conceptual Foundations of Management Accounting*. Reading, Massachusetts: Addison-Wesley Publishing Co., 1980.

Bigger, Charles P. *Participation, A Platonic Inquiry*. Baton Rouge, Louisiana: Louisiana State University Press, 1968.

277

Boone, Louis E. and Donald D. Bowen *The Great Writings in Management and Organizational Behavior.* Tulsa, Oklahoma: Penn Well Publishing Co., 1980.

Bower, Joseph L. *Managing the Resource Allocation Process.* Homewood, Illinois: Richard D. Irwin, Inc., 1970.

Bryk, Anthony S. *Stakeholder-based Evaluations.* San Francisco, California: Jossey-Bass Inc., 1983.

Campbell, Donald T. and Julian C. Stanley *Experimental and Quasi-Experimental Designs for Research.* Chicago, Illinois: Rand McNally and Company, 1966.

Caplan, Edwin H. *Management Accounting and Behavioral Science.* Reading, Massachusetts: Addison-Wesley Publishing Co., 1971.

Caplow, Theodore. *How To Run Any Organization.* Hinsdale, Illinois: The Dryden Press, 1976.

Christopher, William F. *Management for the 1980's.* Englewood Cliffs, New Jersey: Prentice-Hall, Inc., 1980.

Cohen, Jacob and Patricia Cohen *Applied Multiple Regression Correlation Analysis for the Behavioral Sciences.* New York, New York: John Wiley & Sons, 1975.

Costello, Timothy W. and Sheldon S. Zalkind *Psychology in Administration.* Englewood Cliffs, New Jersey: Prentice-Hall, Inc., 1963.

Cummings, L.L. and W.E. Scott Jr. *Readings in Organizational Behavior and Human Performance.* Homewood, Illinois: Richard D. Irwin, Inc. and The Dorsey Press, 1969.

D'Abreo, Desmond. *Ideology and Process of Participatory Evaluation.* New Delhi, India: Indian Social Institute, 1983.

Dermer, Jerry. *Management Planning and Control Systems.* Homewood, Illinois: Richard D. Irwin, Inc., 1977.

Douglas, Jack D. *Investigative Social Research.* Beverly Hills, California: Sage Publications, Inc., 1976.

Drucker, Peter F. *The Practice of Management.* Cavaye, London: Pan Books, 1955.

_____. *Management Tasks, Responsibilities, Practices.* New York, New York: Harper & Row, 1974.

_____. *The Changing World of the Executive.* New York, New York: Times Books, a division of Random House, Inc., 1982.

_____. *Innovation and Entrepreneurship.* New York, New York: Harper & Row, Publishers, Inc., 1985.

Emory, C. William. *Business Research Methods.* Homewood, Illinois: Richard D. Irwin, Inc., 1976.

Erdos, Paul L. *Professions Mail Surveys.* New York, New York: McGraw-Hill Book Co., 1970.

Euske, Kenneth J. *Management Control: Planning, Control, Measurement, and Evaluation.* Reading, Massachusetts: Addison-Wesley Publishing Co., 1984.

Filley, Alan C., Robert J. House, and Steven Kerr *Managerial Process and Organizational Behavior.* Glenview, Illinois: Scott, Foresman and Co., 1976.

Financial Accounting Standards Board. *Accounting Standards Original Pronouncements July 1973-June 1, 1984.* New York, New York: McGraw-Hill Book Co., 1984-85 Edition.

Gambino, Anthony J. and Thomas J. Reardon *Financial Planning and Evaluation for the Nonprofit Organization.* New York, New York: National Association of Accountants, 1981.

Greenleaf, Robert K. *Servant Leadership.* New York, New York: Paulist Press, 1977.

Guba, Egon G. and Yvonna S. Lincoln *Effective Evaluation.* San Francisco, California: Jossey-Bass, Inc., 1981.

Hopwood, Anthony G. *An Accounting System and Managerial Behaviour.* Lexington, Massachusetts: Lexington Books, D. C. Heath & Co., 1973.

_____. *Accounting and Human Behaviour.* London, England: Haymarket Publishing Limited, 1974.

Hutchinson, John G. *Readings in Management Strategy and Tactics.* New York, New York: Holt, Rinehart and Winston, Inc., 1971.

Jellema, William W., ed. *Institutional Priorities & Management Objectives.* Association of American Colleges, 1971.

Jones, W. T. *The Sciences and the Humanities, Conflict and Reconciliation.* Berkeley, California: University of California Press, 1965.

Judd, Charles M. and David A. Kenny *Estimating the Effects of Social Interventions.* Cambridge, England: Cambridge University Press, 1981.

Katz, Daniel and Robert L. Kahn *The Social Psychology Of Organizations.* New York, New York: John Wiley & Sons, Inc., 1966.

Kerlinger, Fred N. *Foundations of Behavioral Research.* New York, New York: Holt, Rinehart and Winston, Inc., 1964.

King, Bert, Siegfried Streufert, and Fred E. Fiedler, eds. *Managerial Control and Organizational Democracy.* New York, New York: John Wiley & Sons, 1978.

Koontz, Harold and Cyril O'Donnell *MANAGEMENT: A Book of Readings.* New York, New York: McGraw-Hill Book Co., 1972.

_____. *MANAGEMENT A Systems and Contingency Analysis of Managerial Functions.* New York, New York: McGraw-Hill Book Co., 1976.

Krone, Robert M. *Systems Analysis and Policy Sciences.* New York, New York: John Wiley & Sons, 1980.

Levinson, Harry. *Organizational Diagnosis.* Cambridge, Massachusetts: Harvard University Press, 1972.

Leys, Wayne A. R. *Ethics for Policy Decisions.* New York, New York: Prentice-Hall, Inc., 1952.

Likert, Rensis. *New Patterns of Management.* New York, New York: McGraw-Hill Book Co., Inc., 1961.

_____. *The Human Organization.* New York, New York: McGraw-Hill Book Co., 1967.

Lofland, John. *Doing Social Life.* New York, New York: John Wiley & Sons, 1976.

Maciariello, Joseph A. *Program-Management Control Systems.* New York, New York: John Wiley & Sons, 1978.

_____. *Management Control Systems.* Englewood Cliffs, New Jersey: Prentice-Hall, Inc., 1984.

McGregor, Douglas. *The Human Side of Enterprise.* New York, New York: McGraw-Hill Book Co., Inc., 1960.

Massie, Joseph L. and Jan Luytjes *Management in an International Context.* New York, New York: Harper & Row, Publishers, Inc., 1972.

Mazmanian, Daniel A. and Jeanne Nienaber *Can Organizations Change? Washington, D.C.:* The Brookings Institution, 1979.

Nadler, Gerald. *The Planning and Design Approach.* New York, New York: John Wiley & Sons., 1981.

Naisbitt, John. *Megatrends.* New York, New York, New York: Warner Books, Inc., 1984.

Newman, William H., Charles E. Summer, and E. Kirby Warren *The Process of Management.* Englewood Cliffs, New Jersey: Prentice-Hall, Inc., 1972.

Nie, Norman H., C. Hadlai Hull, Jean C. Jenkins, Karin Steinbrenner, and Dale H. Bent *Statistical Package for the Social Sciences.* New York, New York: McGraw-Hill Book Co., 1975.

Patton, Michael Q., *Creative Evaluation,* Beverly Hills, California: Sage Publications, 1981.

_____. *Practical Evaluation,* Beverly Hills, California: Sage Publications, 1982.

Paxton, John, *The Statesman's Yearbook,* New York, New York: St. Martin's Press, 1985.

Perrow, Charles. *Complex Organizations, A Critical Essay.* Dallas, Texas: Scott, Foresman and Co., 1972.

Pollard, Harold R. *Trends in Management Thinking 1960-1970.* Houston, Texas: Gulf Publishing Co., 1978.

Ramanathan, Kavasseri V. *Management Control in Nonprofit Organizations.* New York, New York: John Wiley & Sons, 1982.

Rivers, William L. *Finding Facts.* Englewood Cliffs, New Jersey, New Jersey: Prentice-Hall, Inc., 1975.

Roethlisberger, F.J. *The Elusive Phenomena.* Boston, Massachusetts: Division of Research, Harvard University, 1977.

Rossi, Peter H., Howard E. Freeman, and Sonia R. Wright *Evaluation—Systematic Approach.* Beverly Hills, California: Sage Publications, 1979.

Russell, Bertrand. *A History of Western Philosophy.* New York, New York: Simon and Schuster, 1945.

Schiff, Michael and Arie Y. Lewin *Behavioral Aspects of Accounting.* Englewood Cliffs, New Jersey: Prentice-Hall, Inc., 1974.

Simon, Herbert A. *Administrative Behavior.* New York, New York: The Macmillan Co., 1960.

Soderstrum, Edward J., *Social Impact Assessment,* New York, New York: Praeger Publishers, 1981.

Steers, Richard M. *Organizational Effectiveness, A Behavioral View.* Santa Monica, California: Goodyear Publishing Co., Inc., 1977.

Stone, Eugene F. *Research Methods in Organizational Behavior.* Glenview, Illinois: Scott, Foresman and Company, 1978.

Stuckenbruck, Linn C., ed. *The Implementation of Project Management: The Professional's Handbook*. Reading, Massachusetts: Addison-Wesley Publishing Co., 1981.

Tannenbaum, Arnold S. *Control in Organizations*. New York, New York: McGraw-Hill Book Company, 1968.

_____. Tannenbaum, Arnold S., Bogdan Kavcic, Menachem Rosner, Mino Vianello, and Georg Wieser *Hierarchy in Organizations*. San Francisco, California: Jossey-Bass Publishers, 1974.

Thomas, William E. *Cost Accounting, Budgeting, and Control*. Cincinnati, Ohio: Southwestern Publishing Company, 1978.

Thompson, James D. *Organizations in Action*. New York, New York: McGraw-Hill Book Co., 1967.

Walker, Helen M. and Joseph Lev *Statistical Inference*. New York, New York: Holt, Rinehart and Winston, 1953.

Weiss, Carol H. *Evaluation Research*. Englewood Cliffs, New Jersey: Prentice-Hall Inc., 1972.

Wheelen, Thomas L. and J. David Hunger *Strategic Management*. Reading, Massachusetts: Addison-Wesley Publishing Co., 1984.

Zedeck, Sheldon and Milton R. Blood *Foundations of Behavioral Science Research in Organizations*. Monterey, California: Brooks/Cole Publishing Co., 1974.

B. REPORTS

American Institute of Certified Public Accountants. *Objectives of Financial Statements*. New York, New York, New York: American Institute of Certified Public Accountants, 1973.

Buckley, John W.; Buckley, Marlene H.; and Chiang, Hung-Fu. *Research Methodology & Business Decisions*. New York, New York: National Association of Accountants, and Hamilton, Ontario, Canada: The Society of Industrial Accountants of Canada, 1976.

Drew, David E., "Science Development," A Technical Report presented to the National Board on Graduate Education, Report No. 4, June 1975.

O'Connor, Rochelle. *Managing Corporate Development*. A Research Report from The Conference Board. New York, New York, New York: The Conference Board, Inc. 1980.

_____. *Evaluating The Company Planning System and the Corporate Planner*. New York, New York: The Conference Board, 1982.

Population Council. *Studies In Family Planning*. New York, New York: Population Council, 1981.

World Bank, "World Development Report," 1983, Published for The World Bank by Oxford University Press, July 1984.

C. ARTICLES

Adelman, Irma and Cynthia Taft Morris, "Performance Criteria For Evaluating Economic Development Potential: An Operational Approach," *Quarterly Journal of Economics*, Winter 1968, pp. 260-280.

Baumgartel, Howard, Luther E. Dunn, and George I. Sullivan, "Management Education, Company Climate, and Innovation," *Journal of General Management, Winter 1976/77, pp.* 17-26.

Benke, Ralph L. and W. Timothy O'Keefe, "Organizational Behavior and Operating Budgets," *Cost and Management Journal, July-August 1980, pp.* 21-27.

Bernhart, Michael H., "Using Model Projects to Introduce Change into Family Planning Programs," *Studies In Family Planning, October 1981, pp.* 346-352.

Bloom, Howard S. and Susan E. Philipson Bloom, "Household Participation In The Section 8 Existing Housing Program: Evaluating A Multistage Selection Process," *Evaluation Review*, June 1981, pp. 325-340.

Baner, David K., "The Politics of Evaluation Research," *Omega*, The International Journal of Management Science, December, 1974, pp. 763-774.

Booth, John A. and Mitchell A. Seligson, "Peasants as Activists: A Reevaluation of Political Participation in the Countryside," *Comparative Political Studies*, Vol. 12, No. 1, April 1975, pp. 29-59.

Bozeman, Barry and Jane Massey, "Investing in Policy Evaluations: Some Guidelines for Skeptical Public Managers," *Public Management Forum. May/June*, 1982, pp. 264-270.

Browne, Edmond Jr. and John Rehfuss, "Policy Evaluation, Citizen Participation, and Revenue Sharing in Aurora, Illinois," *Public Administration Review*, Vol. 35, No. 2, March/April 1975, pp. 150-157.

Brownell, Peter, "The Role of Accounting Data in Performance Evaluation, Budgetary Participation, and Organizational Effectiveness," *Journal of Accounting Research*, Vol. 20, No. 1, Spring 1982, pp. 12-27.

Bruckman, John C., "Program Evaluation: Myth or Reality?" *National Productivity Review*, Vol. 2, No. 4, Autumn 1983, pp. 371-375.

Buckley, John W., "Accounting Policy and Impact Analysis," Working Paper No. 75-14, Accounting and Information Systems Research Program, University of California, Los Angeles.

Cain, Bonnie J., "Participatory Research: Research With Historic Consciousness," Working Paper No. 3, International Council For Adult Education, 1978.

Camillus, John C. and John H. Grant, "Operational Planning: The Integration of Programming and Budgeting," *Academy of Management Review*, July 1980, pp. 369-379.

Campbell, Donald T., "Focal Local Indicators For Social Program Evaluation," *Social Indicators Research*, 1976, pp. 237-256.

Chacko, Thomas I., Thomas H. Stone, and Arthur P. Brief, "Participation in Goal-Setting Programs: An Attributional Analysis," *Academy of Management Review*, June 1979, pp. 433-436.

Chandler, Robert E., "The Statistical Concepts of Confidence and Significance," *Psychological Bulletin*, Vol. 54, 1957, pp. 429-431.

Clark, Terry Nichols, "Modes of Collective Decision Making: Eight Criteria for Evaluation of Representatives, Referenda, Participation, and Surveys," *Policy and Politics*, Vol. 4, 1976, pp. 13-22.

Cohn, Myrna L., "Crystal Lake: An Evaluation Research Design of an Organization Development Project In A Field Setting," *Academy of Management Proceedings*, 1977, pp. 338-342.

Communications, "Client Participation in the Evaluation of a Residential Treatment Program," *Journal of Applied Behavioral Analysis*, November 1978, p. 124.

Conlon, Edward J. and Gerrit Wolf, "The Moderating Effects of Strategy, Visibility, and Involvement on Allocation Behavior: An Extension of Straw's Escalation Paradigm," *Organizational Behavior and Human Performance*, 1980, pp. 172-192.

Culbertson, Hugh M., "Public Relations Ethics: A New Look," *Public Relations Quarterly*, Winter 1973, pp. 15-24.

Dachler, H. Peter and Bernhard Wilpert, "Conceptual Dimensions and Boundaries of Participation in Organizations: A Critical Evaluation," *Administrative Science Quarterly*, March 1978, Vol. 23, pp. 1-34.

Daneke, Gregory A, "Implementation: The Missing Link Discovered?," *International Journal of Public Administration*, Vol. 2, No. 1, 1980, pp. 25-49.

Daneke, Gregory A. and Patricia Klobus-Edwards, "Survey Research for Public Administrators," *Public Administration Review*, Sept/Oct 1979, pp. 421-426.

Darney, Philip D., "Fertility Decline and Participation in Georgia's Family Planning Program: Temporal and Areal Associations," *Studies in Family Planning*, Vol. 6. No. 6, 1975, pp. 156-165.

Dekbecq, Andre' L., "Negotiating Mandates Which Increase the Acceptance of Evaluation Findings Concerning Demonstration Programs," Academy of Management Proceedings 35th Annual Meeting, August 1975.

Dery, David, "Evaluation and Problem Redefinition," *Journal of Public Policy*, Vol. 2, No. 1, February 1982, pp. 23-30.

Dinkle, Nancy R., Joan Wagner Zinobur, and Eugenie Walsh Flaherty, "Citizen Participation in CMHC Program Evaluation: A Neglected Potential," *Community Mental Health Journal*, Spring 1981, pp. 54-65.

Drew, David E., "Evaluation: A New Discipline," Unpublished paper, March 1979.

_____. "Multivariate Ocularmetrics: Graphing Multiple Time Series Residual Data," Unpublished paper, March 1980.

Drew, David E. and Emmett Keeler, "Algorithms for Health Planners: Vol. 6, Hypertension," prepared for the Health Resources Administration, Dept. of Health, Education, and Welfare, August 1977.

Drew, David E. and Mary Ann Plant Law, "Design of an Evaluation of The Experimental Program to Stimulate Competitive Research in Selected States," Unpublished paper, May 1979.

Dunham, Randall B., Frank J. Smith, and Richard S. Blackburn, "Validation of the Index of Organizational Reactions With the JDI, the MSQ, and Faces Scales," *Academy of Management Journal*, Vol. 20, No. 3, September 1977, pp. 420-432.

Engstrom, Ted, "A Vision For the World," *New Wine*, December 1983, pp. 4-10.

Ernest, Manfred, "Attitudes of Diplomats at the United Nations: The Effects of Organizational Participation on the Evaluation of the Organization,"*International Organization*, Autumn 1978, pp. 1037-1044.

Ertel, Madge O., "A Survey Research Evaluation of Citizen Participation Strategies," *American Geophysical Union*, Vol. 15, No. 4, August 1979, pp. 757-762.

Fabrikant, Richard and Hugh D. Grove, "Outcome Measurement and Resource Allocation in Non Profit Enterprises," Unpublished 1980.

Feuerstein, Marie-Therese, "Participatory Evaluation—An Appropriate Technology for Community Health Programmes," *Contact 55*, February 1980, pp. 1-8.

_____. "Participatory Evaluation: By, With, and For the People," *Idea*, RRDC Bulletin, March 1982, pp. 18-23.

Flaherty, Eugenie Walsh and Charles Windle, "Mandated Evaluation in Community Mental Health Centers: Framework for a New Policy," *Evaluation Review*, October 1981, pp. 620-638.

Flamholtz, Eric G., "The Process of Measurement in Managerial Accounting: A Psycho-Technical Systems Perspective," *Accounting Organizations and Society*, 1980, pp. 31-42.

Franklin, E. Gene, George Hayduk, Michael Corbett, "Public Attitudes Towards Community Service Needs and Government in Indiana," *Midwest Review of Public Administration*, June 1979, pp. 119-131.

Freeman, Howard E. and Peter H. Rossi, "Social Experiments," *Health and Society*, Summer 1981, pp. 340-373.

Gambling, Trevor, "Magic, Accounting and Morale," *Accounting Organization*, and Society, Vol. 2, No. 2, pp. 144-151.

Gardner, Godfrey, "Workers' Participation: A Critical Evaluation of Coch and French," *Human Relations*, Vol. 30, No. 12, 1977, pp. 1071-1078.

Gavin, James F. and S. Morton McPhail, "Intervention and Evaluation: A Proactive Team Approach to OD," *The Journal of Applied Behavioral Science*, Spring 1972, pp. 175-194.

Gottman, John M., Richard M. McFall, and Jean T. Barnett, "Design and Analysis of Research Using Time Series," *Psychological Bulletin*, Vol, 72, No. 4, 1969, pp. 229-306.

Greer, Thomas V. and Joanne G. Greer, "Problems in Evaluating Cost and Benefits of Social Problems," *Public Administration Review*, March/April, 1982, pp. 151-156.

Griesinger, Donald W., "Management Theory: A Cybernetic Perspective," Unpublished paper, January 1986.

Hargrove, Erwin C., "The Bureaucratic Politics of Evaluation: A Case Study of the Department of Labor," *Public Administrative Review*, March/April 1980, pp. 150-159.

Hite, James, "Commentary on Participation in Statewide 208 Water Quality Planning in North Carolina: An Evaluation," by David R. Godschalk and Bruce Stiftel, *Annals of Regional Science*, 1982, pp. 130-131.

Hofstede, Geert, "The Poverty of Management Control Philosophy," *Academy of Management Review*, July 1978, pp. 450-461.

Irland, Lloyd C., "Citizen Participation—A Tool for Conflict Management on the Public Lands," *Public Administration Review*, May/June 1975, pp. 263-269.

Jemelka, Ron P. and Gary D. Borich, "Traditional and Emerging Definitions of Educational Evaluation," *Evaluation Quarterly*, Volume 3, No. 2, May 1979, pp. 263-276.

Johnston, Bruce F. and William C. Clark, "Organization Programs: Institutional Structures and Managerial Procedures," *Redesigning Rural Development*, The Johns Hopkins University Press, Baltimore, Maryland, 1982, p. 311.

Kamieniecki, Sheldon and Michael Clark, "Organization Theory, Evaluation Research, and the Effectiveness of Citizen Advisory Bodies," *International Journal of Public Administration*, Vol. 4, No. 1, 1982, pp. 81-98.

Kaplan, Rachel, "Citizen Participation in the Design and Evaluation of a Park," *Environment and Behavior*, December 1980, pp. 494-507.

Kaplan, Robert S., "The Role for Empirical Research in Management Accounting," Working Paper 9-785-001, Harvard Business School, Rev. 1985.

Kenis, Izzettin, "Effects of Budgeting Goal Characteristics on Managerial Attitudes and Performance," *The Accounting Review*, October 1979, pp. 707-721.

Kerzner, Harold, "Evaluation Techniques in Project Management," *Journal of Systems Management*, February 1980, pp. 10-19.

King, John L., "Cost-benefit Analysis for Decision Making," *Journal of Systems Management*, May 1980, pp. 24-29.

Kinkead, Gwen, "Humana's Hard-Sell Hospitals," *Fortune*, November, 17, 1980.

Knowles, Malcolm S., "Human Resources Development in OD," *Public Administration Review*, March/April 1974, pp. 115-123.

Kovach, Kenneth A., Ben F. Sands, Jr., and William W. Brooks, "Management By Whom?—Trends in Participative Management," *S.A.M. Advance Management Journal*, Winter 1981, pp. 4-14.

Laczniak, Gene R. and Anne Curley, "Public Participation in Rulemaking by the Federal Trade Commission: A Survey of Some Recent Experiences," *The Journal of Consumer Affairs*, Summer 1981, pp. 32-45.

Long, Robert H., "Values Clarification: A Highway to Success," *The Magazine of Bank Administration*, September 1980, pp. 8-12.

Lord, Frederic M., "Do Tests of the Same Length Have the Same Standard Error of Measurement?" *Principles of Educational and Psychological Measurement*, Rand McNally & Company, Chicago, Illinois, 1967, pp. 193-197.

Magee, Robert P., "Equilibria in Budget Participation," *Journal of Accounting Research*, Autumn 1980, pp. 551-573.

Martin, Merle P., "Use of Regression and Correlation-Part 3," *Journal of Systems Management*, August, 1980.

Maynard-Moody, Steven, "Reconsidering Charity: Some Possible Negative Effects of Evaluation Research," *Administration and Society*, February 1982, pp. 379-403.

Mazmanian, Daniel, "Participatory Democracy in a Federal Agency," *Water Politics and Public Involvement*, Harvey Dickerson and John Pierce, (eds), *Ann Arbor Science*, 1976.

McKenna, Eugene F., "An Analysis of Leadership Patterns in the Finance Function," *Accounting Organization and Behavior*, 1980, pp. 297-310.

McPike-Smith, Gerald, "Management Planning Systems and Information Models," *Accountants Record*, August 1980, pp. 8-10.

Merryfield, Merry, "The Challenge of Cross-Cultural Evaluation: Some views from the Field," Unpublished Manuscript, Africa Studies Program, Indiana University, February 1984, pp. 1-46.

Milani, Ken, "The Relationship of Participation in Budget-Setting to Industrial Supervisor Performance and Attitudes: A Field Study," *Accounting Review*, April 1975, pp. 274-284.

Mintzberg, Henry, "Organization Design: Fashion or Fit?" *Harvard Business Review*, January/February 1981, pp. 103-116.

Mock, Theodore J., "Concepts of Information Value and Accounting," *The Accounting Review*, October 1971, pp. 765-778.

Moles, Jerry A., "What Does One Say To A Naked Lady? Validity, Variability, and Data Collection: A Peruvian Example," *Journal of Anthropological Research*, Vol. 34, No. 2, Summer 1978, pp. 263-290.

Neave, Edwin H. and Edward R. Peterson, "A Comparison of Optimal and Adaptive Decision Mechanisms in an Organizational Setting," *Management Science*, August 1980, pp. 810-822.

Nelson, Don A., "More Effective Strategic Planning For Organizations," *The CPA Journal*, May 1984, pp. 18-23.

Newman, D. Paul, "Prospect Theory Implications for Information Evaluation," *Accounting Organization and Society*, Vol. 5, No. 2, pp. 217-230.

Nichols, John M., "Evaluation Research in Organizational Change Interventions: Considerations and Some Suggestions," *The Journal of Applied Behavioral Science*, Winter, 1979, pp. 23-40.

Nunnally, Jum, "The Place of Statistics in Psychology," *Educational and Psychological Measurement*, Vol. 20, 1960, pp. 641-647.

Nutt, Paul Charles, "On the Quality and Acceptance of Plans Drawn by A Consortium," *The Journal of Applied Behavioral Science*, Winter 1979, pp. 7-21.

Oliver, Rodney A., "An Evaluation of the Use Mode of Evaluation Research In A National Tourist Board," *Journal of Marketing Research Society*, October 1977, pp. 151-166.

Otley, David T., "Budget Use and Managerial Performance," *Journal of Accounting Review*, Vol. 16, No. 1, Spring 1978, pp. 122-148.

Pant, Niranjan, "Status, Participation, and Evaluation of Municipal Bureaucracy," *Indian Political Science Review*, February 1976, pp. 216-226.

Perkins, Dennis N. T., "Evaluating Social Interventions: A Conceptual Schema," *Evaluation Quarterly*, Vol. 1, No. 4, November 1977, pp. 639-657.

Peters, Tom and Nancy Austin, "A Passion For Excellence," *Fortune*, May 13, 1985, pp. 20-31.

Plebane, Louis P. and Hemant K. Jain, "Evaluating Research Proposals With Group Techniques," *Research Management*, November 1981, pp. 34-38.

Pratt, John W. and John S. Hammond III, "Evaluating and Comparing Projects: Simple Detection of False Alarms," *Journal of Finance*, December, 1979, pp. 1231-1242.

Putman, Anthony O., "Pragmatic Evaluation," *Training and Development Journal*, October 1980, pp. 36-40.

Ratcliffe, Thomas A. and David J. Logsdon, "The Business Planning Process—A Behavioral Perspective," *Managerial Planning*, March/April 1980, pp. 32-38.

Reen, Martin and Sheldon H. White, "Policy Research: Belief and Doubt," *Policy Analysis*, pp. 239-271.

Reimer, Douglas, "A Control System for Non-profit, Religious, Organizations," Unpublished working paper, 1982.

Ritchie, J. R. Brent, "Roles of Research in the Management Process," *MSU Business Topics*, Summer 1976, pp. 13-22.

Roberts, Paul Craig, "Overpopulation is Not the Third World's Worst Threat," *Business Week*, August 6, 1984, p. 10.

Rogers, H. G., M. A. Ulrich, and K. L. Traversy, "Evaluation in Practice: The State of the Art in Canadian Governments," *Canadian Public Administration*, Fall 1981, pp. 371-386.

Ronen, J. and J. L. Livingston, "An Expectancy Theory Approach to the Motivational Impacts of Budgets," *Accounting Review*, October 1975, pp. 671-685.

Rosener, Judy B., "Citizen Participation: Can We Measure Its Effectiveness?" *Public Administration Review*, September/October 1978, pp. 457-463.

_____. "User-Oriented Evaluation: A New Way to View Citizen Participation," *The Journal of Applied Behavioral Science*, Vol. 17, No. 4, October, November, December 1981, pp.583-596.

Rozeboom, William W., "The Fallacy of the Null-Hypothesis Significance Test," *Psychological Bulletin*, Vol. 57, 1960, pp. 417-428.

Ryan, Joseph E., "Profitability in the Non-Profit Environment," *Journal of Systems Management*, August 1980, pp. 6-10.

Sarsfield, E. William, "Evaluative Research: Progress Through Experimentation," *Government Executive*, March 1976, pp. 33-36.

Sewell, W. R. Derrick and Susan D. Phillips, "Models for the Evaluation of Public Participation Programmes," *Natural Resources Journal*, Vol. 19, April 1979, pp. 337-358.

Snowden, Maurice, "Measuring Performance in Capital Project Management," *Long Range Planning*, August 1980, pp. 51-55.

Sorenson, James E. and Hugh D. Grove, "Cost-Outcomes and Cost-Effectiveness Analysis: Emerging Non-Profit Performance Evaluation Techniques," *The Accounting Review*, July 1977, pp. 658-675.

Sorensen, James E. and A. Ronald Kucic, "Assessing the Cost-Outcomes and Cost-Effectiveness of Community Support Programs (CSP)," Unpublished, July 1981.

Strasser, Stephen, J. D. Eveland, Gaylord Cummins, O. Lynn Deniston, and John H. Romani, "Conceptualizing the Goal and System Models of Organization Effectiveness—Implications For Comparative Evaluation Research," *Journal of Management Studies*, July 1981, pp. 321-340.

Swan, John E., I. Fredrick Trawick, and Maxwell G. Carroll, "Effect of Participation in Marketing Research on Consumer Attitudes Toward Research and Satisfaction With the Service," *Journal of Marketing Research*, August 1981, pp. 356-363.

Swidorski, Carl, "Sample Surveys: Help For The 'Out-of-House' Evaluator," *Public Administration Review*, January/February 1980, pp. 67-71.

Terpstra, David E., "Relationship Between Methodological Rigor and Reported Outcomes in Organization Development Evaluation Research," *Journal of Applied Psychology*, October 1981, pp. 541-543.

Uecker, Wilfred C., "The Effects of Knowledge of the User's Decision Model in Simplified Information Evaluation," *Journal of Accounting Research*, Vol. 18, No. 1, Spring 1980.

Usry, Milton F., "Organizing Capital Expenditure Resource Allocation and Control Systems," *Managerial Planning*, May/June 1980, pp. 16-21.

Weinrott, Mark R, Richard R. Jones, and James R. Howard, "Cost-Effectiveness of Teaching Family Programs for Delinquents," (Results of a National Evaluation), *Evaluation Review*, Vol. 6, No. 2, April 1982, pp. 173-201.

Weiss, Carol H., "The Many Meanings of Research Utilization," *Public Administration Review*, September/ October 1979, pp. 426-431.

Wheelwright, Steven C. an Robert L. Banks, "Involving Operating Managers in Planning Process Evolution," *Sloan Management Review*, Summer 1979, pp. 43-59.

White, Reba, "What is Evaluation Research and Why are so Many Brokers Interested in it?" *Institutional Investor*, May 1977, pp. 37-39.

Willette, Joanne L. and Howard L. Fleischman, "Federal Legislation Accountability: Designing an Evaluation System," *Evaluation Review*, Vol. 6, No. 2, April 1982, pp. 155-171.

Williams, Jerre S., "An Evaluation of Public Participation," *Administrative Law Review*, Winter 1972, pp. 49-65.

Windle, Charles and Nancy C. Pashall, "Client Participation in CMHC Program Evaluation: Increasing Incidence, Inadequate Involvement," *Community Health Journal*, Spring 1981, pp. 66-76.

Wokutch, Richard E., "The Impact of Values on Evaluation Research," *Academy of Management Proceedings*, August 1978, pp. 265-269.

Wolman, Harold, "The Determinants of Program Success and Failure," *Journal of Public Policy*, Volume I, No. 4, 1982, pp. 433-464.

Index

For Product Safety Concerns and Information please contact our EU
representative GPSR@taylorandfrancis.com Taylor & Francis Verlag GmbH,
Kaufingerstraße 24, 80331 München, Germany

Printed and bound by CPI Group (UK) Ltd, Croydon, CR0 4YY
08/05/2025
01864394-0005